DATE DUE

Revolution
in Orange

Revolution in Orange

The Origins of Ukraine's Democratic Breakthrough

Anders Åslund
Michael McFaul
Editors

CARNEGIE ENDOWMENT FOR INTERNATIONAL PEACE
Washington, D.C.

JN
6639
.A5
R48
2006

Carnegie Endowment for International Peace
1779 Massachusetts Avenue, N.W., Washington, D.C. 20036
202-483-7600, Fax 202-483-1840
www.CarnegieEndowment.org

The Carnegie Endowment for International Peace normally does not take institutional positions on public policy issues; the views and recommendations presented in this publication do not necessarily represent the views of the Carnegie Endowment, its officers, staff, or trustees.

To order, contact:
Hopkins Fulfillment Service
P.O. Box 50370, Baltimore, MD 21211-4370
1-800-537-5487 or 1-410-516-6956
Fax 1-410-516-6998

Composition by Stephen McDougal
Maps by Dave Merrill
Photos by *Ukrainska pravda* and AP/Wide World Photos
Printed by Edwards Brothers, Inc.

Library of Congress Cataloging-in-Publication data

Revolution in orange : the origins of Ukraine's democratic breakthrough / Anders Åslund and Michael McFaul.
   p. cm.
   Includes index.
   Summary: "This volume explores the role of former president Kuchma and the oligarchs, societal attitudes, the role of the political opposition and civil society, the importance of the media, and the roles of Russia and the West"—Provided by publisher.
   ISBN-13: 978-0-87003-221-9 (pbk.)
   ISBN-10: 0-87003-221-6 (pbk.)
   ISBN-13: 978-0-87003-222-6 (cloth)
   ISBN-10: 0-87003-222-4 (cloth)
   1. Presidents—Ukraine—Election, 2004. 2. Contested elections—Ukraine.
3. Ukraine—History—Orange Revolution, 2004. 4. Ukraine—Politics and government—1991- I. Åslund, Anders, 1952- II. McFaul, Michael. III. Title.

   JN6639.A5R48 2006
   947.708'6—dc22
                          2005037725

11 10 09 08 07 06   1 2 3 4 5   1st Printing 2006

Contents

Foreword

THE MEANING OF major events unfolds over decades and centuries. Actions that break like waves on the nearest shore hit distant lands later, and the erosion that each wave causes leads to further change years hence. Historians learn by surveying multiple landscapes and by revising and improving accounts as time goes on.

The Orange Revolution in Ukraine was certainly a major historical event. We know this even a year after it happened. In March 2005, hundreds of thousands of Lebanese consciously invoked the Ukrainian example as they peacefully massed in Beirut to demand self-governance. Kyrgyzstan's so-called Tulip Revolution took inspiration from Ukraine, too. Nondemocratic rulers understood the historical significance, as well. In May 2005, Chinese Premier Hu Jintao issued a report to the Communist Party Central Committee outlining policies to "crush U.S. attempts to start a color revolution in China." Zimbabwe adopted new policies cracking down on nongovernmental organizations, which are seen as vectors of peaceful revolution. Eritrea in May 2005 introduced a new law sharply limiting the role of nongovernmental organizations. And, of course, Russia and the neighboring states of Azerbaijan, Belarus, Kazakhstan, and Uzbekistan have tightened controls to prevent a replay of the Orange Revolution in their countries. It is precisely because the Ukrainian events were so historically significant that these nondemocratic governments have acted to prevent their repetition.

The present volume is a pioneering effort to describe and explain the events leading up to and through November and December, 2004—the acts of the "Revolution," as it is called. It is an initial history and analysis. In the years to come, historians will mine this treatment and archives of official documents (if they become available) to fill out the story.

Pioneering always entails risk, just as it carries exceptional rewards. We were confident to undertake these risks because we were led by two exceptional, highly informed, and engaged scholars, Anders Åslund and Michael McFaul. Åslund is not only a renowned economist and McFaul an outstanding political scientist, but both men have spent extensive amounts of time over the years working in Ukraine and establishing connections there. Their close ties to Ukraine—Åslund was in Kyiv during the Orange Revolution—enabled them to identify and recruit the best possible authors for this book. Most of these authors are themselves Ukrainian, while the chapter on Russia's role in this period is written by outstanding Russian scholars from the Carnegie Moscow Center. All of the authors here are not only recognized leaders in their fields, they all had on-the-ground experience interacting with the various Ukrainian, Western, and Russian dramatis personae of the Orange Revolution.

The result is a highly readable, deeply informed, and insightful volume, an invaluable first draft of the history of this remarkable episode.

For making this book possible, we are grateful to the Law Reform Institute, the German Marshall Fund of the United States, the International Renaissance Foundation, and the Chopivsky Family Foundation.

—Jessica T. Mathews
President, Carnegie Endowment for International Peace

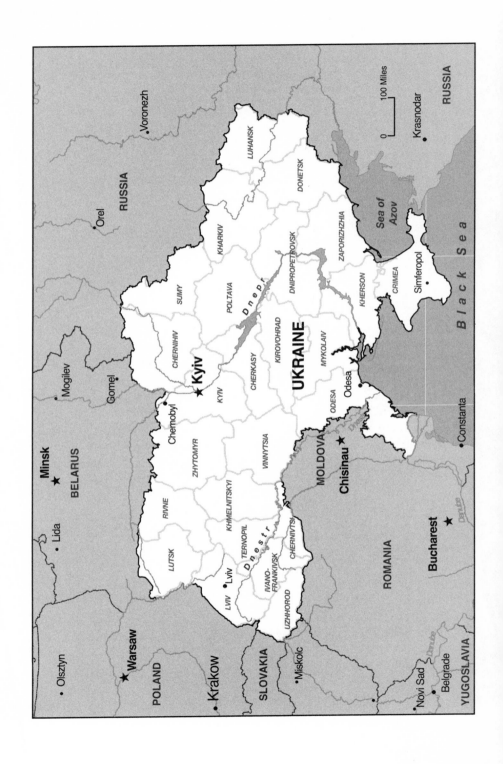

Introduction:
Perspectives on
the Orange Revolution

ANDERS ÅSLUND AND MICHAEL MCFAUL

ON SUNDAY, NOVEMBER 21, 2004, the second round of the highly contested presidential elections in Ukraine took place. The next day, it became clear that President Leonid Kuchma's incumbent regime had crudely rigged the elections to the advantage of its candidate, Prime Minister Viktor Yanukovych. Without hesitation, the challenger, Viktor Yushchenko, a former prime minister, declared the victory had been stolen from him and urged citizens to gather at "Maidan," Kyiv's Independence Square in the center of the city. Yushchenko's call was heard through much of the country thanks to TV Channel 5, which was owned by Petro Poroshenko, a wealthy businessman in Yushchenko's Our Ukraine party. Others stayed connected via the Internet, notably the Web newspaper *Ukrainska pravda*, and also kept in touch on mobile phones. In the freezing morning hours of November 22, thousands gathered at Maidan. Their numbers grew and grew until they finally reached roughly one million. Each presidential candidate declared himself president—a classic situation of dual sovereignty. The Orange Revolution had begun.

The immediate cause of the revolution is abundantly clear: the old regime had brazenly stolen the elections. The opposition—the rightful winners—demanded that the law of the land be obeyed, while the incumbent regime only pretended to do so.

After the first round of the presidential election on October 31, the Central Election Commission, which was effectively controlled by the government, delayed the announcement of the final vote counts for many days, arousing wide-spread suspicion of vote rigging. In the end, however, it announced that Yushchenko had won over Yanukovych by the tiniest of margins. But since neither candidate won an absolute majority, a run-off election was scheduled for November 21. Meanwhile, the failed candidates from the first round of elections threw their support behind Yushchenko, rendering him the obvious favorite in the upcoming run-off. Public opinion polls also pointed to a Yushchenko victory. But, it was also widely expected that the incumbent regime would rig the run-off elections.

Four processes comprise the Orange Revolution. The first and most significant event was the popular protest, which occurred in several major cities throughout Ukraine but was concentrated in Maidan in downtown Kyiv. After the second election, a city of 1,500 tents was swiftly set up on the Khreshchatyk, Kyiv's main thoroughfare adjacent to Maidan. Masses of people roamed the streets at all times, their numbers ballooning to hundreds of thousands every evening when Yushchenko and other revolutionary leaders spoke from a major stage on the square—their demands for democracy and freedom simultaneously televised on Channel 5. The dilemma for the protestors was that they lacked a clear strategy for taking power. Although some protestors called for the seizure of government buildings (similar to what the Georgian protestors did in the Rose Revolution the year before), Yushchenko and most of his close circle of advisors categorically rejected any action that might provoke violence. At the same time, they also worried that the government might outlast the protest and considered a speedy conclusion vital. To this end, protestors blockaded the main government buildings, effectively shutting down the government, and ensuring a prolonged stand off.

The second process at work was the negotiation between the regime and the opposition mediated by Polish President Alexander Kwasniewski, Lithuanian President Valdas Adamkus, the EU's High Representative Javier Solana, and Russian State Duma Speaker Boris Gryzlov. Both Yanukovych and Yushchenko participated in these negotiations, which aimed at compromise and a peaceful solution. The mediators succeeded in helping to structure a dialogue between opposing forces and deterred both sides from taking radical or violent action, but they did not resolve the stand off.

The third process played out in parliament and an array of courts, which handled various complaints about the elections. After the Rada, Ukraine's parliament, refused to ratify the official results released by the Central Election Committee, the matter was handed over to the Supreme Court for adjudication. On December 3, the Supreme Court issued a critical decision when it ruled the second round of the presidential elections null and void. The court decided that a rerun would take place on December 26. While this decision satisfied the Yushchenko camp's desire to reach early closure, the incumbent regime did not benefit in any way. Although this decision was widely welcomed by the opposition, mass demonstrations continued. Something more was needed to bring active protests to an end.

The fourth and final event came in the form of a pact between the incumbents and the opposition that amended the constitution. On December 8, the Ukrainian parliament approved amendments substantially reducing the powers of the president, something of great interest to the current President Kuchma and his colleagues in view of a likely win by the opposition. In return, the parliament also approved changes in electoral law championed by the opposition and intended to reduce opportunities for fraud. With this pact in place, both sides agreed to rerun the second round of elections in December.

Compro mise

This rerun did take place on December 26, 2004. The voting occurred in good order with an extraordinary number of foreign observers on hand. Yushchenko defeated Yanukovych with 52 percent of the votes cast, against 44 percent, which was probably close to the real results of November 21. Yanukovych contested the results in the courts with great vigor, but with weak evidence. Nonetheless, his multiple protests delayed the conclusion of the elections and the inauguration of the new president.

Finally, on January 23, 2005, the Supreme Court certified the results and Yushchenko took the oath of office, inaugurated both in Parliament and at Maidan. The active phase of the Orange Revolution was over. Its most intense period lasted from November 22 until December 8, and Yushchenko's inauguration marked its end.

The name of the "Orange" Revolution comes from the campaign color chosen by the Yushchenko campaign in the summer of 2004. Orange did not have any prior ideological connotation. The alternative would have been the traditional Ukrainian blue and yellow colors, but the greatest threat to Yushchenko's candidacy was to be labeled a radical Western Ukrainian nationalist, when the crucial swing electorate lived in central Ukraine. So the neutral orange was chosen. The Yushchenko campaign's most visible slogan read simply *"Tak!* (Yes!) Yushchenko."* The emphasis lay single-mindedly on democracy and freedom.

Well before the second round, people on both sides of the metaphorical barricades anticipated that they would be compelled to assume physical positions on opposite sides of real barricades. The Rose Revolution in Georgia, which occurred almost exactly one year earlier in November 2003, provided inspiration and a historical model. With the election date set well in advance, there was much speculation about how events would unfold and both sides carefully mapped their strategy. As early as July 2004, conventional wisdom in Kyiv suggested that Yushchenko would win the real election in the second round, but Yanukovych would steal the elections and Yushchenko supporters would take to the streets.[1] The only question was whether the opposition could rally enough protestors to effectively challenge the corrupt election results. Anticipating a similar scenario, the Yanukovych camp pursued its own public relations campaign, essentially arguing that Ukrainians were too docile to pursue a revolution of their own.

Both sides seemed to act in accordance with their long-prepared scripts, but who would prevail was far from certain. Understanding why and how the Yushchenko camp did win—why the Orange Revolution succeeded—is the central purpose of this book. We have focused on eight broad factors that influenced the outcome of the Orange Revolution: the nature of the old regime; the strength, strategy, and tactics of the political opposition; societal attitudes; the role of civil society; the student movement, *Pora* (It's Time); the media; Russia; and the West.

To establish context, in chapter one Anders Åslund discusses the oligarchic nature of Ukraine's old regime. President Kuchma pitted the oligarchs against one another and state power was never fully consolidated. As the economy grew rapidly, the number of successful businessmen grew and they became more assertive and aggressive toward each other. Expanding economic pluralism laid the ground for political pluralism, but competition within the old regime was so severe that there was no coherent response to growing political opposition. Privatization, separation of properties, and consolidation of enterprises gave big businessmen greater security, but did little to mitigate their activism. Thus, great entrepreneurial aspirations and uncertain property rights generated outlandish campaign financing. Ultimately, the economy and society had evolved beyond the old regime.

In chapter two, Adrian Karatnycky discusses the emergence of a
broad-based reformist, democratic opposition in Ukraine. Throughout
the 1990s, the only consistent opposition came from the communists
and socialists. A handful of democratic reformers were present in the
various administrations, but they were few and their participation in
government kept them out of consistent opposition. The first significant
non-socialist opposition emerged under Pavlo Lazarenko after he was
ousted as prime minister in 1997. In late 2000, the murder of journalist
Heorhiy Gongadze and revelations of President Kuchma's involvement
led to three months of street demonstrations in Kyiv under the banner
"Ukraine without Kuchma." Yet the only viable political reform leader
at the time, then-prime minister Viktor Yushchenko, did not join these
protests. Only with the sacking of Yushchenko in April 2001 did the
base for a broad reformist opposition emerge, and Yushchenko successfully led his Our Ukraine bloc in the parliamentary elections in March
2002. The democratic opposition had been formed and the stage was set
for presidential elections in October 2004, with Yushchenko as the dominant opposition candidate.

But what did Ukrainians actually think? Taras Kuzio examines societal attitudes in chapter three. "Kuchmagate," the political crisis resulting from Kuchma's alleged involvement in the murder of Gongadze,
set the stage emotionally. The incumbent regime was perceived as corrupt and criminal, and as time passed these attitudes became more deeply
ingrained. While Ukraine enjoyed high economic growth, people did
not perceive a positive change in their own lives. They believed the
money was flowing to oligarchs and organized crime; therefore
Yanukovych's words about economic success fell on deaf ears. And attempts by the regime and its Russian consultants to use anti-American
propaganda against Yushchenko were equally fruitless. The stark choice
between Yushchenko, who was widely perceived as "clean," and
Yanukovych, who was an ex-convict, made it easy for the opposition to
present the election as a choice between good and evil. Finally, the slogan "Back to Europe!" served to mobilize the West-oriented part of society, while the East did not seem to have much fighting spirit.

Ukraine possessed the most mature civil society of any post-Soviet
state and Nadia Diuk explores this history in detail in chapter four. In
the mid-1980s when it became politically possible, a large number of
civic organizations and initiatives emerged, including broad civil organizations, think tanks, monitoring groups, and media. Civic groups used
the Internet extensively for information and communication. Nongov-

ernmental organizations conducted opinion polls and monitored elections. The one shortcoming was that this strong civil society could not communicate with the regime. Instead, from 2000 a variety of nongovernmental organizations spearheaded the protest movement against the regime by innovative means. By the fall of 2004, they succeeded in getting several hundred thousand people into the street throughout Ukraine. The nongovernmental organizations excelled in peacefulness and they played a decisive role in the Orange Revolution.

In chapter five, Pavol Demes and Joerg Forbrig explore Pora, the group that spearheaded civil action in Ukraine. The authors present a picture of an amazingly capable and timely organization. Founded in March 2004 as a national council of nongovernmental organizations, Pora quickly grew into a countrywide network inspired by similar movements in Georgia, Serbia, and Slovakia. Its campaign consisted of six elements: development of an organizational structure, formation of a campaign strategy, training activists, an information campaign, a response to repression, and mobilization for free and fair elections. Although Pora received a very small amount of foreign funding, the driving force behind Pora was the energy of its own activists.

Olena Prytula, editor-in-chief of the Internet newspaper *Ukrainska pravda*, dissects the role of the media in the Orange Revolution in chapter six. On the one hand, she depicts a media that was rigorously controlled by pro-regime oligarchs. On the other hand, she describes a Ukraine that did maintain independent and opposition media. The opposition had several big newspapers, and *Zerkalo tyzhnia* was an outstanding independent intellectual weekly. Rather surprisingly, the regime allowed the opposition to buy a significant cable channel, Channel 5, which became the voice of the Orange Revolution. Because of the poor quality of most newspapers, the Internet came to play a surprisingly significant role in Ukraine. That was particularly true of the online publication *Ukrainska pravda*, which served as the main news medium of the Orange Revolution. Tragically, this website played an additional role in ending the old regime when the murder of its first editor-in-chief, Heorhiy Gongadze, sparked protest.

In chapter seven, Oleksandr Sushko and Olena Prystayko consider the role of the West in the Orange Revolution. Worried by the role the West played in ousting Eduard Shevardnadze in Georgia a year earlier, the old regime demonized Western involvement. The West did have an interest in the Ukrainian election, namely to promote democratic values, but it was hardly nefarious. The EU was ambivalent and hesitant to begin with because although the new EU member states favored pro-moting democracy in Ukraine, the old EU members began from a Rus-sia-first position. However, as violations of democratic practice became rampant, the EU united around a pro-democracy position. The United States had taken greater interest in Ukraine all along, and it adopted a clear pro-democracy stand, to which it devoted significant resources. Some Western support went to the NGO sector, but it was quite small. The main Western activity was to mobilize an unprecedented number of international election observers. Their role in exposing large-scale elec-toral fraud cannot be underestimated. After the second-round election, individual Western politicians participated in negotiations with the two leading contenders. In the end, the Ukrainian election drama served to unite the West around democratic values.

Russian scholars Nikolai Petrov and Andrei Ryabov consider Russia's role in the Ukrainian presidential elections in chapter eight. In Moscow, the Russian presidential administration defended Russian interests in the Ukrainian elections, allowing neither the security services nor the Ministry for Foreign Affairs to play any role. The authors argue that the Kremlin served Kuchma, having decided early on to back his candi-date, rather than pursuing any political agenda of its own in Ukraine. The Russian state provided the Ukrainian state with ample monetary benefits before the elections and channeled Russian business funds to the Yanukovych campaign. In addition, several Russian political con-sultants worked in Ukraine for Yanukovych (as did a few, less visible ones for Yushchenko) In the second round of the elections, President Putin himself became personally involved in Yanukovych's campaign.

In singling out these key factors, we have deliberately focused on the proximate causes of the Orange Revolution. To varying degrees, all of the chapters discuss the deeper, structural processes at work. But the book's overall contribution is to provide one of the first comprehensive accounts of the short-term variables that combined to produce the Or-ange Revolution.

In the final chapter, Michael McFaul places the Orange Revolution in comparative perspective. In the first part of the chapter, McFaul com-pares the Orange Revolution to other recent electoral breakthroughs in the region—Serbia 2000, Georgia 2003, and Kyrgyzstan 2005—seeking to distinguish what factors were similar and necessary in all of these cases and theorizing about the conditions under which other countries might undergo color revolutions of their own. In the second part of the chapter, McFaul compares the Ukrainian drama of the fall of 2004 to other revolutions more generally, seeking to answer the question: was the Orange Revolution really a revolution?

As all the authors are discussing different aspects of the same events, much of the history is inevitably repeated in the various chapters. As editors, rather than delete this repetition we have let the authors illuminate the same facts from different angles, inspired by Lawrence Durrell in his Alexandria Quartet. We have not tried to tone down differences of opinion, while we have endeavored to verify the facts. Finally, we have established January 23, 2005, as a firm cut-off date, so as not to allow the story of the revolution to be flavored by later events. On that date, the victory of the Orange Revolution was legally concluded and the regime change comsummated. In this book, we refrain from discussing the formulation of the new government of the Orange revolutionaries and its dramas.

Notes

1.   The observation of one of the authors during a visit to Kyiv in July 2004.

---------- CHAPTER ONE ----------

The Ancien Régime:
Kuchma and the Oligarchs

ANDERS ÅSLUND

AT THE OUTSET OF THE Orange Revolution, Ukraine was a highly oligarchic regime, far more so than Russia. It was dominated by three wealthy regional oligarchic groups, which owned large conglomerates. They enjoyed close connections with President Leonid Kuchma, had large party factions in parliament, owned media empires, benefited from extensive governmental privileges, and controlled many important officials, including people in branches of law enforcement.

The enigma of the revolution in Ukraine is how the mighty could lose power through an election without bloodshed. Most of the explanation lies in the very structure of the old regime, reminiscent of how Alexis de Tocqueville explained the roots of the French Revolution.[1] In this chapter, I therefore discuss the nature of the old regime, outlining in the first section the characteristics of the Ukrainian oligarchy. In the second section I show how the relationship between the president and the oligarchs evolved over time, and in the third section I sum up the main oligarchic groups before the Orange Revolution. In the fourth section I analyze how the oligarchic groups engaged in politics. Finally, in

---

I am grateful to Roman Ginzburg and Matthew Gibson, who provided me with research assistance, and to the participants of the book workshop in Kyiv on March 10, 2005, who offered a variety of comments. Especially, I want to thank Michael McFaul, Olena Prytula, and Taras Kuzio for their substantial and helpful comments.

9

the concluding section, I lay out the structure inherent in the old regime that made the demise of the oligarchy possible.

Characteristics of the Ukrainian Oligarchy

The oligarchic groups in Ukraine were formed after the end of communism, though several leading figures had been youth communist (*Komsomol*) officials or state enterprise managers. The oligarchic groups started to emerge in 1992. The groups, their practices, their businesses, and their interactions have changed quickly. Many early stars have disappeared. Some have been murdered, while others have emigrated.

The word *oligarch* expresses a popular concept. Ukraine's oligarchs emerged in parallel to Russia's, who have been more closely studied, and they were quite similar.[2] The popular meaning of *oligarch* is a politically well-connected tycoon, a dollar billionaire, or near billionaire, who is the main owner of a conglomerate and has intimate ties with the president. In traditional parlance, an *oligarchy* implies the rule of a limited group of people, but that concept of oligarchy has rarely been used in Ukraine. One reason is that so much power rested with the president, and another is that the system was reasonably open and competitive. Joel Hellman has coined the phrase *state capture* to characterize the relationship between big businessmen and the state in a country such as Ukraine because the big businessmen have influenced the state by all possible means.[3]

In the 1990s, Ukrainian oligarchs focused on and made most of their money in commodity trading. One leading oligarch, Ihor Bakai, stated in a famous interview in 1998 that "all really rich people in Ukraine have made their money on gas."[4] Other sources of revenue were subsidized state credits, steel exports, the oil trade, coal subsidies, and agricultural and chemical exports. Lucrative commodity trading involved several elements of fraud and *rent seeking*, or skimming. First, oligarchs bought gas at low state-controlled prices and sold them for high market prices. Second, the state usually awarded them a monopoly, and typically a regional monopoly, for gas sales. Third, oligarchs often refrained from paying for their purchases, sometimes passing the bill on to the state, as was notably done with much of their gas bills to Russia. Fourth, even when oligarchs did pay, they extracted substantial discounts in barter deals, typically reducing their tax bills with deliveries in kind. Fifth, the government financed the oligarchs with subsidized loans and other subsidies. Sixth, the oligarchs got away with not paying taxes, thanks to legal exemptions, offsets granting them substantial discounts, or simply nonpayment.[5]

The Ukrainian gas trade was a peculiar business. Each year, a handful of Ukrainian businessmen were given regional trade monopolies, and each made hundreds of millions of dollars through small trading companies. The players tended to change from year to year depending on their standing with the president. Since they made their fortunes on commodity arbitrage, these businessmen ignored both the ownership of big companies and production. It was not surprising that Ukraine's output fell continuously throughout the 1990s.

Since the gas monopolies tended to be regional, the oligarchic groups assumed a regional character. As so much hinged on a single gas contract without any recourse to law, top-level violence mounted in the mid-1990s. The gas oligarchs had armies of up to 150 bodyguards around them, and two top businessmen from Donetsk (Ahati Bragin, also known as Alik Grek, and Yevhen Shcherban) were murdered in 1995 and 1996, respectively, presumably by their competitors, though the cases were never solved. Although the threat of violence remained, the violence among the oligarchs gradually dwindled, as did their number of bodyguards.

The Evolving Relationship between the President and the Oligarchs

The relationship between the president and Ukrainian big businessmen changed amazingly fast, challenging facile generalizations. As discussed below, this relationship changed virtually every year.

The first year of independence under President Leonid Kravchuk brought little but chaos. Leonid Kuchma made his political mark as prime minister in 1992–1993, standing out as a representative of two constituencies—the Dnipropetrovsk region and state enterprise managers—but no real system of power developed.

Prime Minister Kuchma was replaced by the energetic Yukhum Zviahilskiy, another state enterprise manager, but he represented the coal industry and the Donetsk region. Zviahilskiy brought with him a group of state enterprise managers from Donetsk who joined the government to make money on subsidized state credits, state subsidies, and privileged arbitrage between fixed state prices and free-market prices. The coal industry firmly established itself as a rent-seeking machine, living on subsidies. Zviahilskiy himself was later prosecuted for having stolen state gasoline worth $25 million. He simply sold the gas and

requested payment into his personal bank account abroad. President
Leonid Kravchuk does not appear to have been involved in these machi-
nations.

In July 1994, Leonid Kuchma was unexpectedly elected the president
of Ukraine. During his first year in power, he disrupted the old corrupt
networks. Early oligarchs such as Zviahilskiy, media oligarch Vadim
Rabinovich, and gas trader Ihor Bakai were out of favor, and the first
two were even prosecuted. The president pursued energetic market reforms for a year, after which, however, the old oligarchs managed to
mend their fences with the new president. The Kuchma regime had become corrupt.

In 1995, the dominant oligarch in Dnipropetrovsk was its governor,
Pavlo Lazarenko. His closest business partner was Yulia Tymoshenko,
who headed their private company, the Unified Energy System of
Ukraine, which traded primarily in gas. Lazarenko became the prime
minister in the summer of 1996, posing a seemingly serious oligarchic
challenge to President Kuchma. Until Lazarenko was ousted one year
later, he appeared to be more powerful than Kuchma. Lazarenko stood
out as the most corrupt Ukrainian politician to date, making money on
the manipulation of the gas market, agricultural procurement, and
privatization. Even the Ukrainian establishment was stunned by his
greed, which contributed to his ouster. The saying went that Lazarenko
lost out because he did not share with anybody.[6] An important consequence of Lazarenko's rule was the formation of a political party,
Hromada. Arguably, this party was the first purely oligarchic party and
one in opposition to the president. One of the most prominent members
of Hromada, Yulia Tymoshenko, left the party after Lazarenko fled
abroad in February 1999. She founded her own party, *Batkivshchyna* (Fatherland), in opposition to Kuchma.

Lazarenko must have shocked Kuchma, and Kuchma appears to have
decided never to put himself in such a trap again. Since Lazarenko had
been the leader of Kuchma's regional base, Dnipropetrovsk, Kuchma
could no longer trust the region fully. His first lesson was that he needed
a weak but completely loyal prime minister, which led him to choose
the unfailingly obedient Valery Pustovoitenko. Another lesson was that
Kuchma needed to exploit his Machiavellian talents more fully to play
the oligarchs against one another.

Soon, the presidential elections in October–November 1999 became
the dominant political issue, but Kuchma, who had presided over a
steady economic decline, was not very popular. He took his cue from

Russian president Boris Yeltsin and the Russian presidential elections
of 1996. In April 1998, during the approach to the election, a former
chair of the National Bank, Vadim Hetman, fell victim to a contract
murder in Kyiv. The case was never solved. Hetman had been
Yushchenko's confidant and potential campaign leader. After the murder, Yushchenko, who had contemplated running in the 1999 elections,
decided against it. Maneuvering to eliminate other centrist candidates,
Kuchma rendered the election a stark choice between him and the trog-
lodyte Communist leader Petro Symonenko. Like Yeltsin, Kuchma relied upon a handful of oligarchs for massive financing and media support (mainly Viktor Medvedchuk, Ihor Bakai, and Viktor Pinchuk).
Symonenko forced Kuchma to a run-off, but Kuchma won with a reas-
suring majority of 56.3 percent of the votes cast.[7] Even so, Kuchma's
power remained constrained. Together with their allies, the communists held about 40 percent of the seats in parliament. A couple of the
many oligarchic party factions tended to vote with the communists, providing them with a majority. The communists regularly voted for subsidies and regulation, which always benefited some oligarchs. As a result, a stalemate persisted between the president and the parliament,
and minimum legislation was enacted.

By the end of 1999, the mood in Ukraine was more pessimistic than
ever. The country seemed stuck in a morass of corrupt state monopoly
trading. Kuchma and the oligarchs did not appear concerned about the
steady decline in the gross domestic product (GDP), but they were truly
worried about Ukraine approaching external default because they had
seen how their Russian brethren had lost their fortunes and power in
Russia's financial crash in August 1998. They decided that Ukraine's
creditworthiness had to be restored. One of the leading oligarchs and
parliamentarians, Viktor Medvedchuk, assembled ten centrist and rightist party factions to form a government that could save Ukraine from
default. The only credible senior economic politician to be found was
Viktor Yushchenko, who had skillfully run Ukraine's central bank for
seven years. He was widely credited with the country's macroeconomic
stabilization and the successful introduction of Ukraine's national cur-
rency in 1996.

Medvedchuk managed to have Yushchenko approved as prime minister by parliament. Yushchenko's most notable appointment was of
former gas trader Yulia Tymoshenko as the deputy prime minister for
energy. In the late 1990s she had successfully transformed herself from
an oligarch to a politician, opposing the remaining oligarchs, though

widespread suspicion constrained popular support for her. For the rest, the government remained dominated by civil servants. Yushchenko did exactly what was required of him. In the course of the first four months of 2000, he restored Ukraine's creditworthiness, but he did so with a vengeance directed against the oligarchs. Immediately, he enacted a law that abolished 270 legislative acts involving subsidies and tax or regulation privileges for concrete businesses. He swiftly uprooted barter and offsets by demanding cash-only payments to the state. In the energy sphere, the gas trade with Russia was reformed, and the oligarchs were forced to pay for the deliveries they received. A large number of big companies were privatized. Many were sold to Russian businessmen, who were prepared to pay more than the Ukrainian oligarchs were. Moreover, a land reform broke up the old collective and state farms, giving the land to the peasants.[8]

By raising state revenues, Yushchenko turned a budget deficit in 1999 to a surplus in 2000 and reduced the state's foreign debt. To an amazing degree, the playing field had been leveled. As a consequence, the Ukrainian economy turned around. For the first time, independent Ukraine recorded economic growth of no less than 5.8 percent in 2000.[9] By May 2000, the oligarchs understood that Yushchenko had saved them and that they no longer needed to accept the hardship he had imposed upon them. Because of political vagaries, however, they failed to sack him until April 2001, which was too late for the oligarchs. The clock could not be turned back. Ukraine had changed for good, and the old oligarchic system, dominated by rent seeking, could not be restored. The gas trade was no longer a bonanza, and several major energy traders vanished. Instead, the owners of steel mills became the richest and most powerful oligarchs. The oligarchs had been transformed from rent seekers to producers.

Economically, the year 2000 marked a definite break with the old parasitical rent-seeking machine. At long last, a reasonably free market economy, with predominantly private ownership, had been established. As a consequence, the dependence of businessmen on the state diminished, allowing them to act independently. After their ouster in early 2001, Yushchenko and Tymoshenko stood out as strong political leaders in opposition to the oligarchs. Until then, many had wondered whether the two were fish or fowl.

In November 2000, socialist leader Oleksandr Moroz revealed that audiotapes existed that had been made by Kuchma's bodyguard, Mykola Melnychenko. These tapes suggested that the president had given his

Gongadze

consent to the murder of a muckraking journalist, Heorhiy Gongadze. Kuchma's popularity plummeted to single digits, never to recover. A broad opposition movement, "Ukraine without Kuchma," was formed that organized prolonged street protests, which continued for several months. The action came to a sudden end on March 9, 2001, when a demonstration in Kyiv turned violent. Several young nationalists were arrested and sent to jail, while the opposition claimed that the demonstration was a government provocation. The outbreak of violence shocked the opposition, bringing its protest actions to an end, but Kuchma's claim to legitimacy was no longer credible.

Beginning in 2001, Kuchma had to rely all the more on his skills as a conspirator, playing powerful figures against one another without alienating them. He became a godfather, the ultimate arbiter in a world without formal laws, providing the last recourse for complaints against arbitrary government actions.[10] The more arbitrary the application of law was, the greater the power of the arbiter became. Kuchma responded to his experience with the combative reformist Yushchenko government by appointing a neutral government of civil servants under Anatoliy Kinakh, the chair of the Party of Industrialists and Entrepreneurs and a decent technocrat. Still, the Yushchenko reforms were not reversed.

The next big political event was the parliamentary elections in March 2002. After having been ousted as prime minister, Yushchenko assembled a broad coalition in an electoral bloc of liberal, nationalist, and rightist parties running against Kuchma and his oligarchic regime. In the proportional balloting part of the election,[11] his Our Ukraine party obtained 24 percent of the votes cast. A number of big businessmen (mini-oligarchs) who had made their money on cooperation with the old regime now changed sides and joined Yushchenko. Yulia Tymoshenko ran with her own bloc, supposedly because their electorates were disparate and did not like one another. The opposition, comprising Our Ukraine, the Yulia Tymoshenko bloc, the Socialist Party, and the Communist Party, initially had a majority in parliament, but it failed to act fast enough to seize power. Besides, Our Ukraine and the communists stood far apart. With bribery and threats of economic repression, the regime soon broke the opposition's majority. In fact, the new parliament was more oligarchic than ever. Half of parliament comprised loose oligarchic factions. Even so, the spell of the oligarchs was broken. Everyone was just waiting for the presidential elections in October 2004, which were presented as a showdown between Yushchenko and an as-yet-unknown oligarchic candidate.

In November 2002, Kuchma sacked Kinakh's government for passivity and appointed for the first time a coalition government of politicians
from the nine oligarchic factions in parliament. Also for the first time,
the government was dominated by oligarchs. The choice of a prime
minister, Viktor Yanukovych, was obviously a choice for the presidential candidate. Yanukovych represented the strongest oligarchic clan,
Donetsk, and he was seen as Rinat Akhmetov's foremost politician. Although he had been convicted for violent crimes twice in his youth, he
appeared to be the only oligarchic candidate who could muster more
than a 6 to 7 percent popularity rating, and it continued to rise.
Medvedchuk had long given up his hope of becoming president since
he could gain no popular support. The main politician from
Dnipropetrovsk, Serhiy Tyhipko, had a weaker political base than
Yanukovych. Tyhipko tried to launch his presidential bid by becoming
the chair of the National Bank of Ukraine but failed to rise in the opinion polls, leaving Yanukovych as the only plausible candidate from the
oligarchic camp.[12]

Ironically, just before its demise, the oligarchic regime was stronger in
terms of formal powers than it had ever been. It dominated the parliament, controlled the government, including law enforcement, and ruled
the media. Yet the oligarchs were by no means united, and that would
cause their downfall. The last two years of the old regime were characterized by the oligarchs' frantic desire to seize as many assets as possible
while the going was good. Even so, the economy boomed as never before.

A little-noticed aspect of Ukrainian politics is that relationships among
the power elite have changed amazingly fast since independence, leaving everyone uncertain. At one time, opportunistic behavior and complete flexibility had been the keys to success. The oligarchs got used to
exploiting the uncertainty of property rights to extend their own properties and to ensuring their own property rights by investing in politics.

Part of the explanation of how the mighty oligarchic system could
fall so swiftly lies in the relationship between the president and the oligarchs. The formal powers of the president had been rather limited, but
he cleverly reinforced his power by playing both oligarchs and governmental agencies, especially law enforcement, against one another. He
did so increasingly, but as his wiliness became obvious, his popularity
declined, prompting him to rely more upon authoritarian measures. In
doing so, Kuchma exceeded his formal powers and resorted to old com-
munist-style telephone commands. As the president persistently

violated laws, corrupt practices became prevalent. Although Kuchma did not care much about the law, he insisted on his prerogatives. To make the most of his powers, he made sure to appear entirely unpredictable, rendering his public statements almost stochastic. In this way, Kuchma tried to increase the insecurity of oligarchs and officials. It would be inaccurate to describe President Leonid Kuchma as dominated by the oligarchs, in spite of their close links or the oligarchs' being far richer than he. Their relationship was rather one of symbiosis.

The Main Oligarchic Groups

To understand the oligarchs, we need to describe the top groups as they were on the eve of the presidential elections in 2004. Prime Minister Viktor Yanukovych was effectively supported by three oligarchic groups: Rinat Akhmetov's System Capital Management (SCM), in Donetsk; Viktor Pinchuk's Interpipe, in Dnipropetrovsk; and the Kyiv-based group of Hrihoriy Surkis and Viktor Medvedchuk, which is usually not identified with any specific enterprise or holding company.[13]

System Capital Management is by far Ukraine's biggest company, with about 160,000 employees. It is a holding company almost completely owned by Rinat Akhmetov, controlling a conglomerate. It is a vertically integrated company, mainly producing steel, but expanding upstream into coal and iron-ore mining. It owns some machine-building plants, primarily to service its steel production and mining industries. System Capital Management also owns a brewery and regional media. Akhmetov rules as the king of Donetsk with control over the regional administration, which was run by Viktor Yanukovych until November 2002.[14]

Viktor Pinchuk's Interpipe might be the second wealthiest company in Ukraine, but its number of employees is much smaller. It is based in Dnipropetrovsk and specializes in the production of steel pipes and railway wheels, that is, of high value-added steel products. Besides steel, Pinchuk owns three medium-size television channels (ICTV, *Novy Kanal*, and STB) and Ukrsotsbank.[15] Pinchuk is married to Kuchma's only daughter.

Both SCM and Interpipe appear to be normal corporate structures, while the third oligarchic group, the Surkis-Medvedchuk group, lacks any central company or transparency. It is sometimes called the Dynamo group, after the famous soccer club in Kyiv controlled by Surkis, and sometimes the Kyiv group, after its seat. Many of their companies are owned by others, notably the state, but also by partners, and group ownership is concealed in offshore companies. The group controls nine regional electricity distribution companies, substantial real estate in Kyiv, forests in Transcarpathia, and effectively the three biggest television channels: Inter, 1+1, and the state-owned First National Channel (UT–1). Medvedchuk has been a full-time politician for many years. He was the first deputy speaker of parliament, and in 2002–2004, he was the head of the presidential administration, which raised queries over whether government was his main business. Medvedchuk controlled a large number of governmental appointments, notably in the Ministry of the Interior and in regional administrations.

After these three major groups, several large and well-connected groups follow that appear to have maintained political neutrality. Privat Group, in Dnipropetrovsk, might be the biggest. It is headed by three partners: Ihor Kolomoyskiy, Gennady Bogoliubov, and Alexei Martynov. Privat Group controls a large bank (Privatbank), a vertically integrated oil company (Sintoza and semi-state-owned Ukrnafta), a vertically integrated mining-and-steel company, and large electricity holdings. Like the Surkis-Medvedchuk group, Privat Group does not have clear corporate structures, and much of its ownership is hidden in offshore companies, partly to escape antimonopoly measures. Officially, Privat Group keeps a low profile. It competed with, and lost to, Interpipe in a high-profile 2003 privatization move in the Dnipropetrovsk region for the Nikopol Ferroalloy Plant. Commercially, it is close to the Surkis-Medvedchuk group, with which it shares numerous electric companies, but it also has a major joint venture with SCM: Ukrrudprom, a large iron ore mine.[16]

The traditionally preeminent group in Donetsk was the Industrial Union of Donbas (ISD). Unlike all the other groups, its main owners, Vitaly Haiduk and Serhiy Taruta, are former state enterprise managers from the metallurgical industry. This large conglomerate has ninety thousand employees and is focused on steelworks, though it has many other enterprises as well. Unlike SCM and Privat, which have opted for vertical integration upstream, ISD has chosen downstream vertical integration, investing extensively in steelworks in Central Europe. Previously, SCM and ISD shared the ownership of many steelworks, but they have increasingly divided their properties. Since SCM received most of them, ISD appeared to be squeezed out. It still shares the ownership of some machine-building plants.[17]

Other large enterprise groups in Ukraine are Alexander Yaroslavsky's Ukrsibbank in Kharkiv and the Zaporozhstal group owned by three young men in Zaporizhzhia. Ukrsibbank is a mixed conglomerate and private investment group, while Zaporozhstal is primarily a metallurgical company. Strikingly, at least six of Ukraine's biggest enterprise groups are metallurgical companies, and, not surprisingly, are located in the east of the country. Politically, only the first three groups—SCM, Interpipe, and the Surkis-Medvedchuk Group—really supported Yanukovych openly, while the others were more or less neutral. The overwhelming majority of Ukrainian businessmen supported Yushchenko against the major oligarchs.

An important development in the March 2002 elections was that several big businessmen joined the opposition. In particular, Petro Poroshenko (Ukraine's chocolate king, with the company Roshen, who also has interests in agriculture and the Leninska Kuznia shipyard); David Zhvanya and Mykola Martynenko (focused on state-owned Atomenergo); and Yevhen Chervonenko (a major trucker from Lviv) were elected to Our Ukraine. They stayed with Yushchenko despite extensive harassment from authorities, such as tax audits, innumerable inspections, and repeated arrests of their executives. It seemed they thought a Yushchenko victory would provide them with sufficient financial payback, although Poroshenko alleged that his opposition cost him no less than two-thirds of his wealth over four years.[18] Yet they held out and eventually won with Yushchenko, and they remain conspicuously wealthy.

Big Ukrainian business went through a great transformation in the early 2000s that had political consequences. First, enterprises were increasingly privatized, which gave the businessmen an interest in acquiring companies and defending their properties rather than sitting on state enterprises and parasitically tapping their cash flows while extracting state subsidies, as was the case in the 1990s. Therefore, they started caring about production and investment.

Second, big businessmen have progressively separated and consolidated their holdings. Ukrainian corporate legislation is so rudimentary that a partner or minority shareholder has minimal legal rights. Since the courts work poorly, most enterprises opt for far-reaching vertical integration to reduce their dependence on subcontractors. As a consequence, Ukrainian enterprise ownership appears to be more concentrated and consolidated than in Russia. Most of the five biggest groups nonetheless have some major properties in common.

Third, since big businessmen separated their properties from one another, they have become competitors. It is common to speak of the Donetsk and Dnipropetrovsk groups, but the two biggest enterprises in Dnipropetrovsk—Interpipe and Privat Group—compete ferociously, as do SCM and ISD, the two biggest corporations in Donetsk, though SCM is by far the more powerful of the two. Both in Dnipropetrovsk and Donetsk, large metallurgical companies of roughly equal size stand against one another, evidencing that Ukraine was by no means monopolized by the top oligarchs. In the 1990s, by contrast, big Ukrainian businessmen were so interdependent that they had to be highly secretive and extremely careful not to criticize one another.

Fourth, as rent seeking faded, businessmen became more independent from the state, particularly after the great liberalization of 2000. They had to focus on production instead.

Fifth, greater mutual independence and competition among the big businessmen intensified their competition over property rights, which contributed to extraordinary political campaign financing. According to the Yushchenko campaign, as early as July 2004 the Yanukovych campaign had planned financing of $600 million, half of which was to come from Russian enterprises and half from Ukrainian oligarchs, primarily from Rinat Akhmetov.[19] Later, some even talked about total campaign funding of $900 million. David Zhvanya, the chief fundraiser for the Yushchenko campaign, has stated that his presidential campaign and the protests they organized cost more than $150 million, which was provided by Ukrainian businessmen.[20] This means that the Ukrainian presidential elections cost more than 1 percent of the GDP, or more than one hundred times as much as the simultaneous U.S. presidential elections in relation to the GDP.[21] One of the owners of Privat Group, Bogoliubov, argued that democracy in Ukraine could be formed only after privatization had been completed. Until then, Ukrainian politics would be dominated by businessmen driven by their aspiration to grab state assets.[22]

Sixth, all these developments have contributed to much greater openness and transparency. Until 2000 it was exceedingly difficult to figure out who owned what. Ownership was hidden in offshore companies, and the big groups had no clear corporate structures. Now the leading companies have set up holding companies, clarified their corporate structures, and are publishing extensive organizational charts of the biggest enterprise groups.[23]

How Ukrainian Oligarchs Engage in Politics

Another key to understanding the Ukrainian oligarchs is to examine with which state institutions they have interacted most intensely.

The president and the presidential administration have been central to all oligarchic struggles. Serious oligarchs must have access to the president, and many oligarchs have served as presidential advisors or in senior positions in the presidential administration. Notably, Medvedchuk was the head of the presidential administration during Kuchma's last two years in power. The president has been so important because of his considerable constitutional powers and his even greater informal powers.

The second stage for big businessmen has been parliament and not the government. Their share of the deputies has expanded continuously, though the parliamentary elections in March 2002 might have marked a peak. Oligarchic parties supporting Kuchma held approximately half the seats in parliament in about nine party factions, but the other parties included many big businessmen too. The Ukrainian parliament is a millionaires' club (as the U.S. Senate was called in the 1880s). It is commonly said that 300 of the parliament's 450 deputies are dollar millionaires.[24] In the 2002 elections, "safe" seats on party lists were sold for up to $3 million.[25] Literally all big businessmen in Ukraine, with the exception of Rinat Akhmetov and the owners of Privat Group, are members of parliament. The political strength of the oligarchic groups could be judged by their parliamentary numbers. By the summer of 2004, Akhmetov's Donetsk faction, the "Regions," had sixty-six members of parliament, and Pinchuk's Dnipropetrovsk Labor Ukraine party had some forty members of parliament, as did the Surkis-Medvedchuk "(United) Social Democratic Party of Ukraine." The names did not reflect their political orientation, though several oligarchic parties used social democratic rhetoric to camouflage their demand for state intervention in favor of their business interests. Both the number of factions and their sizes varied swiftly. Smaller oligarchic groups had factions of fifteen to twenty members of parliament.

Evidently, top businessmen considered membership in parliament vital to their business interests. It gave them legal immunity, although their managers were often arrested when the principals misbehaved politically. The businessmen-parliamentarians also extracted state benefits, such as tax exemptions, subsidies, trade barriers, and privatization deals. They easily blocked any undesirable legislation. Membership in parliament also guaranteed them high-level governmental access. Finally, the Ukrainian parliament performed many of the functions of a stock exchange, being the meeting place and trading floor of Ukraine's big businessmen.

Given the importance of state largesse and state capture, one would expect the government to be a major target of oligarchic intrusion, but that has largely not been the case. The main exceptions were the governments of acting prime minister Yukhum Zviahilskiy in 1993–1994 and of Pavlo Lazarenko in 1996–1997. Both, however, fell into disgrace after their dismissal and were prosecuted for large-scale misappropriations. Serhiy Tyhipko became the deputy prime minister of economy in 1997 while one of the partners in Privat Group, but he soon divested his share in that company. Until 2002 the Ukrainian cabinet of ministers was dominated by civil servants, with only a sprinkling of politicians and hardly any businessmen. Oddly, the main economic bodies, the Ministry of Finance, the Ministry of Economy, the central bank, and the State Property Fund, did not house any oligarchs.

Everything changed in November 2002 with the formation of Viktor Yanukovych's government, which brought two important novelties. First, it was a political coalition representing party factions holding a majority in parliament. Second, top figures from the oligarchic groups joined the government personally. The Donetsk group dominated the government with Prime Minister Viktor Yanukovych (formerly the governor of Donetsk oblast), First Deputy Prime Minister and Minister of Finance Mykola Azarov (formerly the longtime head of the State Tax Administration), and Deputy Prime Minister for Energy Andriy Kliuev (a big businessman from Donetsk). Eight other oligarchic groups had also been represented in Kuchma's last government. That government of oligarchs had many strong and forceful personalities, but coordination was nearly impossible. By coming out into the open, the oligarchs exposed themselves and became responsible.

In a nearly lawless country like Ukraine, law enforcement bodies are important. For much of Kuchma's reign, these enforcement bodies had been dominated by three people: Minister of the Interior Yuriy Kravchenko, Security Minister Leonid Derkach, and Mykola Azarov, then the head of the State Tax Administration. All three were often considered oligarchs in their own right, and Kuchma played them against one another as he maneuvered among the oligarchs. Kuchma sacrificed both Kravchenko and Derkach in the aftermath of the Gongadze murder scandal, and Azarov lost control of the tax service to Kravchenko when he joined the government in November 2002. During the last two years of the old regime, the oligarchs appear to have strengthened their role in law enforcement. Medvedchuk played an especially prominent role in the multiple special forces of the Ministry of the Interior. The prosecutor general was usually a part of all political persecution. Yet law enforcement had never been consolidated under unified central control as it was in President Putin's Russia. Each oligarch appears to have had some part of law enforcement working for him, and parts of law enforcement leaked information extensively to the opposition. Strangely, the Security Service of Ukraine (SBU), the former KGB, was perceived as being little involved in oligarchic strife.

The oligarchs mainly played their game at the national level. The regional governors were not all that significant in highly centralized Ukraine, as they were not elected but were appointed by the president. A governor was typically a senior official who had suffered a serious setback in Kyiv. For instance, after Yuriy Kravchenko was sacked as the minister of the interior for seeming to be responsible for the Gongadze murder, he served briefly as the governor of the Kherson region before becoming the head of the State Tax Administration. Admittedly, in Donetsk the regional governor (Yanukovych) was little but a servant of Rinat Akhmetov, and their Regions party won elections overwhelmingly. In Dnipropetrovsk the governor was appointed by President Kuchma and frequently replaced, and several governors seemed independent from both Interpipe and Privat Group, though Labor Ukraine held the region. Although Kyiv was the seat of the Surkis-Medvedchuk group, Surkis humiliatingly failed twice to win mayoral elections in Kyiv.

What Made the Demise of the Oligarchy Possible?

A critical question in the context of this book is to explain how the demise of the oligarchy was possible. Several partial reasons are to be found in the nature of the old regime. The overall explanation is that pluralism and competition had increased both among the elite and in society. We can sum up our observations in seven general conclusions.

First, the chief feature of Ukraine's old regime was that President Kuchma played everybody against everybody else in a duplicitous fashion. His dilemma was that his power was more limited than he desired, and he successfully extended it by acting as an arbiter. As a consequence, state power was not consolidated, and both oligarchs and law enforcement bodies watched one another. This internal division of the regime implied a certain instability. The old elite was too divided to collude successfully.

A second, related characteristic of Kuchma's rule was that, with the rapid structural modernization of the economy, the oligarchic groups became increasingly aggressive in their competition. Privatization promoted not only economic but also political pluralism. Ukrainian businessmen separated their holdings from one another and consolidated their holdings, which became increasingly transparent. With deregulation, businessmen extended their economic freedom from the state. In short, privatization and market reform made businessmen more secure, which emboldened them to protest.

A third feature of the regime was that even its closest supporters were more focused on fighting one another than the opposition. Yanukovych was the candidate of the Donetsk clan rather than of the whole Kuchma regime. Pinchuk made no secret of his low regard for Yanukovych, and his three television channels appeared to be almost neutral until Yushchenko started campaigning for the reprivatization of Kryvorizhstal, the steelworks that Pinchuk and Akhmetov had bought together in a sweetheart deal. Medvedchuk appeared so focused on enhancing his influence over law enforcement that suspicion arose that he was preparing to take over by force. Another suspicion was that Kuchma wanted to have the presidential elections declared null and void to stay in power a bit longer. The leaders of the old regime were all preoccupied with one another and had little time for the opposition. The opposition, on the contrary, was convinced that it was now or never.

A fourth hallmark of the old Ukrainian regime was that various branches of law enforcement were combating one another as well. Repeated leaks of important secret information were one indication.[26] If someone had a problem with one branch of law enforcement, he or she could turn to another branch, as was illustrated by the legal wrangling over the validity of the 2004 presidential elections. Actual repression was limited in its severity, which limited the offender's fear of the authorities. In the end, the SBU tried to spread the impression that it had revolted against the Ministry of the Interior and blocked the use of force.[27]

A fifth characteristic of the Kuchma regime was its disregard for the law. As noted earlier, Ukraine has fairly rudimentary corporate legislation, lacking even an elementary law on joint stock companies. The legal system is in sad shape, and no real judicial reform has been undertaken. Rather than pursue any legal reform, President Kuchma exploited the lawlessness of the old communist system, which allowed him and the staff of his vast presidential administration to call any official and order him or her to make a decision in violation of the law.[28] Kuchma did not satisfy demands from the rising entrepreneurial stratum for a rational legal system.

A sixth feature of the old system was the complex status of property rights. On the one hand, privatization, the separation of properties, and the consolidation of enterprises had given big businessmen enough security to embolden them to show their political muscle. Those dismayed with unjust losses of property went into opposition to recover their losses. A common view in Kyiv was that the Donetsk clan would take over much of the property in the capital if Yanukovych were to win the election. This threat helped to mobilize the Kyiv middle class behind Yushchenko. On the other hand, property rights remained sufficiently weak and contested to prompt businessmen into politics to mitigate such risks. Their two contrary ambitions, to ensure property rights and to seize property, contributed to an extraordinary level of campaign financing.

The seventh and final feature of the old regime was that economic growth had been so high for so long that it was taken for granted. Alexis de Tocqueville pointed out that the French Revolution did not happen when things were getting worse, but when they were getting better.[29] Likewise, the Orange Revolution took place amid an unprecedented economic boom. For five years Ukraine's gross domestic product had risen by an annual average of no less than 9 percent, and it surged by a stunning 12.1 percent in 2004.[30] Although the standard of living increased even faster, with the real wage skyrocketing by 24 percent in 2004, people were dissatisfied.[31] As in de Tocqueville's France, the problem was not the economic efficiency of the old system, but that its injustices had become less tolerable. "Although inequality of taxation prevailed all over Europe, there were few countries in which it had become so flagrant and so much detested as in France." Furthermore, "There was nothing new in these delinquencies on the part of the administration; what was new was the indignation they aroused."[32] High economic growth appears rather to have convinced people of the obsolescence of the political system. A Marxist would say that the economic base had outgrown the political superstructure, and rising prosperity undoubtedly enhanced the self-confidence of the surging middle class.

Two constant features of the old system contributed to the revolution as well. First, Ukraine had had a constitution since 1996, and certain formal rules were perceived as vital: notably, that elections should be

held and that they should be held on time. Official respect for the for-
malities of the elections was the focal point of opposition activity.

Another peculiarity of the old Ukrainian regime was the great political influence of Ukraine's various regions. Most Ukrainian elections have
been characterized by strong tension between east and west. At the time
of independence, westerners held sway, but not for long. Dnipropetrovsk
dominated under prime ministers Kuchma, Lazarenko, and
Pustovoitenko. Donetsk people came to prominence with prime ministers Zviahilskiy and Yanukovych. Admittedly, Yushchenko comes from
Sumy, and Kinakh from Mykolaiv, but neither really represents his region. Ukraine's regional rivalries have not destabilized the Ukrainian
state but rather contributed to its pluralism, as Stephen Sestanovich has
suggested: "Ukraine's very dividedness has turned out to be a crucial
ingredient of its emergent democratic success. . . . The country's divisions give losers a political base that can't be taken away. National disunity guarantees contested elections in practice, but poll results suggest
that Ukrainians have gone further, embracing pluralism as a principle."[33]
The opposition was able to control several of the western provinces even
under Kuchma. Strangely, the country's extreme centralization of state
power has not mitigated this regional rivalry.

The Ukrainian revolution was no surprise. The possibility of a regime change in the presidential elections of 2004 had been intensely
discussed ever since the parliamentary elections in March 2002. Thousands of people had been working for that aim. In August 2004, the
Yanukovych campaign argued intensely that there would be no "Chest-
nut Revolution" or a repetition of the Georgian Rose Revolution in
Ukraine. Nevertheless, the old regime was peacefully defeated in the
scheduled elections. This oversight by the old regime can be explained
not only by the strength and determination of the revolutionaries, but
partly by Kuchma's reluctance to give up his old game, partly by the
hubris of the old regime, and also by the obstacles to collusion among
the competitive Ukrainian elite.

Notes

1. Alexis de Tocqueville, *The Old Regime and the French Revolution* (New York: Doubleday, 1955 [1856]). Valerie Bunce has made a similar argument about the end of communism; see Bunce, *Subversive Institutions: The Design and the Destruction of Socialism and the State* (New York: Cambridge University Press, 1999).
2. See two excellent studies: Chrystia Freeland, *Sale of the Century: Russia's Wild Ride from Communism to Capitalism* (New York: Crown Business, 2000); and David Hoffman, *The Oligarchs* (New York: Public Affairs, 2002).

3. Joel S. Hellman, "Winners Take All: The Politics of Partial Reform in Postcommunist Transitions," *World Politics*, 50 (1998): 203–34.

4. Viktor Tymoshenko, "Vse bogatye lyudi Ukrainy zarabotali svoy kapital na rossiyskom gaze" [All Rich People in Ukraine Made Their Capital on Russian Gas], *Nezavisimaya gazeta*, October 16, 1998.

5. Anders Åslund, "Why Has Ukraine Failed to Achieve Economic Growth?" in Anders Åslund and Georges de Ménil, eds., *Economic Reform in Ukraine: The Unfinished Agenda* (Armonk, New York: M. E. Sharpe), 255–77.

6. Åslund, "Why Has Ukraine Failed?"

7. Robert Kravchuk, *Ukrainian Political Economy: The First Ten Years* (New York: Palgrave MacMillan, 2002), 81.

8. Anders Åslund, "Ukraine's Return to Economic Growth," *Post-Soviet Geography and Economics*, 42 (5) (2001): 313 28.

9. *Economic Statistics*, International Centre for Policy Studies, Kyiv, January 2005.

10. Cf. Diega Gambetta, *The Sicilian Mafia* (Cambridge, Mass.: Harvard University Press, 1993).

11. Half of the 450 seats was allocated through a proportional electoral system with party lists. The other half was won through majority votes in one-man constituencies.

12. Intelligent observers argue that Tyhipko would have been a much better candidate, but I am not aware of any opinion poll recording more support for him than 4 percent, and he had had ample opportunity to boost his public standing.

13. A general source on the biggest businessmen and their holdings is *Investgazeta Top 100*, June 24, 2003.

14. Interview with Rinat Akhmetov, December 8, 2004; Kerstin Zimmer, "The Captured Region: Actors and Institutions in the Ukrainian Donbas," in Melanie Tatur, ed., *Making Regions in Post-Socialist Europe: The Impact of History, Economic Structure, and Institutions—Case Studies from Poland, Hungary, Romania, and Ukraine* (Opladen: Leske & Budrich, 2003); Adrian Karatnycky, "A Ukrainian Magnate Tries to Mend Fences," *Wall Street Journal*, January 14, 2005; and Yevhen Dubohryz, "More-or-Less Civilized," *Kontrakty*, January 17, 2005.

15. Interview with Viktor Pinchuk, March 2003.

16. Interview with Gennady Bogoliubov, March 2003; "Sekrety gruppy 'Privat': Mesta starta kar'ery Tigipko" [Secrets of the Privat Group: The Starting Place of the Career of Tyhipko], *Ukrainska pravda*, August 3, 2004; "Semeniuk suditsya za sobstvennost' Pinchuka, Akhmetova, Privata i Ruslana" [Semeniuk Is Suing for the Property of Pinchuk, Akhmetov, Privat and Ruslan], *Ukrainska pravda*, February 9, 2005.

17. Interview with Serhiy Taruta, December 2004; Zimmer, "The Captured Region"; Dubohryz, "More-or-Less Civilized."

18. Serhiy Leshchenko, "Interview with Petro Poroshenko," *Ukrainska pravda*, January 5, 2005.

19. Interview with a senior member of the Yushchenko campaign, September 2004.

20. "Business Bankrolled Orange Revolution," Agence France-Presse, Kyiv, February 17, 2005.

21. The George W. Bush 2004 campaign is officially assessed to have cost $670 million.

22. "Sekrety gruppy 'Privat'" [Secrets of Privat Group].

23. *Investgazeta Top 100*, June 24, 2003.

24. Yulia Tymoshenko and Petro Symonenko have used this number.

25. Personal information from insiders at the time.

26. At least top Yushchenko aides Oleh Rybachuk and David Zhvanya enjoyed substantial access to covert information from the SBU. Interviews with both. *Ukrainska pravda* has repeatedly published vital leaks from the secret service.

27. C. J. Chivers, "How the SBU Averted a Crackdown in Late November," *New York Times*, January 17, 2005. This version is widely disputed by Ukrainians as successful disinformation from the SBU.

28. De Tocqueville described a similar state of affairs in France before the revolution: "There we have the old regime in a nutshell: rigid rules, but flexibility, not to say laxity, in their application. . . . under the old regime everything was calculated to discourage the law-abiding instinct." *The Old Regime,* 67.

29. Ibid., 176.

30. *Economic Statistics*, International Centre for Policy Studies, April 2005.

31. See chapter three in this book.

32. Ibid., 87 and 178, respectively.

33. Stephen R. Sestanovich, "Ukraine's Democratic Strengths," *Washington Post*, November 19, 2005.

The Fall and Rise of Ukraine's Political Opposition: From Kuchmagate to the Orange Revolution

ADRIAN KARATNYCKY

THE ROOTS OF THE Orange Revolution extend back much further than the year 2004 and Ukraine's turbulent fall and winter. Indeed, Ukraine's broad-based political opposition was many years in the making. Still, it can even be said that—apart from the Communist Party and, to a lesser degree, the Socialist Party—until the late 1990s, nothing resembling consistent opposition operated in Ukraine. A systematic reformist democratic political opposition did not emerge until the close of the year 2000.

From Cooperation to Opposition

Why was there no consistent reform opposition in the early years of Ukraine's independence? In the latter part of the 1980s, under Mikhail Gorbachev's rule, Ukraine, much like the Baltic states and other Soviet republics, saw a proliferation of independent civic groups. The most notable of these was the People's Movement of Ukraine, *Rukh*, which served as an umbrella group for hundreds of local and national civic, cultural, political, and human rights organizations. Established by reformist writers and former political prisoners, Rukh organized mass demonstrations involving tens and even hundreds of thousands of participants in the years 1989–1991. It actively campaigned and helped elect noncommunists and anticommunists to the Ukrainian SSR's Supreme

Soviet. In the legislature, it created a coalition faction, the Democratic bloc, with dissidents from the Communist Party's Democratic platform.

After the breakdown of the USSR, the collapse of the communist system, and the emergence of independent post-Soviet states in the aftermath of the failed August 1991 coup, the unity of Rukh as a civic-political coalition began to erode, and new political parties started to proliferate on the Ukrainian landscape.

Thus, nongovernmental reformist parties—many of them arising from a splintering of Rukh—existed in the early years of independence, but their challenges were primarily focused on elections. They were not consistently articulate beyond short electoral periods. Although both in the 1991 and 1994 presidential elections reform candidates ran for the country's highest office, their candidates never achieved significant support. The high-water mark came in 1991, when Vyacheslav Chornovil of Rukh obtained 23.2 percent of the vote. In the 1994 presidential elections, Oleksandr Moroz (of the then-statist socialists) obtained 13.3 percent, while independent reformer Volodymyr Lanoviy attained 9.5 percent. In 1999, Moroz was again the main opposition force (with 11.3 percent support) in the presidential election won by President Kuchma. Despite a significant presence of reformist legislators in Rukh, the top leadership posts were consistently held by ex-communists, many with a *nomenklatura* past. In the parliamentary electoral process, opposition politics were encumbered by half of the seats being constituency-based, according to the law reform introduced in 1998. These seats were usually won by nominally independent candidates linked primarily to the ruling administrative elite and loyal to the incumbent executive.

In his three years as president, Leonid Kravchuk established the practice of cooperating with noncommunist and anticommunist reformers, as well as placing them in governmental leadership posts. While power was firmly in the hands of Kravchuk's intimates, who were mainly former Communist Party officials, high-ranking posts were also shared with national democratic leaders and reform democrats. For example, Ihor Yukhnovsky served as first deputy prime minister in 1992–1993, while in 1992–1993 Rukh leader Oleksander Lavrynovych was the acting director of the Central Election Commission.

This practice expanded under President Leonid Kuchma (1994–2004). Leaders such as Serhiy Holovaty of the Reform group (which had emerged in large measure from the milieu of Rukh activists) became the justice minister from 1995 to 1997; Yuriy Kostenko (a leader of the Rukh group in parliament) served as environment minister from 1995 to 1998;

and Viktor Pynzenyk (also of the Reform group) was intermittently deputy prime minister for economic affairs from 1995 to 1997.

It is hardly surprising that this phenomenon of "cohabitation" and participation became widespread. After all, reformist political parties were weak and undisciplined. They were sometimes pressed to join the government by Western democracies eager to install reformers in key ministries to ensure momentum for the economic and political reform process. Moreover, the contours of high corruption and criminality associated with President Kuchma's inner circle were largely unknown beyond the realm of suspicion and supposition. The ruling elite had not yet consolidated itself into disciplined financial-political parties, which would then emerge only with the rapid rise of oligarchic groups in the late 1990s. Independent political parties found it difficult to maintain a political *apparat* in the absence of independent private-sector support and with most of their supporters impoverished. In addition, the vast powers of the presidency (which came into effect with the constitutional reforms of 1996) made the head of state the key power broker, limiting the importance of parliament and parties within the legislature.

This constitutional reform also made governorships subject to presidential appointment, eliminating another potential base for independent political patronage and support. Finally, the Kuchma administration skillfully used governmental posts to blunt or diffuse continuing opposition and to co-opt potential political opponents.

If we exclude the communists (who were antireform) and the socialists (who were never participants in the Kuchma leadership), the factors I have listed contributed to the absence of consistent reformist political opposition to incumbent power in the first decade of Ukraine's independence.

Thus, with the exception of the socialists, among today's incumbent "Orange" coalition parties,[1] there is no important political grouping that was not linked to high government service in the Kuchma years. Current top officials who served in high office during those years include President Yushchenko, who was the prime minister under Kuchma; Prime Minister Yulia Tymoshenko, who was the deputy prime minister; First Deputy Prime Minister Anatoiy Kinakh, who is a former prime minister; Deputy Prime Minister Oleh Rybachuk, who was the chief of staff to Prime Minister Yushchenko; Foreign Minister Borys Tarasyuk, who had already served as the foreign minister; and Finance Minister Viktor Pynzenyk, who had repeatedly been the deputy prime minister.

What led the migration of these leaders into open political opposition? What events triggered the creation of the political network of opposition forces that advanced the Orange Revolution?

The emergence of a consolidated opposition took many years and was advanced by multiple factors. The passage of a new constitution in 1996 rendered the presidency an inordinately powerful post, but it also made the president and his inner circle the objects of all negotiation and eventually the focal point of all blame and opposition. With the passage of constitutional reform, all Ukrainians knew that "the buck stopped" in Kuchma's office (usually before making its way to a numbered offshore account).

At the same time, insider privatization, macroeconomic stabilization, and an end to hyperinflation created a new set of political actors: powerful and prosperous oligarchic groups. The increasing influence of these largely regional elites became felt with the arrival to power of Pavlo Lazarenko, the former governor of Dnipropetrovsk. As first deputy prime minister and as prime minister, Lazarenko was widely believed to be involved in the accumulation of vast personal economic wealth, corroborated by evidence presented at his U.S. trial.

Lazarenko's rule aroused growing worries about the role of political-economic groups and their patrimonial links with the government. Those concerns became the natural focus of the disaffection of displaced ministers, who became increasingly critical toward Kuchma. The rise of oligarchic interest groups structured regional, economic, and political interests. While certain groups surged as powerful political insiders, some former political insiders were transformed into political outsiders and unswerving political opponents. As a result of Lazarenko's expulsion from the top leadership, he and his backers (including Yulia Tymoshenko) were transformed into a clear political opposition force against the president. Other officials who were forced out of the government also joined the opposition to the Kuchma administration.

The Years 2001–2002: The Opposition Falters

Before 2000, civic groups, represented by voter-monitoring groups, civic alliances, think tanks, and independent media (chiefly Internet journals and newsweeklies) formed the mainstay of consistent criticism of the Kuchma presidency. Many of them, however, were on the periphery of party political life.

In 2000, the first triggers of persistent antigovernment opposition came with the abduction and murder of opposition investigative journalist

Heorhiy Gongadze. The journalist's disappearance became an international cause célèbre, but it would have led nowhere if not for the defection of Major Mykola Melnychenko and the revelation that he and some cohorts had recorded more than one thousand hours of President Kuchma's private conversations. In those conversations, Kuchma demanded Gongadze's abduction, discussed the criminal harassment of political opponents, engaged in high-level corruption, and revealed himself to be at the center of a criminal and corrupt system of rule.

Protests were launched under the "Ukraine without Kuchma" and "For Truth" banners, representing the two coalitions uniting opposition youth and civic and political organizations. These groups held a series of demonstrations (and later a petition campaign) aimed at pressing for Kuchma's impeachment and removal from office. While students and civic activists were highly active in the effort, the "Ukraine without Kuchma" movement also included leaders and activists from a number of political parties, including the Socialist Party, Yulia Tymoshenko's Batkivshchyna Party, the Rukh Party, and the *Sobor* Party. Key leaders of the Orange Revolution took part in the 2000–2001 protests, including Socialist Party official Yuriy Lutsenko (now Ukraine's interior minister), Taras Stetskiv (who in 2004 served as a coordinator of the Maidan protests), as well as the future leaders of the Pora youth movement, which was established in 2004.

Several leaders of the anti-Kuchma movement of 2000–2001 had earlier cut their organizational teeth on the mass protests of 1990, when students and workers forced the resignation of the Ukrainian SSR's retrograde prime minister, Vitold Fokin. Anti-Kuchma protests crested in the winter of 2000–2001, but crowds in Kyiv never exceeded fifty thousand. On March 9, 2001, with protests ebbing, police suppressed an antigovernment rally and demolished a "camp city" in Kyiv. Most protests had been nonviolent, though agents provocateurs had engaged in violent attacks on the militia.

Yet the consolidation of a broad-based opposition element in 2001 was complicated by a set of complex situational factors. First, the main source of support, the reformist political establishment, represented by then–prime minister Viktor Yushchenko, had adopted a stance of neutrality dictated by its participation in the government. Second, the eruption of violence among the demonstrators had deterred much of Kyiv's and Ukraine's middle class and intelligentsia from comfortably supporting the "radical" opposition. Third, the Kuchma government cowed potential proponents from the business elite from supporting opposition groups through tax harassment and criminal processes—the most

notable being that against former deputy prime minister Yulia
Tymoshenko, who was held in jail in February and March 2001. Fourth,
the Communist Party, an inconsistent and unreliable opponent of the
Kuchma regime, still commanded a fair amount of public support, which
was to erode significantly by 2004.

The failure of the civil opposition was underscored by its inability to
secure high-level support from a broad spectrum of democratic-reform
politicians. This began to change with the dismissal of Viktor
Yushchenko as prime minister in April 2001. By October 2001, with
Yushchenko and his circle of supporters removed from power (though
still ambivalent in their stance toward President Kuchma), opposition
leader Tymoshenko, who had worked successfully alongside
Yushchenko in the government, called for the creation of a broad political alliance that would link her Front for National Salvation, the socialists of Oleksandr Moroz, and Yushchenko's emerging Our Ukraine coalition. Tymoshenko declared, "It is exactly this bloc, according to my
deep conviction, that will claim a victory in [next year's] parliamentary
elections and install in power honest politicians who are able to intro-
duce order in the state. . . . " Otherwise, she warned, there "will be a
parliament controlled by oligarchic, antidemocratic, and antireformist
forces that will continue with the shameful practice of suppressing
people, stealing national wealth, and ruining the independent state."

This idea of coalition politics was broached by Yushchenko himself
in the fall of 2001, but Tymoshenko and other opposition leaders worried that the ex-prime minister was ready to make common cause with
some pro-Kuchma groups.

The 2002 Parliamentary Race: The Opposition Revives

Although the opposition parties campaigned separately, in the March
2002 parliamentary elections, parties and blocs opposing President
Kuchma did well in the proportional party list vote, with Our Ukraine
receiving nearly 33 percent of those seats. The Tymoshenko bloc and
the socialists each won nearly 10 percent of the seats. This vote demonstrated the unified opposition's potential, which was manifest in the
presidential campaign of 2004.

Still, the ruling elite's political bloc, "For a United Ukraine," managed to win the lion's share of the seats apportioned by majority vote in
individual constituencies, where significant falsification occurred. This,
coupled with pressure on independent candidates, led to the creation of

Table 2.1. Composition of Ukraine's Parliament (The Rada)

	Votes on Party Lists (%)	Results for Party Lists (no. seats)	Single-Mandate Districts (no. seats)	Total Seats (March 31, 2002)	Total Seats (January 15, 2004)
Opposition Factions					
Our Ukraine	23.57	70	42	112	102
Communists	19.98	59	6	65	59
Tymoshenko bloc	7.26	22	0	22	19
Socialists	6.87	20	2	22	20
Subtotal				221	200
Pro-Presidential Factions					
For a United Ukraine	11.77	35	86	121 (split after elections)	
Regions of Ukraine (joined by European Choice faction in November 2003)					67
Labor Ukraine					42
Democratic Initiatives					18
People's Power					22
Agrarian Party					14
People's Democratic Party					16
People's Choice					14
(United) Social Democratic Party of Ukraine	6.27	19	8	27	36
Subtotal				148	229
Deputies from other parties and independents			80	80	20
Total in Parliament				449[a]	449[a]

[a]One seat remained vacant.

Official data from www.rada.gov.uka and www.cvk.ukrpack.net. Allegiances and descriptions reflect the state of affairs on the dates indicated. After the Orange Revolution and Yushchenko's election victory, some pro-Kuchma parties dissolved, and many voted for the Yushchenko-nominated government.

a pro-Kuchma majority under parliamentary speaker Volodymyr Lytvyn, the former head of the presidential administration.

After the Our Ukraine bloc failed in its bid to form a parliamentary majority with "moderate centrists" and the forced defection of some of the elected supporters to the Kuchma camp, Yushchenko adopted an increasingly oppositional stance and began to cooperate with the radical opposition represented by the Tymoshenko bloc and the socialists.

This political migration into outright opposition was reinforced by the president's appointment in June 2002 of Social Democratic leader Viktor Medvedchuk as the head of the presidential administration. Under Medvedchuk, the government's control of the media was strengthened. Yushchenko and other political leaders were either taken off the airwaves or became the subject of unrelenting media attacks on national television.

Medvedchuk understood well that Yushchenko had the best chance to be elected as the successor to President Kuchma, but because of their mutual antipathy, Medvedchuk launched an all-out long-term effort to preclude rapprochement between Yushchenko and segments of the ruling elite. Instead, with Kremlin support, he backed the heretofore-obscure governor of the Donetsk oblast, Viktor Yanukovych, an ex-convict who in November 2002 became prime minister and the presidential standard-bearer of the ruling elite. (Some believe that Medvedchuk harbored hopes of a third term for President Kuchma, but there is no question that in the end he threw in his lot with Yanukovych.)

The parliamentary election of March 2002 was a dry run for the Yushchenko presidential campaign of 2004. It reinforced the idea among radical oppositionists and moderate reformers that Yushchenko had broad-based support and enough backing to win the presidency. Yushchenko's personal popularity, reflected in numerous polls throughout 2003–2004, was important in building a widening and cohesive coalition. Discipline within the disparate opposition elements was easier to maintain because the prize of political power seemed to be within reach. This meant that Yushchenko could exert continuing influence over his alliance.

Under increasing pressure and attack from the Kuchma administration, Yushchenko moved toward cooperation with the more radical opposition. Thus he could augment his own base with growing support from new business and financial interests and substantial staffing from the radical anti-Kuchma network. This network included large numbers of opposition civic groups, activists from minor political parties, and organizers of the large antigovernment protests during 2000–2001.

By the summer of 2004, Yushchenko had made a pact with Yulia Tymoshenko, creating the People's Power Coalition. The pact included an agreement, subsequently honored by Yushchenko, to nominate Tymoshenko for prime minister in the event of his victory in the presidential race.

Table 2.2. Percentage of Voter Support for Leading Candidates in Ukraine Elections, 2003–2004

	June 2003	January 2004	April 2004	June 2004
Yushchenko	35.4	33.9	29.1	35.5
Yanukovych	13.8	13.8	21.9	24.0

Source: Democratic Initiatives Foundation/SOCIS Polling Data (available in Ukrainian at www.dif.org.ua).

Note: Following Western practice, I have provided the distribution of votes for the two main rivals among voters who expressed a preference, a practice Democratic Initiatives/SOCIS did not follow. Typically, most polls indicated between 25 percent and 35 percent of the electorate showing no preference among many candidates.

The coalition with Tymoshenko was of crucial importance, for it cemented Yushchenko's credibility with radical oppositionists and grassroots civic activists. The relentless media attacks on Yushchenko by the hated Kuchma media *apparat* reinforced this support, as did, ultimately, the attempt to assassinate Yushchenko (or to knock him off the campaign trail) by poisoning him. In early September 2004, the poisoning had a catalytic effect on civic and political activists.

Minigarchs vs. Oligarchs

Yushchenko launched his election campaign in the summer of 2004 and was determined to base it at the grassroots level. He made full use of his political partner, the charismatic Yulia Tymoshenko, with her help effectively doubling his outreach. The campaign used a distinctive political color, the now-famous orange hue, and a catchy campaign slogan: *"Viryu, Znayu, Mozhemo"* (I believe, I know, We can do it). The slogan created a sense of mission for the election. It suggested idealism ("I believe"), a voter's discernment and access to real information ("I know"), and unbridled confidence ("We can"). Yushchenko's campaign frequently attacked Kuchma and his opponents (especially after the attempt to poison Yushchenko), focusing on their rampant corruption, which, Yushchenko charged, impaired the fair distribution of the bounties of a growing economy. His campaign, however, also advanced a positive agenda of hope and reminded voters of Yushchenko's solid record as prime minister, during which he made up wage arrears, increased pensions, and squeezed the oil and gas barons to enhance the public treasury.

By contrast to Yushchenko's smart opposition campaign, Yanukovych's campaign traded on his status as prime minister and focused on official events that reflected incumbent power. It was redolent of the Soviet past: there were the obligatory factory meetings, staged ribbon cuttings, and the like. While the economy was expanding rapidly, Yanukovych, encouraged by his Russian campaign advisors, placed greater emphasis on the issues of state status for the Russian language and integration with Russia as key themes of his campaign. As though to underscore this connection subliminally, Yanukovych's campaign literature used the white, red, and blue colors of the Russian state flag.

Although the polls showed that many Ukrainians were in favor of closer links with Russia, President Putin damaged Yanukovych's chances by overplaying his hand. The Russian president increased the pace of bilateral meetings with Ukraine's leaders and regularly visited Kyiv and the Crimea. Yet these frequent official appearances in Ukraine served not only to underscore a link between the Kremlin and candidate Yanukovych, but also reminded the public of Yanukovych's close link to the unpopular president Kuchma, who by protocol was present at most of those meetings. A June 2004 poll showed that less than 10 percent of the voters fully trusted the lame-duck incumbent president, while nearly 56 percent did not trust him at all.

Despite a huge disadvantage in media, financing, and administrative resources, plus falsifications, Yushchenko came out on top in the first round of the presidential race by a margin of 39.9 to 39.2 percent— just ahead of Prime Minister Yanukovych—in a crowded field of twenty-four candidates. This, too, helped in the further consolidation of political support and the broadening of the opposition coalition. Financial and economic groups, which emerged as a result of the Yushchenko-inspired boom with an average growth rate in the gross national income of 9 percent since the year 2000, had created a new generation of "minigarchs." They resented rampant corruption in tax administration and government and were angry at the plunder of the country by a narrow group of oligarchic billionaires backing the incumbent power elite and its candidate, Yanukovych. Yushchenko's first-round success also helped set in motion negotiations with other candidates and the further broadening of his coalition. Notably, Yushchenko gained the support of socialist Oleksandr Moroz and the candidate of the Party of Industrialists and Entrepreneurs, ex-prime minister Anatoliy Kinakh.

The process of civic revolutionary consolidation proceeded and widened in the three weeks before the second round of the presidential election. In the aftermath of the electoral fraud of November 21–22, it would reach its apogee. According to independent exit polls, Yushchenko had won the second-round vote by a margin of 10 percent, and the Central Election Commission's unofficial tally showed Yanukovych as the winner by a margin of 49.5 to 46.6 percent. In the end, public anger over mounting evidence of voter fraud led to the Orange Revolution and forced a rerun of the second round. On December 26, the results closely resembled those of the November 21 exit poll. Yushchenko had won by a margin of 52 to 44 percent.

The Orange Revolution, which featured seventeen days of mass rallies in Kyiv and other major cities, succeeded because it benefited from a series of tactical decisions made by the Yushchenko camp. One decision, made in the summer of 2004, was to launch a grassroots campaign of public meetings and mass rallies with the presidential standard-bearer. Yushchenko and many of his political allies crisscrossed Ukraine in an impressive daily regimen of campaign rallies. According to Yushchenko's then-chief of staff, Oleh Rybachuk, Yushchenko typically held four to five meetings a day, one in a major urban center, and several others in neighboring towns and villages. These rallies by the candidate were compounded by the brisk schedule of meetings undertaken by Yushchenko's backers: Yulia Tymoshenko, Borys Tarasyuk, and Yuriy Kostenko, who themselves addressed scores of rallies in July, August, September, and October.

Blocked from the airwaves and from most of the media, the Yushchenko campaign also created its own distribution network of activists, who disseminated campaign literature, including a mass-circulation election newspaper and special expanded editions of independent opposition papers, some of them printed in editions of as many as five to six million copies. Such grassroots activists, who engaged in organizing rallies, disseminating posters, and distributing campaign literature, were also trained to assume the role of election monitors later at tens of thousands of polling stations during the three stages of presidential voting.

Yushchenko further benefited from the significant growth of independent civic life and the emergence of an array of skilled civic organizers, some of whom had honed their skills in previous protest movements. Many of these civic activists had helped organize the "Ukraine without Kuchma" and the "For Truth" movements, including Vladislav Kaskiv and Mykhailo Svystovych, who became key leaders in the two wings of the Pora civic youth movement. Although Pora was organized around civic education and election-monitoring efforts, its activists also had significant contact with Georgian and Serbian (as well as Slovak and Romanian) civic activists and developed organizing and civic action techniques used in those earlier democratic transitions. In the summer of 2004, Pora activists were also trained in organizing techniques and in nonviolent civic protest, such as crowd control and the logistics of organizing mass protests, skills that were intended to be deployed in the event of voter fraud.

The Orange opposition was a mass movement led by a broad-based political umbrella coalition. The People's Power Coalition, founded on the Yushchenko–Tymoshenko alliance, was expanded with the participation of the Party of Industrialists and Entrepreneurs and the Socialist Party. After the regime had sought to falsify the November 21 second-round election results on a grand scale, Yushchenko's People's Power Coalition was strengthened by grassroots structures, financial resources, and the leaders of a wide array of civic groups. These united in the Committee for National Salvation, the umbrella coalition for the Orange Revolution. Cultural figures, mayors and other local officials, militia and military officers, and unions and worker collectives, all flocked to Yushchenko's side, as did the international community.

Although Western financial support had provided training and supported election monitoring, exit polls, and civic-education work, the various components were strictly nonpartisan, and the Yushchenko campaign was financed entirely by Ukrainians. Millions of dollars poured in to fund the establishment of a large tent city, to supply food for the tens of thousands of regular demonstrators, and to provide heat as the temperatures dropped in November and December. Local entrepreneurs fed and housed thousands of demonstrators. The local city administration of Kyiv also loaned its resources to support the popular power movement.

Yushchenko's longtime popularity (as reflected in polling data and in large public rallies) and his significant chance for victory yielded an additional benefit, the desire of many security and military officials to remain neutral in the campaign. Yushchenko's years in government had fostered numerous relationships with security, police, and military officials. These informal contacts became important channels of communication in the period before the election and increased after Yushchenko's poisoning, which some professional security service officials resented as further evidence of the criminalization and degradation of their services.

Segments of the SBU wiretapped the offices of the Central Election Commission and recorded the conversations of high government and presidential administration officials associated with voting fraud. That the Orange coalition was led by seasoned former government officials and prominent business leaders and was supported by many local government officials facilitated splits within the ruling coalition. The Orange coalition could bargain with members of the establishment and count on support from democratically oriented officials.

Western diplomatic pressure and international media attention, cultivated diligently by the opposition as the events in Ukraine became the globe's top international story, were also part of the arsenal of the political opposition. Finally, the opposition was helped by a media revolt against state censorship by journalists at virtually all Ukraine's national television stations. The independent Channel 5 (carried mainly on cable) and ERA television, whose news and commentaries had recently adopted a pro-opposition tone, played crucial roles.

The Orange Revolution: The Opposition Triumphs

All these factors contributed to the peaceful and successful democratic outcome of the Orange Revolution, but the emergence of a broad, unified coalition committed to nonviolent action appears to have had the greatest significance. The unity of the opposition is vital in most successful transitions from authoritarianism to democracy. Equally important is the conscious commitment of civic groups to nonviolent means of struggle and pressure.

When the protests erupted on the morning of November 22 and the Orange Revolution was launched, significant advance preparation had been made for the demonstrations. Support for the mass protests came from domestic Our Ukraine donors, who were mainly the country's emerging upper middle class and new millionaires. Civic forces formed a common front with the political opposition only after it had become clear that the authorities were ready to accept the election fraud and proclaim Viktor Yanukovych the winner of the second round of voting.

Taras Stetskiv, one of the four coordinators of the protests in Independence Square, in a Canadian Broadcasting Corporation documentary, said that he had received approval from the Our Ukraine leadership to organize the infrastructure for postelection protests in the likely event of a voter fraud. That decision, however, came only after Yushchenko's poisoning, which convinced the opposition standard-

bearer that his opponents were ruthless and capable of holding power
by any means necessary. This decision provided access to crucial funds,
which were used to build the infrastructure of the demonstrations, including the stage, sound system, musicians, tent city, canteens, communications equipment, and security.

Another crucial factor was the November 20 decision of a court in
Kyiv's Shevchenko district to turn down the city administration's request to ban the protest rally at Maidan or relocate it to a remoter point.
That last-minute decision, which came on the afternoon before election
day, was vital to the opposition's success. Maidan itself is ideally suited
for a long-lasting winter protest. First, it is within minutes of the parliament, the Council of Ministers building, and the presidential administration, allowing for the rapid deployment of protestors. Beneath Maidan,
a warren of underground passages, walkways, plazas, shops, and cafés
enables protestors to descend to recover from the winter cold. This, as
much as the tent city, which housed tens of thousands of demonstrators, ensured a large, steady public presence in the square throughout
seventeen days of protest.

But the Orange Revolution could not have succeeded without public
opprobrium and civic anger. No matter how much preparation or training there was, no one could guarantee the massive participation of the
people of Kyiv, and later, of much of Ukraine. People were mobilized
by the personal popularity of Yushchenko, their growing awareness of
the criminality and corruption of the incumbent ruling elite, and the
spread of a democratic consciousness that had developed over Ukraine's
thirteen years of independence.

On November 22, the Orange Revolution drifted dangerously away
from constitutionalism when Yushchenko took the oath of office and
declared himself president. Soon after, however, it became clear that
Yushchenko's action had been intended as a means of increasing pressure, and the preferred course was to work through existing constitutional structures. Rada's decision to annul the second round and order a
rerun of the election, together with the legislative framework for new
elections adopted by Rada, was essential in the transformation of a
people's revolution into a constitutional process.

In securing the bargain to hold a repeat of the second-round vote,
Yushchenko and his circle made a grand bargain: the reshaping of constitutional order, with a reduction in presidential power, which is to
take effect no later than January 2006. There are good reasons why this
bargain made sense.

1. A large, supportive parliamentary majority was created through compromise.
2. Ukraine's presidency had been unchecked and far too powerful, and its powers needed to be reduced.
3. Decentralization of the strengthening of local government is critical for long-term democracy and stability.
4. The March 2006 parliamentary elections are likely to result in Rada with a "pro-Orange" majority, and President Yushchenko—acting through his Our Ukraine bloc—will likely play a pivotal role in shaping a majority and in determining both the next, more powerful, prime minister and the next, more powerful parliamentary speaker.

Prospects for Ukraine after the Orange Revolution

In the end, Ukraine's secure transition to democracy will be determined as much by the nature of the opposition to Yushchenko as by the internal political evolution of Our Ukraine and other Orange parties. This is why it is essential that politicians linked to high corruption and electoral falsifications be ostracized from opposition groups and denied a place in Ukraine's politics. What Ukraine above all needs is a "non-Orange" opposition that can be trusted to preserve democratic practices when it eventually comes to power.

What, then, is the likely future of Ukraine and the legacy of the Orange Revolution? A recent study by Freedom House of sixty-seven transitions from authoritarian rule since 1972 may offer an answer.[2] The study found that of the thirty-six "free" countries post-transition, twenty-four (67 percent) had strong civic movements; eight (22 percent) had moderately strong civic movements; and only four (11 percent) had civic movements that were weak or absent in the two-year period before the opening came for transition. By contrast, the distribution of those forces among "partly free" countries was eight (36 percent), "strong"; seven (32 percent), "moderate"; and seven (32 percent), "weak or absent." Among "not free" countries, the distribution was zero, "strong"; three (33 percent), "moderate"; and six (67 percent), "weak or absent."

The study also found that there is a multiplier effect in the combination of a strong civic coalition and a transition environment in which violence is absent. When those two characteristics—namely, transitions that have strong nonviolent civic coalitions and transitions that were themselves nonviolent or mostly nonviolent—were combined, eighteen transition countries satisfied both criteria. In the year before their transitions, zero countries had been rated as free, nine were partly free, and nine were not free. After the transition, seventeen (94 percent) of the countries were free, one was partly free, and there was no not-free country. Transition countries in which the two criteria were present in the two years before the political opening also saw their post-transition score improve from an average of 5.47 to 1.53, a gain of 3.94 points on a seven-point Freedom House scale, which is a dramatically positive effect.

Ukraine's transition was led by a nonviolent broad-based civic-political coalition and occurred in conditions of nonviolence. Thus the evidence of recent history suggests that the course consciously taken by Ukraine's Orange opposition in its march to power was also the optimal course for securing a durable democracy in the long term. This is perhaps the most important legacy of the leaders of the Orange Revolution and its participants.

In the meantime, optimistic prognoses notwithstanding, Ukraine's Orange opposition now confronts the complex and difficult challenges of securing democracy, combating crime and corruption, reinforcing the rule of law, and strengthening economic growth.

Notes

1. The Orange Revolution was steered by the Committee of National Salvation, which comprised a wide array of political parties, civic organizations, and local authorities. After the triumph of the civic nonviolent protests of November and December 2004, newly elected president Yushchenko put in place a coalition government that included the following representative political parties and blocs: the Our Ukraine bloc and its partners: the Reform and Order Party, the Rukh Party, and the Ukrainian National Party; the Yulia Tymoshenko bloc; the Socialist Party; and the Party of Industrialists and Entrepreneurs.
2. See "How Freedom Is Won: From Civic Resistance to Durable Democracy," www.freedomhouse.org.

CHAPTER THREE

Everyday Ukrainians and the Orange Revolution

TARAS KUZIO

IN THE FOUR YEARS leading up to Ukraine's 2004 presidential elections, the country suffered from an acute political crisis that had begun in November 2000 when the Kuchmagate crisis began. It culminated exactly four years later with the Orange Revolution. The crisis was revealed in low trust in state institutions, low popularity for President Leonid Kuchma and high support for his impeachment, a growing gulf between the ruling elite and society, heightened opposition activity in the streets and in parliament, and international isolation. Seventy-two percent of Ukrainians wanted Kuchma to leave office early, and 53 percent supported his impeachment.[1]

This was the backdrop to the events that unfurled in the last two months of 2004. Ukraine's ruling elite had been living in a world separate from society. In that world, they were forced to deal with Ukrainian citizens only periodically, in presidential and parliamentary elections. As they had done in the former Soviet Union, they had been reasonably successful in dealing with the elections in 1998 and 1999 by manipulating them. In 2002, however, they had their first shock when the opposition won control of half of the parliamentary seats. Viktor Yushchenko's Our Ukraine party created the largest faction after the elections, which was the first time the Communists had been pushed into second place.

Mobilizing the opposition was important but insufficient in a country where the regime was prepared to use every means available to prevent Yushchenko's victory. During most of the 2004 election campaign, from July onward, the popular mood was that Yushchenko was likely to win but that the authorities would nevertheless declare their candidate president. During the elections, the portion of those who believed Yushchenko would win grew from 19 to 45 percent, while the portion of those who thought Yanukovych could win declined by 23 percent.[2]

Following the election violations of 2002, only 20 percent of Ukrainians trusted the authorities to hold free and fair elections in 2004, and 58 percent believed that elections would not be free or fair.[3] This view was reinforced by the April 2004 mayoral elections in Mukachevo when the Our Ukraine candidate won, but the authorities' candidate was declared the duly elected mayor. Yushchenko at the time predicted that the election would be a "repetition of that which could take place in October if the Mukachevo question is left without an adequate reaction from [Ukrainian] society and the world." The authorities had "demonstrated all their technologies that they [were] willing to use in the (presidential) election."[4]

This mood gradually changed during the long election campaign because of three factors. First, Yushchenko himself became a radical after he was poisoned in September. The act of poisoning Yushchenko in itself was a sign that the authorities would not let the opposition win. Second, the authorities were forced to concede a narrow Yushchenko victory in round one. This changed the mood to one of "He can do it!" and led to fence sitting by state officials who previously had been ordered to back Viktor Yanukovych. Third, after round one, many voters saw the halting of the election of Yanukovych as of equal importance as the election of Yushchenko.

Polls conducted before election day showed that Ukrainian society was ready to protest in the streets against election fraud. Eighty-four percent of Ukrainians agreed that they had a right to protest publicly in the event of election fraud. Only 6 percent disagreed.

Experts at the Center for Economic and Political Studies of Ukraine, known as the Razumkov Center, cautioned that not all favorable respondents would automatically hit the streets to protest. At the same time, they warned, "It would be naïve to hope that the authorities could without limit discredit themselves in the eyes of their own population without an outcome that could turn out to be fatal to themselves."[5]

Another poll conducted by the Democratic Initiatives Foundation and the Sotsis Institute found that 18.1 percent of Ukrainians were ready to take part in protests against election fraud, as opposed to believing they had a right to do so, as in the Razumkov Center poll. Some 10.6 percent would strongly protest if their candidate did not win the election.[6]

The Ukrainian authorities warned against such "revolutionary'" activities while repeatedly dismissing the notion that Ukrainians would follow Georgia's 2003 revolution. Statements by the security forces, Yanukovych, and Kuchma all denounced plans for protests. Kuchma badly misjudged the popular mood when he categorically said on state Channel 1 television, on the eve of round two, that there would be no revolution in Ukraine. "The authorities will never allow an aggressive minority to dictate political logic," Kuchma reiterated, since revolutions are carried out by fanatics and that "it is scoundrels who reap the benefits."[7] Unless Kuchma was aware of upcoming plans for election fraud, it is unclear how he knew that the opposition would lose the election, thereby becoming the minority, since Yushchenko had, after all, won round one.

The opposition hoped to draw upon one hundred thousand supporters as crowds approaching this size had been mobilized in the campaign, but they knew they needed far more people to be successful in blocking election fraud. Ultimately, both sides miscalculated the popular mood; the authorities' arrogance and belittling of the *narod*—the people—as passive subjects proved to be as wrong as the opposition's underestimation of the deep changes that had taken place in Ukrainian society since 1991, coupled with a profound desire to be treated by their rulers as human beings, that is, as European citizens.

In this chapter, I consider society's views, interactions with, and participation in the Orange Revolution from six perspectives. In the first section I survey the important role of the four-year political crisis as a precursor to and facilitator of the revolution. Next, I discuss how the Orange Revolution differs from those in Serbia and Georgia in that Ukraine had a functioning state and a strong economy. Economic issues in themselves did not play a significant role in the elections. Nevertheless, issues indirectly related to economics, such as popularly perceived unjust privatization, the rise of the oligarchs, and corruption each played a role.

Other factors include the yawning gulf between the ruling elite and the population, with the authorities living in a separate world, and the youth, who constituted most of the participants in the Orange

Revolution, playing a crucial part in the elections. Many young people were politicized and mobilized during the Kuchmagate crisis preceding the 2004 elections. Below I discuss the key personalities in the elections and the mistake the authorities made in choosing Yanukovych as their candidate. Finally, I look at why the Yushchenko camp was far more successful in mobilizing civil society during the Orange Revolution than his opponent, Yanukovych, was.

Political Crisis as a Prequel

Without a four-year political crisis,[8] it is doubtful that there would have been a Yushchenko victory in either the 2002 or 2004 elections. Kuchmagate began in November 2000 and ended exactly four years later during the Orange Revolution. Yuriy Lutsenko, a "Ukraine without Kuchma" and Orange Revolution activist as well as interior minister explained during the repeat vote of round two that a "Ukraine without Kuchma" was now over.[9]

The crisis generated an internal revolution among Ukrainians, as anti-Kuchma protestor and youth activist Volodymyr Chemerys described the situation that evolved during the Kuchmagate crisis. Kuchma continued to remain in power but in the minds of Ukrainians, psychologically, he had already left office.

The authorities ignored the people, who reciprocated by ignoring the *vlada* (the authorities). This internal revolution was crucial in bringing out the large numbers of Ukrainians in the Orange Revolution who otherwise would have continued to adhere to the proverb "It's not my business." During and after round two of the election, many hitherto apolitical Ukrainians joined the Yushchenko camp and the Orange Revolution. The 2004 Eurovision song winner, "Ruslana," the Klitschko boxer brothers, and rock bands such as Okean Yelzy are evidence of this change in attitude.

The crisis also stirred young people from their traditional political apathy in Ukraine and the Commonwealth of Independent States (CIS). Young activists formed the backbone of the activity of nongovernmental organizations (NGOs) in civil society against corruption (*Chysta ukraina* [Clean Ukraine]), in election monitoring (*Znayu!*), and in radical political activity (Pora) groups. Pora received training and advice from Serbia's *Otpor* and Georgia's *Kmara* youth activist groups.[10] The anti-Kuchma protests of 2000–2003 and the 2002 elections were formative for these young activists. Although ostensibly politically neutral the youth tended to sympathize with Yushchenko. Calls for free and fair elections were in Yushchenko's interest as they would automatically benefit him over Yanukovych.

Economy, Corruption, and Oligarchs

Economic issues as such did not play a major role in the 2004 elections; if they had, Yanukovych may have won. Ukraine was different from both Serbia and Georgia in that it had a strong state and a rapidly growing economy, with the highest growth rate in Europe in 2004. Issues related to economics, such as popular perceptions of unjust privatizations and the rise of Ukraine's oligarch class, did play a role because voters looked at the elections as a referendum on the previous decade, not from the short-term perspective of how good the economy was during the elections.

As Michael McFaul points out in the conclusion, the body of literature on democratization stresses how economic crises inevitably lead to general crisis in a regime and the ouster of the ruling elite. The CIS proved to be different from this norm. Since 1989 all CIS (except in Moldova and Belarus) had suffered an acute economic depression, yet it did not lead to counterrevolutions and a return of Soviet and neo-Soviet groups to power. Ukraine proved to be different because an acute political crisis had dominated Ukrainian politics since the fall of 2000. In addition, economic growth was not being felt by the population but was still being largely squandered through growing levels of corruption. From 1994 to 2002, the largest influence on society had consistently been the mafia and organized crime, up from 34 to 38 percent.[11]

Of Ukrainians, 77–85 percent wanted change and did not back a continuation of the status quo.[12] On the eve of the 2004 elections, 55.7 percent of Ukrainians did not believe that Ukraine was moving in the right direction.[13] In Ukraine at that time, it would have been unrealistic for any incumbent to argue in support of his or her anointed successor continuing the status quo since most Ukrainians looked negatively at the 1990s as a decade of the "primitive accumulation of capital" ("bandit capitalism"). Ukrainians wanted change. The question was, what kind of change? Change in Ukraine had been associated *primarily* with Yushchenko and not with Yanukovych.[14] Yushchenko's campaign was premised on his being in opposition to the "bandit regime," while Prime Minister Yanukovych defended his government's record and called for the continuation of the "successful" policies undertaken to date by him and Kuchma. Yanukovych attempted to distance himself quietly from Kuchma and to present himself as a change candidate, but the fact that he was Kuchma's chosen successor dogged him throughout rounds one and two. It was only in round three, when Yanukovych felt betrayed by the Kyiv elite for not having followed through on the plan to install him as president, that he attempted to change himself into an opposition candidate. By then, however, it proved to be too late. He could not change his image to that of an oppositionist in the repeat of the second round on December 26. Indeed, as Yushchenko pointed out, how could a prime minister be in opposition?

Kuchma praised the laying of the foundation for a national economy as his achievement, something he reiterated when he was first elected in 1994. Ukraine had been on the verge of disaster and possible disintegration in 1993, which had been a year of hyperinflation. Kuchma also praised the economic growth of the previous four years as laying the basis for Prime Minister Yanukovych's election program.

These claims ignored a vital factor in public perceptions of socioeconomic conditions in Ukraine. Ukraine returned to economic growth under Yushchenko in 2000–2001. Polls showed that, of Ukraine's ten prime ministers since 1991, he was regarded as Ukraine's most successful. Yushchenko was given credit for relaunching economic growth and for repaying wage and pension arrears.

The same was not true of Yanukovych's government. Populist attempts to win votes by increasing pensions and student stipends on the eve of election day largely backfired as polls showed that most Ukrainian voters understood the move to be an election tactic. Communist voters, who are largely pensioners, would have defected to Yanukovych even without any pension hike. The Yanukovych election campaign frequently complained that voters were *not* giving them credit for Ukraine's economic boom. In 2002, 81 percent of Ukrainians *perceived* that their standard of living had declined since 1990.[15] A year later, 86 percent still believed that the economic situation was very bad or bad, with only 9 percent stating it was good. Record economic growth was not denting this decade-long perception of a poor economic situation.[16]

The attempt to attract support for Yanukovych based on credit for high economic growth proved insufficient to attract Ukrainian voters. Although Ukraine's economy had Europe's highest growth rate in 2004, it failed to improve the popularity of the authorities significantly. The majority of Ukrainian voters did not believe that Ukraine was heading along the right path, a result of the large gulf between declared

Table 3.1. Percentage of Economic Growth Rates in Ukraine, 2000–2004

Year	2000	2001	2002	2003	2004
GDP growth	5.9	9.2	5.2	9.4	12.1

Source: International Centre for Policy Studies, *Economic Statistics,* June 2005.

objectives and reality. Ukrainians did not feel that high economic growth had translated into a higher standard of living. Positive changes, such as economic growth, had occurred despite government policies, not because of them. Ukraine's public mood was one of not being thankful to the authorities while at the same time expecting nothing. Public perception of the authorities as incompetent, corrupt, and uninterested in the plight of the average citizen was widespread, leading to a lack of faith and trust in the government.

In 2002, 73 percent of Ukrainians feared unemployment, 71 percent feared a rise in prices, 65 percent feared the nonpayment of wages, and 51 percent worried about famine.[17] The parliamentary ombudsman for human rights estimated that 5.7 million Ukrainians had been forced to seek work abroad. In addition, the Ukrainian population had shrunk by 5 million, a demographic disaster following 7 million deaths in the 1933 artificial famine (Stalin's campaign of mass starvation) and 6 million in World War II.

The huge social consequences of the past decade's transition were felt by most Ukrainians, most of whom had family members working abroad or who had emigrated. Opinion polls on the eve of the elections showed that a third of young Ukrainians were ready to leave Ukraine, an exodus that would have taken place in the event of a Yanukovych victory. Ukrainians constituted, along with Russians, Indians, and Afghans, one of the four national groups that made up the greatest number of migrants in the world. Between 2002 and 2004, one-third of Ukrainians wanted to emigrate.

Long-term trends associated with the 1990s also proved problematic for the authorities. Two areas that were important in shaping social attitudes in an election year were the growth of oligarchs and widespread, high-level corruption. Privatization was publicly believed to have benefited only a small group of former Soviet *nomenklatura* who were accountable to no one.

Parliamentary speaker Volodymyr Lytvyn told a congress of his Agrarian Party, which officially backed Yanukovych but in reality sat

on the fence, that "Ukraine is close to becoming a totally corrupt country ruled by oligarchs and party-clan groups."[18] Most Ukrainians believed that the "mafia and organized crime world" was the most influential group in society.

In Yanukovych's first speech as a candidate he also, like Lytvyn, denounced the lack of impact of countless decrees and programs to fight
corruption in Ukraine. As a candidate, Yanukovych had little choice but
to condemn corruption, but that did not mean that most Ukrainians
believed he would do anything about the problem were he to be elected.

The ruling elite had already suffered from an identity crisis common
to all oligarchs in the CIS who had emerged in the 1990s. Ukrainians
perceived the accumulated wealth of oligarchs as illegitimate, taken at
the expense of the people and the state. The authorities praised the rise
of a "pragmatic and patriotic" "national bourgeoisie" that had allegedly come to realize that the era of "wild capitalism" was over with the
end of the Kuchma era.[19] They therefore unsuccessfully attempted to
project the view that a Yanukovych victory would *not* mean a return to
the 1990s and would instead signal the emergence of a new elite conscious of its duty to the citizens and the state.

This promise would have been readily accepted by society if the authorities' candidate had been Serhiy Tyhipko, Lytvyn, or even Viktor
Pinchuk, who had sought to gentrify himself and divorce politics and
business. Yet the promise did not wash with Yanukovych. Despite his
criminal background, Yanukovych was chosen because he had proved
his loyalty to Kuchma in the 2002 elections when he, as the governor of
Donetsk, had ensured the For a United Ukraine bloc came first with
37 percent, the only oblast where it did so. Yanukovych had also become the candidate by default because other centrists (that is,
Medvedchuk, Lytvyn, and Tyhipko) and Kuchma himself—whom the
constitutional court had permitted to run in the 2004 elections, claiming
that his first term did not count because it had begun before the 1996
constitution was adopted—all had very low ratings in opinion polls of
less than 5 percent.

Yanukovych could not win using positive arguments about his candidacy. He was hampered by being associated with Kuchma, and he
failed to convince most voters that he should be given credit for economic growth. This left the Yanukovych campaign and its Russian political advisors with little option but to rely on a large volume of negative media attacks against Yushchenko as a "Nazi," a "nationalist," and
an "American puppet." Much of this anti-American and antinationalist

propaganda resembled Soviet-era denunciations against "bourgeois nationalism" that had targeted Ukrainian diaspora and dissident groups. The vilification of Yushchenko undoubtedly dented his support in eastern Ukraine by making him a negative "other" candidate for "Russophones" and communist voters. Many of Yanukovych's voters joined him in the last few months of the campaign, convinced by such campaign rhetoric.

Such anti-Yushchenko propaganda undoubtedly affected Communist and Regions of Ukraine voters most, both of whom are heavily concentrated in the Donbas (Donetsk and Luhansk oblasts) and the Crimea. Yushchenko's Our Ukraine had failed to cross the 4 percent threshold in the 2002 elections in Donbas and Sevastopol. Most of the 20 percent Communist vote obtained in the 2002 elections went to Yanukovych early in round one of the elections, as seen in Communist leader Petro Symonenko, who came in fourth, with only 4.5 percent. In round two and the repeat vote, the communists had refused to endorse either of the two candidates officially. Nevertheless, all of this traditional 20 percent Communist vote probably went for Yanukovych, accounting for half of the votes for him.

Razumkov Center analysts ruled out the view that oligarchs could support the rule of law, civil society, European values, or democratization. "Oligarchs, by their very nature, are incompatible with democratization and are not influenced by societal interests," they argued. Their sole purpose was to enrich themselves with the assistance of the state. It would be naïve, policy makers polled by the Razumkov Center concluded, to believe that Ukraine's oligarchs supported transition to democratic rule after they had arrived at the conclusion that bandit capitalism was now over.

The Ruling Elite in Its Separate Reality

By the 2004 elections, Ukraine's ruling elite was out of touch with reality. Seventy percent of Ukrainians felt they had no influence on the authorities, and 92 percent felt that their human rights were regularly being infringed. During the elections 10 percent of Yushchenko voters were afraid of revealing their preferences, compared with only 2 percent of Yanukovych voters. In some regions of Ukraine, 70 percent were afraid to answer opinion polls.[20] The majority of Ukrainians lived a life separate from those of their rulers. Kyiv Mohyla political scientist Rostyslav Pawlenko found that "citizens have the role of statistics—[being] either listening consumers of manipulated programs or being inundated with *kompromat,* or brazen lies."[21]

After Medvedchuk became the head of the presidential administration, alternative channels of information to Kuchma were blocked. Kuchma's official statements, interviews, and speeches during the six-month election campaign, where he repeatedly "guaranteed" free elections and condemned attempts at inciting interregional splits, were those of someone who was cut off from the daily reality of the dirty tactics that were being used by *his* side. As the Yushchenko camp argued and Ukrainian voters felt, it was as though the Ukrainian constitution had been suspended during the elections.

Living in a separate reality removed from the lives of ordinary citizens led to erroneous policy decisions. Ukraine's ruling elite severely misjudged the mood of society. It repeatedly ruled out a Georgian-style revolution, claiming that Ukrainians were not Georgians because they are more passive, less hot-headed, and willing to accept fate. This national character was nicely summed up in the proverb *Moja khata z kraju* (literally "My house is on the side" but really meaning "It's not my business"). These views of passive Ukrainians by the ruling elite were compounded by three other factors.

The first factor was a Soviet-style disrespect for Ukrainians as subjects who were easily molded to the whims of the authorities. This view may have been held in the Donetsk region, which is dominated by one party (the Regions Party), one oligarch (Rinat Akhmetov), and one television station (TRK Ukraina). It was not true of the remainder of the country. Orange Revolutionary songs repeatedly condemned the authorities' view of the Ukrainian public as *bydlo* (scum) or *kozly* (bastards), the latter term being from Yanukovych's depiction of his opponents.[22] The Orange Revolution's hip-hop anthem by the Ivano-Frankivsk band *Hrandzoly* (Sleigh), which was Ukraine's entry in the 2005 Eurovision song competition in Kyiv, stated categorically that "We are not *bydlo!* We are not *kozly!* We are Ukraine's sons and daughters!" The Orange Revolution demanded that the authorities treat Ukrainians as citizens—not as *bydlo* or *kozly*—whereby the state would serve citizens, as in Europe, and not as subjects serving the state (as in the CIS and former USSR).

Second was the arrogance of the elite, which was tied to its contempt for the people. Former President Leonid Kravchuk believed that "the population will believe every line they are being fed."[23] Presumably, this would also apply to the regime enforcing a falsified result that elected

Yanukovych as president. Ukraine's ruling elite never envisaged that they could ever lose the elections. The shock of facing an Orange Revolution, votes by parliament and Rada denouncing the second round, and a likely Yushchenko victory in the repeat vote on December 26 led to the disintegration of the centrist camp. Parties in power, by their very nature, are not able to become the opposition.

The third factor was contempt for the opposition's ability to put people in the streets. The "Ukraine without Kuchma!" and "Arise, Ukraine!" protests of 2000–2003 attracted twenty to fifty thousand participants. Such numbers were insufficient to remove Kuchma from power and would have been even less sufficient to facilitate a revolution. Kuchma ridiculed the opposition's prediction that they would put two hundred thousand protestors in the streets. His ridicule backfired after round two when the crowds peaked at one million.

Kuchma's contempt for the opposition, the arrogance of the elite, and his disrespect for the people led to the government's biggest blunder: a lack of planning to block the movement of the protestors in the two days immediately following round two of the elections (November 22–23), when the Orange Revolution could have, ostensibly, been nipped in the bud. Instead, Kyiv's residents and hard-core activists took to the streets on Monday (November 22). Beginning on Tuesday, November 23, they were joined by others from the provinces, particularly by western Ukrainians.

Kuchma was also praised by his allies for his role in state building, including the adoption of Ukraine's 1996 constitution. What this praise failed to acknowledge, however, was that Ukraine's semipresidential constitutional system had been parliament's compromise. Kuchma's 1996 draft of the constitution, which he threatened to put to a referendum, would have created a "superpresidential system." It also ignored the disastrous public view of state institutions. After all, what would have been the point of the emergence of such institutions if they had no public support?

By the 2004 elections, trust in state institutions was low. In fact, the public's trust in state institutions was lower than for astrologers, according to a survey by the Academy of Science's Institute of Sociology.[24] Sixteen percent of Ukrainians trusted astrologers, while only 13 percent trusted the president. Fifty-five percent of Ukrainians said they would never vote for Kuchma, and a higher number said they would like to see him impeached. By the eve of the 2004 elections, the authorities were not trusted, not respected, not believed, lacked legitimacy, and lived separate lives from the lives from the people.

The Energy of Youth

Young Ukrainians born in the 1980s grew up in the 1990s. They are not afraid of the authorities in the same manner as their elders, who experienced Soviet rule. They look westward, not northeast, for culture, music, fashion, and intellectual inspiration. They have traveled as tourists, illegal workers, and with student exchange programs to the West rather than to the CIS. Ideologically, they want Ukraine to be part of Europe.

The Kuchmagate crisis stirred young people to move from political apathy to political activism. The threat of Yanukovych coming to power, which would have undermined their vision of Ukraine's European future, sparked them into putting all their energy into election activity and into the Orange Revolution, where they represented upward of two-thirds of the participants.

The caricaturing of Yanukovych did much to undermine his popularity among young Ukrainians, who were involved in civil society, election projects, and radical youth groups.

The youths were also able to take advantage of modern communication methods to a far greater extent than were other segments of Ukrainian society. The Yanukovych camp failed to appreciate the importance of Western public opinion, publishing only one op-ed piece in *Wall Street Journal Europe*, compared with numerous submissions by Yushchenko.

Large television screens were used on the Maidan to broadcast to large crowds what was being said by speakers on stage, as well as important news from Channel 5. The impact of those broadcasts on Channel 5's popularity was huge. During the Orange Revolution, its ratings increased from very low (owing to its being a cable channel that was not permitted to broadcast in some regions, such as Donetsk) to third place.

In Ukraine young people were experts with cell phones, which were extensively used. Some cell phones also have video cameras, which were used by students to video unsuspecting professors illegally agitating for Yanukovych during class.

Young people were also expert in using the power of the Internet to communicate with one another and as an information source.[25] Internet usage had grown since 2000 in Ukraine and had especially come into its own in the 2002 and 2004 elections.[26] The authorities had never appreciated the power of the Internet and had never been able to compete in Internet publications. The Internet provided an alternative to state and private television stations, which were hostile to the opposition. Sixty-eight percent of Ukrainians believed there was political censorship in

Ukraine, particularly on television, which was trusted by only 21 percent of the people.[27]

The threat to the authorities from young people could be seen on the eve of the first round of elections when they accused NGOs of being terrorists after the authorities clumsily planted explosives in NGO offices. A similar tactic was used in Serbia in the 2000 elections against Otpor. In both cases the accusations backfired. Neither the Serbian nor the Ukrainian public believed the authorities when they accused "young kids" of being terrorists. Security service officers privately communicated to NGO leaders that the operation had nothing to do with them but was one ordered by the executive office and implemented by the interior ministry. These accusations of terrorism simply increased public attention upon the NGOs and led to an influx of new volunteers.[28]

Personalities and Humor

For the success of the Orange Revolution to be achieved, two types of candidates were needed to face each other in the second round. The choice between Yushchenko and Yanukovych in round two was for many Ukrainians a stark choice of good versus evil.[29]

A "clean," charismatic candidate is an asset for the opposition because he or she can take the high moral ground. Viktor Yushchenko fit that requirement perfectly. He did not have a corrupt background, and he had served as a successful chair of Ukraine's central bank and as prime minister.

Yushchenko's opponent ideally should be someone whom the opposition would find it easy to mobilize against. Yanukovych fit the bill perfectly because of his criminal record (of two sentences), his origins in Ukraine's most criminalized region (Donetsk), and the widespread perception that he was intellectually challenged.[30]

Yanukovych's criminal record damaged his support in the security forces. Military, interior ministry, and security service officers found it incredible that their next president and commander-in-chief could be an ex-convict. This undermining of support may have been a contributing factor in the security forces either defecting or staying neutral during the 2004 elections and Orange Revolution. The security service disliked Yanukovych as a candidate and illicitly taped his unofficial (dirty tricks) campaign headquarters.[31] The audio tapes were handed to the Yushchenko camp after round two.

Young people were particularly good at turning Yanukovych's flaws into humor. On weekends, Kyiv's main thoroughfare, Khreshchatyk, is closed to traffic, making it an ideal location for election campaigning. Young Pora! and Znayu! activists dressed in prison uniforms and campaigned on behalf of Yanukovych. They became a regular tourist spectacle attracting Kyivites and tourists alike, who were encouraged to believe that prisoners had been let out for the weekend to campaign for one of their own. On occasion, they "campaigned" next to the official Yanukovych election bus.

This humorous image spread. A cartoon printed for the repeat election in the mass-circulation newspaper *Silski visti* (December 23, 2004), a newspaper sympathetic to the Socialist Party, showed two prison guards talking to each other outside an empty prison cell. One asks the other, "Where are the brothers [as in criminal brotherhood]?" The fellow officer replied, "Don't worry. They will soon return. They have just gone out to campaign for their own . . ." (namely, Yanukovych). Another commonly heard anecdote asked why relations in prison had improved recently. The answer: because each prisoner is concerned that his or her neighbor could be the next president.

The idea of Yanukovych being intellectually challenged led to the emergence of an entire subculture in the opposition campaign. With educated Ukrainians, students, and intellectuals tending to favor Yushchenko over Yanukovych, it is not surprising that Yanukovych became the butt of jokes. Mikhail Brodsky and Yulia Tymoshenko have now admitted that they were behind many of those jokes.[32] On the eve of the repeat vote of round two, a book of *Yanukdote* (anecdotes about Yanukovych) was published in Kyiv.[33]

This humorous subculture took off in September 2004 after Yanukovych's visit to Ivano-Frankivsk. During the visit he was hit by an egg thrown by a student. He looked at the egg and then fell over, apparently in agony. The entire episode was broadcast by opposition channels, which undermined the government's claim that Yanukovych had, in fact, been hit by a brick. This attempt to draw publicity away from the poisoning of Yushchenko earlier in the month backfired completely.

Television, and then the Internet, began to ridicule the event: how could the large, tough-looking Yanukovych be knocked over by a small egg? Websites began to appear that included a rapidly growing number of egg jokes. There were series of egg cartoons, including "Merry Eggs"(*Veseli yaytsa*), in which two funny eggs sing songs and joke.

Yanukovych's intellectual ability was also ridiculed because of his frequent use of criminal slang and his illiteracy. Numerous spelling and grammatical mistakes were found in his candidate-registration documents. One particular mistake (signing his name "Proffessor") came to haunt him throughout the elections. A thirteen-episode Internet film ("Operation ProFFessor") was produced. It comprised excerpts of popular Soviet comedies performed by impersonators of well-known politicians dubbing the voices of the characters. The series was a massive hit.[34]

Yanukovych's wife received the same treatment. During the separatist congress held on November 28 after round two, she accused the organizers of the Yushchenko tent city of distributing oranges injected with narcotics to force protestors to stay there. She also claimed that *valenki* (knee-high winter boots) had been sent free of charge from the United States, a hint that the CIA was behind the Orange Revolution. Satirical songs immediately appeared that poured ridicule on these claims by interlacing her comments with other words. The tent city began to hang up *valenki* with the words "Made in USA" scrawled on them.

As a successor candidate, Yanukovych's bid for election carried with it baggage from a decade of Kuchma in office and three years of the Kuchmagate crisis. As Yushchenko pointed out, and as his supporters undoubtedly believed, Yanukovych represented both a continuation and an entrenchment of the status quo as "Kuchma-3."

As parliamentary speaker and head of the People's Agrarian Party Lytvyn pointed out, it might have been better if Yanukovych were a self-declared candidate rather than the government's candidate as Kuchma-3.[35] The authorities had very low popularity ratings, and any association with Kuchma would negatively influence a candidate's ratings.[36]

Great hostility toward the authorities made it impossible for Communist Party leader Petro Symonenko to advise his voters to back Yanukovych in round two. By election day, after months of an incessant media barrage against Yushchenko depicting him as a fascist and American stooge, the majority of Communist voters voted for Yanukovych (which was really a vote against Yushchenko) in round one, putting Symonenko in fourth position. This factor, together with Socialist Party leader Moroz's backing for Yushchenko in round two, provided Yanukovych with no additional left-wing support to draw upon in the second round, placing him at a disadvantage compared with Kuchma in 1994, who drew on left-wing votes.

In that round, voters of the left and the right who did not like the government had an easy choice: to vote for the authorities (Yanukovych) or a candidate opposed to the government (Yushchenko). It is that factor that made the 2004 elections different from those in 1994 (which was a choice between two branches of the party of power, Kravchuk and Kuchma) and 1999 (Kuchma versus the Communists).

Public hostility to the oligarchs was high, and Yushchenko capitalized on that hostility. A Razumkov Center poll found that 67 percent of Ukrainians supported moves against the oligarchs.[37] It is little wonder that Ukraine's oligarchs hid from the limelight. Only Medvedchuk played a prominent public role as the head of the presidential administration, a position that had a detrimental effect upon his own image and upon that of the (United) Social Democratic Party that he leads. Yanukovych was able to conceal some of his oligarch background because he was the "front man" as head of the Regions Party for the real power behind the Donetsk clan, Ukraine's wealthiest oligarch, Rinat Akhmetov.

Some members of the centrist camp understood these social views and acted accordingly. Although their political parties officially backed Yanukovych's candidacy, in reality they sat on the fence and ignored how their members backed Yushchenko. Typical of these fence-sitters was Lytvyn, who warned that tensions were high on this issue: "Sooner or later Ukraine will arrive at the idea of an anti-oligarch coup. Better it was done as soon as possible without revolution [or] tension and in a civilized manner."[38]

The views of Ukraine's leading policy makers were highly negative about Yanukovych. Many of them are based in Kyiv, where Yanukovych failed to win many votes in any of the three rounds of elections. Yanukovych was seen as the candidate least likely to spread European values, according to a Razumkov Center poll.[39] Ukraine's elite policy makers saw Moroz and Yushchenko as being the only two leading candidates who would, if elected, promote European values.

Suspicion was raised by the fact that Yanukovych's project for Ukraine too closely resembled the "managed democracy" model found throughout the CIS. With half of his voters coming from the Communist Party, their support was premised on the need to block the election of the "nationalist" Yushchenko. For them, Yanukovych's criminal record and links to corrupt oligarchs did not override the fact he was the lesser of two evils since any of his faults were outweighed by Yushchenko not being a valid alternative. Such negative voting was magnified by Donbas voters, who both wanted to block (as did Communist voters) a Yushchenko victory and to support their local boy.

This view of Yanukovych's authoritarian instincts was reinforced by Russia's massive intervention in support of Yanukovych and President Putin's two strategically timed visits in rounds one and two of the elections to back Yanukovych publicly. Yanukovych's speeches and election program stressed economic growth and higher standards of living but were conspicuously silent on democratization. His inaugural election speech in Zaporizhzhia completely ignored the issue.[40] Yanukovych's program seemed to confirm the CIS managed democracy model of an economically liberal but politically authoritarian state. A common refrain at the time in Kyiv was, "At least if Yushchenko wins, I know there will be another election."

The managed democracy model was at odds with Ukrainian voters, 75 percent of whom desired greater democratization.[41] Fifty-nine percent did not believe that Ukraine was a democracy, with only 16 percent agreeing to this proposition.[42] These high levels of support for democratization were undoubtedly influenced by the deep political crisis that dominated most of Kuchma's second term.

The Razumkov Center poll asked which candidates were imbued with high morals and standards. One of the issues that this referred to was whether candidates would defend society and Ukraine's national interests above those of their own clans. Moroz, followed by Yushchenko, came at the top of the list in terms of placing society and Ukraine's interests first. When people were asked which candidates were professional and had a good intellect, Yushchenko came first, followed by Moroz. Unlike Yanukovych, Yushchenko was seen as intellectually astute. Yanukovych and Yushchenko were also contrasted by their hobbies, with the former a fan of hunting and the latter interested in more cultured pastimes, such as collecting art, woodcarving, and beekeeping. In the Razumkov Center poll, Yanukovych came at the bottom of both lists of which candidates were imbued with high morals and a good intellect.

If Yanukovych were elected, especially in the manner undertaken in round two, through massive fraud, it would be catastrophic for Ukraine, argued Mikhail Brodsky, the leader of the Yabluko Party. It could lead to "the threat of a criminal-bandit revolt."[43] For many Ukrainian voters it was as important for Yanukovych not to be allowed to win as it was for Yushchenko to win. The popular song "Spovid" (Confession) interlaced Yanukovych's words from different speeches so that he admitted to being crooked. The song began with the words, "I am the most criminal, honest citizen." The song ends with the words of the song's composers advising listeners: "Ukrainians, now make your choice" (that is, after listening to Yanukovych's alleged confession).

What would happen in the event of a victory by Yanukovych? Ukraine's policy makers believed that the status quo would be conserved, that morality would sink lower, and Yanukovych would favor the Donetsk clan. Only the left or right opposition candidates would provide change, which the overwhelming majority of Ukrainians desired.

How was change understood? Although on the whole change was associated with Yushchenko, not all those who desired change voted for him. Some Ukrainian voters for Yanukovych would have preferred the status quo (oligarchs), while others voted against Yushchenko (the communists, who accounted for half of the Yanukovych vote). But a small minority were seemingly convinced that Yanukovych also represented a Putin-style generational change to Kuchma, which would result in policies that would bring order to the country.

Civil Society Mobilization

A final crucial factor in Ukraine was the importance of "Back to Europe!" civic nationalism as a mobilizing force for civil society. Western and Ukrainian scholars had previously suggested that a strong link existed in Ukraine between national identity and civil society.[44] This greater opposition influence in western-central Ukraine was evident in the 2002 elections, where the non-Communist opposition defeated pro-Kuchma parties and blocs.

This close relationship was clearly confirmed in the Orange Revolution by comparing the staying power of Yushchenko supporters who backed the revolution with Yanukovych voters who were dispatched to Kyiv to oppose that revolution. The latter lasted at most two days in the cold in Kyiv and either defected to the Yushchenko tent city or returned to Donetsk, seeing their journey as merely a free two-day holiday in Kyiv. Donetsk protestors sent to Kyiv did not possess a fire in their bellies about the issues, something that strongly differentiated them from participants in the Orange Revolution, where adrenaline and energy were fever-pitched.

Although east Slavic views were quite popular at the mass level, they have proved difficult to use as a rallying point. Ukrainians with a more pro-European national identity have been easier to mobilize than those with an eastern Slavic identity. Russophones have been notoriously impossible to marshal in the former USSR.[45]

Political observer Stephen Shulman believes that Ukraine has two competing national identities: ethnic Ukrainian and eastern Slavic, which closely resemble Yushchenko and Yanukovych, respectively.[46] If Ukraine were to be built around an ethnic Ukrainian core or an east Slavic center, this choice would then influence the country's foreign-policy orientation. Yanukovych's "eastern Slavic" identity promotes economic liberalism, state paternalism, political authoritarianism, and a pro-Russian orientation. The stronger this identity, the less likely there will be support for democratic reform, Shulman believes.

Kuchma balanced both of Ukraine's identities throughout his decade in office and therefore satisfied both camps at different times. The victory of Yanukovych would, however, have meant the coming to power of a more avowedly east Slavic identity, a step too far for many Ukrainian voters and members of the ruling elite. Yushchenko's "ethnic Ukrainian" identity (in Shulman's definition) was associated with democratic reform and a "returning to Europe." This identity was far better at mobilizing the population and giving a fire-in-the-belly energy to create the Orange Revolution.

Yanukovych's background from Donetsk and his views on nationality issues also turned nationally conscious Ukrainians against him. Donetsk has long had an association as Ukraine's "Belarus," where discrimination is rife against nationally conscious Ukrainians and the Ukrainian language. The proportion of education facilities using the Ukrainian language in Donetsk is as low as that in the Crimean Autonomous Republic.

These suspicions of Yanukovych's weak support for issues central to nationally conscious Ukrainians were deepened when he played the Russian language and dual citizenship cards on the eve of election day. It is doubtful whether these two issues added many votes for Yanukovych or simply confirmed the defection of Communist voters to him in round one of the elections and solidified the Donbas vote for him.

The authorities wanted to repeat Kuchma's successful use of the language card in 1994. But even when this tactic was successfully used in 1994, it gave Kuchma only a only 6 percent lead over "nationalist'" Kravchuk. What the authorities ignored was that Kuchma's 1994 victory occurred a decade earlier. Since then, nation building had taken place. In addition, there had been the rise of a younger generation no longer negatively disposed to the Ukrainian language. Raising the issue of the Russian language may have brought him more Communist votes, but it also negatively affected Yanukovych's popularity in central Ukraine, an area that decides Ukraine's elections and that Yushchenko won comfortably.

The 2004 elections proved to be very different from those held in 1994 when President Leonid Kravchuk lost to Kuchma in central Ukraine. In the 2002 parliamentary elections, Our Ukraine and the Socialists (who were also Yushchenko's allies in round two of the 2004 elections) won fifteen oblasts in western, central, and northern Ukraine. Our Ukraine, the Socialists, and the Yulia Tymoshenko party, who were allies after round one of the 2004 elections, together polled 38 percent, giving them a solid starting base for winning seventeen oblasts in all the rounds of the 2004 elections. (Anatoliy Kinakh's Party of Industrialists and Entrepreneurs was a member of the pro-Kuchma For a United Ukraine bloc in 2002 but allied itself to Yushchenko in round two of the 2004 elections.)

In the 2004 elections Yushchenko won a greater share of votes in central and northern Ukraine than did Kravchuk in 1994, which enabled him to defeat Yanukovych. The national democrats had progressively expanded their area of support throughout the post-Soviet era, which was a product of nation building and the emergence of a post-Soviet young generation that was more likely to vote for a candidate representing European values (namely, Yushchenko). The younger generation was also less apathetic than it had been in earlier elections because of its politicization during Kuchmagate and in response to the strategic nature of the 2004 elections in determining Ukraine's medium-term future.

The authorities also miscalculated when they believed that all Russophones would back the upgrading of the Russian language to an official language. What they failed to appreciate was that language issues were low on the list of concerns for voters. They also misjudged the mood of Russophones since not all of them support such moves. The education system in Kyiv has been conducted mainly in Ukrainian since 1992, which sits comfortably since the city is still largely a Russian-speaking city. Although Russophones and Ukrainophones are roughly equal in Ukraine, a sizable portion of the former claim Ukrainian as their native language and therefore have a sentimental attachment to it.[47]

Orange Revolution music, which was continually played in Maidan either by live bands or on compact discs, also touched upon different themes related to the national question. As with the name of Yushchenko's bloc, Our Ukraine, many songs energized Ukrainians to demand the return of what was understood to be their stolen country.

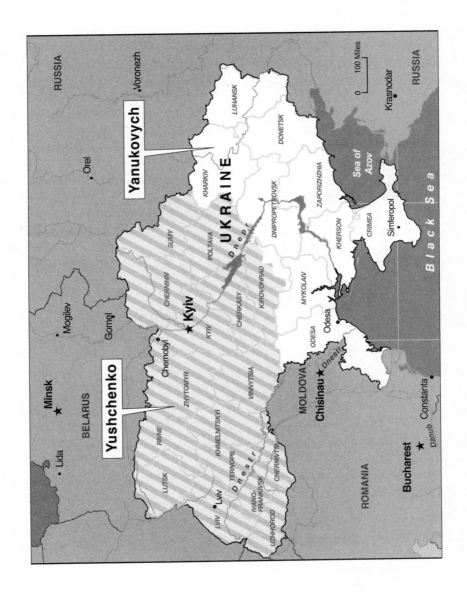

The sentiment expressed was that "this is Our Ukraine, which has been taken over by a small group of usurpers; it is time for it to be returned to its rightful owners: Ukraine's citizens." These usurpers were depicted as a de facto foreign occupation army.

Orange Revolution songs also demanded that Ukrainians not contemplate passivity, because the stakes were too high. Some songs openly called for an uprising, such as Okean Yelzy's "Vstavay!" (Stand up!), which, although written before the elections, became popular during the Orange Revolution.

Songs such as "Ukraina" by the well-known band Mandry called upon Ukrainians to look at their ancestors, who were looking down upon them at this critical time. The option of staying passive was morally wrong because too many Ukrainian intellectuals had already suffered and died. The insinuation was that with the election of Yanukovych, their Ukraine, from a nationally conscious point of view, would be irrevocably lost.

Orange Revolution music called upon Ukrainians to rush to Kyiv to defend this sacred city from a Yanukovych victory. Everyone should travel to Kyiv as soon as they could, by any means possible and, if no other way was available, on foot. The threat of a Donetsk takeover of Kyiv was portrayed in a Pora poster as the equivalent of the Nazis taking over Kyiv in World War II. As Ukrainians had then defeated that attempt, Pora stated that they would also defeat this attempt on this occasion.

Okean Yelzy, one of Ukraine's most popular bands, was typical of the apolitical Ukrainians who became politicized during the elections and the Orange Revolution. Okean Yelzy singer Sviatoslav Vakarchuk was made an advisor to President Yushchenko. The group played the Maidan throughout the Orange Revolution. One of their new songs gave hope to the protestors that spring was very close at hand. "Spring" was understood to be Yushchenko's victory.

Conclusions

The necessary factors for the success of the Orange Revolution included a gestation period before the elections when a political crisis eroded public support for the regime and the ruling elite. The strategic significance of the elections was also crucial. These were not just elections but a strategic turning point that could go toward either a consolidated autocracy or a consolidated democracy. Two other necessary factors were a politically mobilized youth to provide foot soldiers for the revolution and a pro-European civic nationalism that would be far more capable at mobilizing the population than would east Slavic nationalism.

Contributing factors included the authorities choosing an odious candidate, such as Yanukovych. It would have been more difficult to mobilize against Tyhipko, the head of the Yanukovych campaign, or parliamentary speaker Lytvyn. In both Serbia and Georgia, the economies were in a state of freefall within two failed states. That was not the case in Ukraine, which has a functioning state and had experienced strong economic growth. The problem for the authorities was that the state was disliked by its citizens (as represented by their low trust in institutions), while the Yanukovych government was not credited with having achieved economic growth.

Notes

1. Poll cited in *Zerkalo tyzhnia*, August 15, 2002.
2. Polls cited in *Ukrainska pravda*, November 9 and 30, 2004.
3. Poll cited in *Zerkalo tyzhnia*, April 27, 2002.
4. www.razom.org.ua, April 20, 2004.
5. Poll cited in *Ukrainska pravda*, August 5, 2004.
6. Poll cited in *Unian*, July 23, 2004.
7. The speech was reprinted in *Ukrainska pravda*, November 20, 2004.
8. The only lengthy study of the Kuchmagate crisis prequel to the Orange Revolution is Myroslava Gongadze and Serhiy Kudelia, *Rozirvanyi Herb. Khronolohiya Hromadskoho Protestu* [Chronology of civic protest] (Kyiv: Open Society Foundation, 2004).
9. Television station 1+1, December 26, 2004.
10. Pora went public in March 2004 and had a black banner, similar to Otpor. A copycat Pora, with a yellow banner, emerged a month later and was an outgrowth of the Freedom Coalition bloc of NGOs. See www.kuchmizm.info (Black Pora) and www.pora.org.ua (Yellow Pora).
11. Academy of Sciences poll cited in *Suchasnist*, April 2004, 82.
12. A Razumkov Center poll cited by *Zerkalo tyzhnia*, July 3, 2004, and Rakesh Sharma and Nathan van Dusen, *Attitudes and Expectations: Public Opinion in Ukraine in 2003* (Washington: IFES, 2004).
13. Rostyslav Pawlenko in *Ukrainska pravda*, May 25, 2004.
14. Poll cited in *Ukrainska pravda*, November 15, 2004.
15. *Zerkalo tyzhnia*, August 15, 2002.
16. Sharma and van Dusen, *Attitudes and Expectations*.
17. *Suchasnist*, April 2004.
18. *Kyiv Post*, July 1, 2004.
19. www.temnik.com.ua, July 12, 2004.
20. Poll cited in *Unian*, October 27, 2004.
21. Polls cited in *Zerkalo tyzhnia*, August 15, 2002, and *Ukrainska pravda*, May 25, 2004.
22. During the second television debate between Yushchenko and Yanukovych on December 20, Yushchenko asked how his opponent could depict millions of Ukrainians as "bastards."
23. Interviewed in *Den*, September 17, 2002.

24. *Suchasnist*, April 2004.
25. Black Pora discussed tactics and strategy on a server located outside Ukraine that required coded access. This was to prevent infiltration by the security service.
26. See Taras Kuzio, "The Internet: Ukraine's New Samizdat," *RFE/RL Media Matters*, January 4, 2002; and "The Internet and Media Freedom in Ukraine," *Russia and Eurasia Review*, 2 (14) (July 8, 2003).
27. Polls cited by *Zerkalo tyzhnia*, August 15, 2002; and *Interfax*, October 23, 2002.
28. See Taras Kuzio, "Ukrainian Authorities Target Student and Youth Election-Monitoring Groups," *Eurasian Daily Monitor*, 1 (104) (October 13, 2004); and "Ukrainian Leaders Crack down on Youth Groups ahead of Election," *Eurasian Daily Monitor*, 1 (109) (October 20, 2004).
29. See the Pora! election poster at http://vybir.yarema.info/displayimage.php?album=10&pos=13.
30. See Taras Kuzio, "Yanukovych Tries to Clean up His Image," *Jamestown Foundation Eurasian Daily Monitor*, 1 (21) (June 1, 2004).
31. See the large exposé in the *New York Times*, January 17, 2005, about the role of the security service in the Orange Revolution and the poor relations between them and Yanukovych.
32. *Ukrainska pravda*, March 18, 2005.
33. www.yanukovich.nm.ru.
34. See websites http://eggs.net.ua and www.ham.com.ua.
35. See the cartoon at http://mignews.com.ua/mult/4.htm.
36. *Zerkalo tyzhnia*, June 26–July 2, 2004.
37. *Ukrainska pravda*, June 25, 2004.
38. Ibid., July 2, 2004.
39. *Zerkalo tyzhnia*, July 3-9, 2004.
40. *Ukrainska pravda*, July 3, 2004.
41. *Zerkalo tyzhnia*, July 3, 2004.
42. Poll cited in *Den*, November 3, 2000.
43. *Ukrainska pravda*, July 12, 2004.
44. See, for example, Mykola Riabchouk, "Civil Society and Nation Building in Ukraine," in Taras Kuzio, ed., *Contemporary Ukraine: Dynamics of Post-Soviet Transformation* (Armonk, N.Y.: M.E. Sharpe, 1998), 81–98.
45. See Taras Kuzio, "Russians and Russophones in the Former USSR and Serbs in Yugoslavia: A Comparative Study of Passivity and Mobilisation," *East European Perspectives*, 5 (13–15) (June 25, July 9, and July 23, 2003).
46. See Stephen Shulman, "National Identity and Public Support for Political and Economic Reform in Ukraine," *Slavic Review*, 64 (1) (spring 2005), 59–87.
47. See Anna Fournier, "Mapping Identities: Russian Resistance to Linguistic Ukrainianisation in Central and Eastern Ukraine," *Europe-Asia Studies*, 54 (3) (May 2002), 415–33.

CHAPTER FOUR

The Triumph of
Civil Society

NADIA DIUK

REVOLUTIONS ARE DIFFICULT TO PREDICT. The art lies in the spectrum of skills of political scientists and astrologers. Political scientists will point out retrospectively all the quantitative factors that led to the revolution, and astrologers can show how all the stars were aligned to enable the event to happen. Yet perhaps both are required to explain the phenomenon of revolution and the "self-organization" of a society. Two years before the Orange Revolution, public-opinion polling among the youth of Ukraine and Russia revealed similar attitudes on many issues but no particular information that would indicate that Ukrainian youth would be the vanguard of activists who would launch the Orange Revolution and bring down the government.[1] And so it is with "civil society." Of all the elements that are important in creating context and providing the foot soldiers for a revolution, Ukraine's civil society may be the most important, but it is also the most difficult factor about which to compile empirical evidence and to draw direct conclusions. With such amorphous facts and figures available, it might pay to have a background in astrology!

The role of civil society in any democratic transition is crucial in two key areas. First, there is a correlation between the level of maturity of civil society and the level of its organization, the way public protests are conducted, and the outcome.

In Georgia (2003) and Ukraine (2004), where civil society organizations and well-formed coalitions and activist networks had been working for years toward the democratization of society, the protests were peaceful yet forceful. They ended in the complete legitimization of the process of bringing a new government to power. In Kyrgyzstan (2005), where civic groups were not so well organized and where coalitions had barely had time to become established, instances of looting and violence took place, and the transition was not as smooth. The second area where the role of civil society is crucial is in the eventual outcome of a transition. An organized civil society often determines how quickly democratic practices are absorbed into the new political system and the speed with which the consolidation of democratic institutions takes place.

There are other factors common to such "democratic revolutions." Each of the most recent transitions has been precipitated by an election where credible evidence exists (usually collected by well-respected civic groups) that the government has subverted the process and that there has been widespread fraud. With enough free media to inform both the local population and the international community and then a well-organized protest movement to bring people out onto the streets in peaceful protest, a mass protest may be launched. Other common elements of such "revolutions" include some agreement with the security forces with guarantees that they will not shoot at unarmed citizens and a sympathetic attitude from the municipal authorities of the capital city. By definition, the conditions for these factors to be present can exist only if the political system is a soft or semiauthoritarian state, where the emergence of a political opposition and the growth of a civil society are allowed.

Despite the points of similarity, however, each "revolution" has been unique. An examination of the historical roots of civil society in Ukraine and how it evolved and participated in the revolution will give some answers to the key questions always asked: Why did the people take to the streets and why did the revolution proceed the way it did?

Some definition of the term *civil society* should be given here. The historic use of the term generally has been to describe that part of a polity that is the mechanism comprising civic groups, nongovernmental organizations (NGOs), associations, trade unions, political parties, movements, and other freely associating collectives of citizens that interact with institutions of the state for the greater good of the citizen and the state. Since a wave of democratic transitions began with Poland in the 1980s, the term has more often been used simply to describe various types of nongovernmental groups. In this chapter, I show

how the revolution in Ukraine came about when "civil society" according to the second definition was no longer able to express or contain the aspirations of the citizens involved to strive toward a society wherein the first definition of "civil society" is the norm, as it is in most Western democracies.

Civic Groups in Ukrainian Society

Ukraine's uniqueness, especially when broad comparisons are made with Russia, starts with the very concept of civil society. It is conventional wisdom among historians and academics that Ukrainians perceive the state differently from Russians. Throughout Russian history "the state" in its various forms has been the concept around which all ideology and values revolve. Russians have either venerated it or tried to decapitate it, but it has remained a fixture in Russian political consciousness up to the present day.

Ukrainians, inasmuch as such generalizations may be made, have avoided a strong state in favor of loose communities of individuals within the structure of the Zaporizhzhian *Sich* for Cossacks in the seventeenth and eighteenth centuries, or a federalized state, as proposed by the Ukrainian historian Mykola Kostomarov and political publicist Mykhailo Drahomanov in the nineteenth century. The concept of *hromada* (society) was well understood by the Ukrainian intelligentsia of the mid-nineteenth century when they referred to their intellectual circle in Kyiv as the *Hromada*.[2] Even today, civic groups in Ukraine are more often referred to as *hromads'ki orhanizatsii* (civic organizations) rather than by the literal translation of nongovernmental organization, as they are in Russia.

As soon as it became possible to register NGOs under the new policies of glasnost and perestroika in the mid-1980s, civic organizations immediately began to spring up in what was then the Ukrainian Soviet Socialist Republic. The premier civic group, the Popular Movement in Support of Perestroika, or *Rukh*, as it came to be called, was launched in 1989, but there were many others, such as the *Studentske Bratstvo* (Student Brotherhood) and *Tovarystvo Leva* (Lion Society) in Lviv. Those organizations provided an example and paved the way for many civic organizations that emerged in the 1990s. Organizations of youth, women, groups working on ecological problems, and all kinds of charitable and humanitarian organizations were established at that time. As in all countries, Ukraine now has a broad spectrum of civic groups that focus on everything from cultural and sporting matters to social and political problems.[3]

When on considers the path to revolution, however, there are distinct types of civic groups that form the active part of a civil society. The more politically oriented groups become important in the prerevolutionary environment. These groups often respond to the conditions involving elections. Ukraine had a full range of such civic groups, and they created the foundation on which the popular revolution was launched.

Since the early 1990s, Ukraine has developed a type of civic organization that has generally been referred to as a "think tank." A more accurate description might be "analytical center," although the hybrid nature of such a group in Ukraine does not fit Western terminology well. Often being collections of young analysts, these groups have not only provided policy analysis and research into the political situation in the country, they have also been on the front line, organizing other civic groups into coalitions and activist networks. By definition, in a semiauthoritarian country such as Ukraine, any nongovernmental analytical center will be critical of the government. Ukraine's premier think tank is the Center for Economic and Political Studies of Ukraine (or the Razumkov Center), and there are many other centers, such as the Europe XXI Foundation, the Ukrainian Center for Independent Political Research, the Democratic Initiatives Foundation, the Institute for Euro-Atlantic Cooperation, the International Center for Policy Studies, and the Center for Peace, Conversion, and Foreign Policy of Ukraine.[4] Although most of these centers are located in the capital city, after 2000, many of them expanded their programs to include seminars and roundtables in the regions and extended their information dissemination and collection programs throughout the country.

Other organizations attuned to the political environment included monitoring groups of various types. Some focused on the parliament, keeping account of how deputies were voting and whether they were representing their constituencies and voters effectively, such as the Open Society Foundation. Others, as, for example, the Equal Access Committee, monitored the media to show the public how the media—especially television and radio—were dominated by the pro-governmental forces and how audiences were manipulated. In Ukraine, where press freedom had been in decline since the mid-1990s, this was a crucial service.

By the end of the 1990s, as the media came increasingly under the control of a handful of oligarchs close to President Leonid Kuchma (see chapter six) and objective information about the political situation became harder to come by, civic groups themselves took on the role of providing information and acting as centers that collected and disseminated news, information, and analysis. Several Internet sites were established around this time; the best known was *Ukrainska pravda* (www2.pravda.com.ua) launched in 2000. Many sites were offshoots of civic groups or else created virtual civic organizations in cyberspace, such as the website *Maidan* (http://maidan.org.ua/). The dividing line between activist organizations, civic groups, and media outlets blurred during this period. One thing that united them, however, was the understanding that they and the citizens of Ukraine were not faring well under the increasingly corrupt regime of President Kuchma.

Civic Groups and Elections

The past ten years have seen the growth of another type of civic organization that deals directly with election campaigns and the electoral process. Western organizations, such as the International Republican Institute and the National Democratic Institute, have been active since the mid-1990s in providing training in get-out-the-vote techniques and voter education and have distributed materials and inspired indigenous groups to conduct the same kind of programs in elections. Ukraine's largest and most successful election-oriented civic group, the Committee of Ukrainian Voters, was established in 1994 and has trained and sent domestic observers to each national election in Ukraine since then.[5] With a core membership of around twenty thousand, this group is one of the few that can claim to be truly national. Although its membership has fluctuated depending on the immediate need for independent observers, its representatives have often been the most active and civically oriented young people around the country—young people who want to be involved in the political process but who prefer not to join a political party. The Democratic Initiatives Foundation is also noteworthy as the civic group that pioneered the use of the exit poll as a way to counter the falsifying of elections.[6] This group has been conducting exit polls in Ukraine since the 1998 parliamentary elections. By the time of the March 2002 parliamentary elections, the Democratic Initiatives Foundation, together with other polling organizations, accurately polled the results and announced them immediately at the close of the polls, throwing an obstacle to the authorities. Many analysts believe the government wanted to announce different, falsified, results.

Another important feature of civic life in Ukraine in the four years or so preceding the Orange Revolution, and key to the success of the opposition, was the increasing tendency to form coalitions. Whereas the civic groups of the 1990s only sometimes cooperated with one another, many remained sufficiently insecure to be jealous of their foreign contacts and relationships with donors. This insecurity often prevented the groups from creating real coalitions with coordinated activities. The positive example of Slovak civic groups may have helped in the 1998 bid of the civic groups to prevent President Vladimir Meciar from manipulating the elections. The earlier experiences of the Bulgarian civic groups may also have persuaded the Ukrainians that coalitions would enhance their effectiveness.

Attempts to create coalitions were made in the 1999 presidential elections, but the impulse came far too late. The March 2002 parliamentary elections saw the Freedom of Choice coalition come to fruition as well as others. The success of a cooperative approach was demonstrated in results, proved by the exit polls. For the next two years, until the October 2004 presidential elections, coalition building took on more urgency and was carried out with greater commitment. Several coalitions emerged during this period. Two "civic forums" took place, gathering a large number of NGOs, the first in February 2002[7]—partly as a response to the government-controlled civic forum that had taken place in Moscow in November 2001, but also as a way of gathering civic groups from the regions and once more encouraging joint activities and cooperation. The Soros-funded International Renaissance Foundation created a framework for coalitions to emerge in its funding for an election monitoring committee.

By the 2004 elections, a loosely coordinated group of nongovernmental organizations called the Democracy League that had monitored different aspects of democratic development in Ukraine, evolved into yet another coalition: the New Choice 2004 coalition. This group included several of Ukraine's prominent think tanks, including Democratic Initiatives and the Committee of Voters. New Choice produced an analytical document, "Khartia pro chesni vibori (charter on fair elections)," in preparation for the elections (www.monitor.org.ua/?do=1).

By the October 2004 presidential elections, Ukraine was covered with networks of civic groups, many of which had become increasingly radical as the government's pressure tactics of low-level harassment through the frequent deployment of tax police and other repressive methods took effect. Even the parliament, the most democratically inclined institution in Ukraine, created a commission under the leadership of the Communist Valeriy Mishura to investigate the activities of nongovernmental organizations.

For the most part, these groups conducted civic and social activities with an emphasis on monitoring and often challenging the authorities, but already their capacity for influencing the government was diminishing as it became more reckless in its corruption and flouting of democratic principles. Anyone who had visited Ukraine between 2002 and 2004 could feel the almost palpable polarization between a society that was now well informed and angry about the government's misdemeanors but whose civic groups, or fledgling civil society, was not able to be the instrument to change the government. A fully functional civil society would have provided the channels of communication to the government with the expectation of a purposeful response to expressions of discontent or complaints of the citizens.

In Ukraine, as in many countries where a nascent civil society exists with a semiauthoritarian government still in power, increasingly sophisticated networks of civic groups had fulfilled their potential in monitoring the government and in aggregating the complaints of the citizens, but were unable to establish a final link to the government to provide the interaction that would help solve citizens' problems and give a sense that they could influence the government. In that way, Ukraine's civic groups failed to function within the normal operations of a society as a "civil society." Of all the post-Soviet states, however, Ukraine's emerging civil society was the most developed and sophisticated, and also the closest to being a counterweight to the Kuchma government. When citizens are unable to have their problems routinely resolved through civic groups acting as intermediaries, the next stage is to take to the streets.

Civic Groups in the Streets

Several factors came together in the period 2000 to 2004 to bring the people into the streets. The first came at the end of 2000, when the political situation looked as though it were spiraling out of control with the release of the Melnychenko tapes.

As President Kuchma and his top officials circled the wagons to defend themselves, it became clear that Ukrainian society was becoming increasingly polarized. Opposition politicians saw how the regime was becoming more authoritarian and felt their influence diminishing, especially regarding Heorhiy Gongadze, whose disappearance and murder came as a shock, particularly for journalists. They had felt a creeping censorship during the previous two or three years and, for the first time in years, a sense of corporate interest and ethics united them. They rallied around *Ukrainska pravda* in protest and outrage against their colleague's fate and the situation of the media in Ukraine.

The general public was well informed about the Gongadze affair and the allegations of corruption (bootlegged copies of excerpts from the "Melnychenko tapes" could be purchased on the street in Kyiv at the time), even though the official press and television were silent on all these issues. With the parliament in a stalemate with the government, and the organs of law enforcement under the control of the president, there seemed to be no way to channel or resolve increasing citizen discontent. At that point, toward the end of 2000 and beginning of 2001, there appeared to be only one alternative: to take to the streets in protest.

The first mass demonstration took place in mid-December 2000 when youth from the Socialist Party pitched tents in Maidan and were quickly joined by other, more radical groups from both the left and the right, such as the Ukrainian National Assembly and the Young Communists. These protests were conducted under the slogan "Ukraine without Kuchma," which became the name of one of the protest movements. Another group of youth organizations including Young Rukh, the youth wing of the Congress of Ukrainian Nationalists, the Association of Ukrainian Youth, the Ukrainian Students' Union, and others coalesced around the group "For Truth" (*Za Pravdu*). This new group reunited some of the original student hunger strikers from the 1990 student protests.

With the dismissal and surprise imprisonment of Deputy Prime Minister Yulia Tymoshenko in February 2001,[8] the political atmosphere became even more charged and resulted in the emergence of yet another opposition group: the Committee for National Salvation. When Prime Minister Viktor Yushchenko was dismissed through a vote of no confidence in the parliament in April 2001, departing the building with the words: "I'm leaving but only to return," the scene was set for a dynamic development of both civil society and a vigorous protest movement. For the first time in years, there was real political opposition.

The period between April 2001 and the parliamentary elections of March 2002 was characterized by the growing relationship between civil society organizations and the political opposition. Even though the political opposition was in the process of consolidation and did not reach out consciously to civil society, the nongovernmental sector was already far ahead in its strategies for parliamentary elections. It was preparing to support electoral campaigns that were to be conducted without access to television or other mass media. These strategies also included the expectation that the government would attempt to falsify the elections.

The March 2002 parliamentary elections turned out to be a dry run for the presidential elections. The overwhelming results for the opposition parties felt very much like a victory. Civil society organizations had helped to get people out the vote, monitored polling stations, and conducted parallel vote counts and an important exit poll. The disillusionment that set in when the opposition political parties and blocs—Our Ukraine, Yulia Tymoshenko's bloc, and the Socialist Party— were outmaneuvered in the distribution of key posts in parliament, was widespread. It led to the conclusion among many opposition politicians and activists that extraordinary methods would be needed to take on the pro-presidential forces next time.

A very high level of civil society activity in Ukraine characterized the months between mid-2002 and the presidential election campaign of 2004. New types of groups emerged, particularly among the youth, which took as its main premise for organization that the upcoming presidential elections were of critical importance to the future of Ukraine and, moreover, that the elections would not be conducted freely or fairly.

Failing in their ability to influence government through pressure and the usual instruments at their disposal, it was inevitable that civil society organizations would also turn to the street and mass gatherings.

Youth groups such as Pora, *Chysta ukraina*, and *Znayu* (I Know) emerged at this time. These groups were often composed of young people who had taken part in the *Za Pravdu* campaign or who were active in other youth organizations such as *Plast* (a Ukrainian Scouting Organization) and the Ukrainian Youth Association. Implicit in their strategies was the assumption that they would have to adopt new, more active, and directly confrontational methods. Dispute continues around the genesis of the youth group "Pora" and which wing—the "yellow" or the "black"—is the authentic group. The activists of Black Pora came together in 2003 with the explicit aim of challenging the government's authority, which they labeled with the catchy term *kuchmizm*. Taking up some of the more aggressive techniques of civil disobedience practiced by the Serbian youth group Otpor, Black Pora promised to be on the front lines against the government. The leadership of Yellow Pora came out of the Freedom of Choice coalition and tended to see the role of its group as an organizer of youth and trainer of activists to ensure the integrity of the electoral process. These differences turned out to be academic, however, as both wings joined in street actions together, attended training camps in the Crimea and in the Carpathian Mountains, and generally acted in concert throughout the electoral campaign and in the Orange Revolution.

The countdown to the presidential elections took a significant turn over the mayoral election in Mukachevo in March 2004. Despite the best efforts of many civil society organizations that conducted monitoring and exit polls, and with the help of a large contingent of parliamentary deputies from the opposition, no one could prevent gross falsifications and violations of the process and results, as well as pure thuggery from unknown assailants at many of the polling stations. It became clear that the authorities would stop at nothing to maintain their control over the presidential elections. This realization served to radicalize many in the opposition as well as in civil society.

From March until October, Ukraine's youth groups, including Pora, brought thousands of students and young people into the streets all over the country to protest against the government. In June 2004, for example, Pora organized a weeklong event throughout the country under the banner "10 years of *Kuchmizm*" that included a ceremonial presentation of a copy of the Ukrainian constitution to government officials to remind them of their duty to the nation. In July and August, student strikes were organized under the banner "Student Solidarity" to support the students in Sumy who had been struggling for months against the wanton liquidation of the independence of higher educational institutions by the authorities. Ten thousand students converged on Kyiv on October 16, 2004, gathering in the four geographical corners of the city to march in protest. They headed toward the center for a *Studentske Viche* (student rally) as a symbolic depiction of national support for Viktor Yushchenko.

People Take to the Streets

As the electoral campaign progressed, though polling showed Viktor Yushchenko in the lead in September 2004, the potential response of the citizenry to a fraudulent election was still an unknown, even with the large number of Ukrainians working in civil society organizations and in the opposition. There were individuals within the opposition, however, who were developing a strategy to get the people out into the streets in support of opposition candidate Viktor Yushchenko.

Former opposition parliamentarian Taras Stetskiv became a spokesperson for the team of strategists in the Yushchenko campaign who claim that plans for mass demonstrations were started a year before the election.[9] The voting public had been prepared by information from civil society organizations to believe that Yushchenko would win in a fair electoral fight but that the authorities would most likely use all means to prevent it. The Stetskiv team within Viktor Yushchenko's campaign developed a two-pronged strategy: first, to train thousands of activists to lead protest actions, and, second, to devise ways to bring concerned citizens of Ukraine out into the streets to defend their vote.

The first mass rally for Yushchenko took place in Kyiv in the *Spivucha ploshcha* (Singing Field), where he announced his candidacy on July 4, 2004. Thousands of people from all over Ukraine traveled to be present at the announcement, arriving in buses and carrying banners announcing their place of origin. The rally was deliberately organized in the mode of a pilgrimage. The planned procession from the Singing Field to the offices of the Central Election Commission blocked the streets of Kyiv for hours. Such scenes were repeated all over Ukraine as Yushchenko's campaign unfolded around mass rallies and face-to-face meetings in the absence of access to the mass media.

Another mass event was organized on September 18, 2004. A mass and "virtual" rally were held simultaneously in twenty-five oblasts. Yushchenko's campaign speech was beamed by satellite to twenty-five giant screens throughout the country to deliver his message to thousands of assembled voters. On October 23, a living circle of people gathered on the streets of Kyiv to surround the downtown government buildings—to give a sense that the people were encircling and closing in on the government.

Thousands of volunteers were recruited and trained throughout the summer and early fall, mainly under the auspices of Yellow Pora. Despite the much touted meetings with Serb and Georgian activists, Stetskiv and other leaders gave much more weight to the instinctive understanding of clandestine and underground organizing techniques developed by the Organization of Ukrainian Nationalists in the 1930s to the 1950s. These techniques were brought to the campaign by the young people from western Ukraine and by the desire of students from the east to emulate their Cossack ancestors, who were able to organize a "fighting" force. The idea of such skills coming from both the east and west of Ukraine was particularly effective in reinforcing a sense of unity in the opposition.

In preparation for what was envisaged as a prolonged protest, the Yushchenko team was also buying up tents, mobile military kitchens, and old buses to use as barricades if necessary.

Maidan as a Microcosm of Civil Society

When it became clear on the evening of November 21 that the election results were being falsified and that the government was not about to give up its power, the machinery of mass protest that had been carefully prepared over the previous months swung into action. The Yushchenko campaign determined that the best location for a mass protest was Maidan, where hundreds of student hunger strikers had set up their tent city under the shadow of the Lenin statue in 1990. During the day of Sunday, November 21, 2004, several opposition parliamentary deputies had a platform constructed at one end of Maidan. By evening, a group of Pora activists were pitching tents at the other end. The symbolic number of twenty-five tents was chosen—one for each administrative region of Ukraine—with the nominal purpose of providing a focal point for information on the opposition's parallel vote count.

Hearsay has it that even at that stage, from Sunday evening, November 21, to the Monday morning, November 22, neither Yushchenko nor his campaign knew how many people would turn out to protest. When Yushchenko issued a plea to the nation on Monday morning to come to Maidan on whatever transport was available—cars, trucks, bicycles, or donkeys—about five thousand bodies were at Maidan, mainly Pora activists. There was no guarantee as to how many more would come to join them.

Exact figures differ on how many people came to Maidan, but by Tuesday, as people from Kyiv came out and people from numerous other cities arrived, the numbers gradually climbed to well over three hundred thousand. By week's end, on Saturday, November 27, the Orange Revolution was in full swing. Estimates ranged to well over one million people in or around Maidan.

The seventeen-day protest was a rare phenomenon. The attention of the world focused on the center of Kyiv, where hundreds of thousands of people gathered day after day and where many took up temporary residence, all without violence. Moreover, they did so with extraordinary bursts of creativity and goodwill emanating from the crowd.

This type of protest creates a qualitatively new kind of civil society, one that transcends the need for a connection with the state or government because it has its own form of self-organization. Echoes of the Polish Solidarity movement's concept of a self-organized, self-governing, and self-limiting society, independent of Communist control, could be felt in Maidan. An infrastructure of communal facilities developed to feed and house the protestors and a system of self-policing and security emerged.

There were several different groups present in Maidan—all intermingled. As the number of tents increased thanks to generous contributions from the military, the number of people *living* in the tents grew. The core had originally comprised members of Pora, but many others came to show their solidarity and moved in. Early in the protests, Pora had also established another tent city next to the *Verkhovna Rada*, the supreme council building. The principle of organization within the tent city was taken straight from the organizational structure of the Ukrainian Cossacks, with a "commandant" in charge and a number of *sotnyky*, in charge of a hundred people, *desyatnyky*, who were in turn in charge of ten people, and so on. Another group was made up of local Kyivites, who came to Maidan every day, often as families with children and pets in tow, and returned home every evening. Yet another group was the thousands of people who traveled from other cities, all needing food and shelter once they arrived in Kyiv. The presence of many civil society groups, particularly youth groups, in Kyiv made the challenge of housing and finding food for thousands of people easier. Each of the many youth groups coordinated its activists. For example, activists went door to door asking whether families could provide accommodation, and then, using mobile phones and computers, they compiled databases of available places to house people.

The Significance of the Orange Revolution

The significance and impact of the days of the Orange Revolution in Maidan are likely to be felt throughout Ukrainian society long after the politicians it brought to power revert to the day-to-day battles that are part of politics. It is often difficult to quantify and capture the drive and inspiration that draw people to the streets during such periods of "people power." And it is easy in the process of analyzing the events to lose sight of the extraordinary achievement of the citizens and the society involved.

The most striking aspect of the Orange Revolution was the level of mass participation—not only in Maidan—but also the millions of people who followed events by watching Channel 5, listening to Radio Era, or hearing from friends and relatives in Maidan. For weeks, almost the entire population was caught up in the atmosphere of the revolution, watching developments hour by hour. Many people who had never had strong opinions on the use of the Ukrainian language nor felt a strong sense of identity as Ukrainians suddenly joined the revolution simply by sporting the color orange. Even the use of the color was a stroke of genius for the Yushchenko campaign. Not only did the turning autumnal colors of all the trees in Ukraine at the time of the presidential election give a sense that all Ukraine was bedecked in orange, the color itself created a sense of new identity. This identity was one step beyond the blue-and-yellow variety that had primarily mobilized the regions of western Ukraine during the struggle for independence. This was a new identity that eastern Ukraine could also identify with.

Uniting east and west, it was reinforced by the sheer numbers involved in the protests and by the revolution's slogan, *Razom nas bohato* (Together, we are many), repeated in the catchy rap-songs that entertained the revolution in the streets. Another feature of the revolution was the extraordinary burst of creativity it triggered, with numerous "revolutionary" songs composed for and performed at Maidan, which also reinforced the feeling of the creation of a new popular consciousness. For the first time, many citizens of Ukraine were made aware of what it meant to be Ukrainian. All these elements went into the emergence of what should be considered a new civic nationalism, one that had not existed in Ukraine as a nationwide phenomenon before this event.

No survey of civil society during the Orange Revolution would be complete without a comment about funding and finances. A common question has been: what was the role of foreign assistance and advice in the organization of civic groups for the Orange Revolution? It is true that civic groups working on pro-democracy issues in Ukraine have relied heavily on international sources of funding to operate and form the foundation for the popular movement that became the Orange Revolution. Without years of foreign support of Ukraine's nascent civil society, it remains a question whether the past two years of political campaigning would have had such a result. Yet the notable feature of the events of the past year has been the extent to which internal funds—primarily from Ukraine's rising middle class—provided financial support.

Conclusions: A Substantial and Mature Civil Society

A review of civil society in Ukraine at the time of the Orange Revolution provides quite an impressive picture. Without doubt, Ukraine has had the most mature civil society of any post-Soviet state. A large number of civic organizations and initiatives had emerged since it became politically possible in the mid-1980s. All kinds of different civic organizations were formed: broad civic organizations, think tanks, monitoring groups, and media. The Internet was extensively used for information and communication. Nongovernmental organizations were both undertaking opinion polls and monitoring elections. They were not monopolistic, but they did cooperate. The one shortfall was that the strong civil society could not communicate with the regime. Instead, beginning in 2000, a variety of nongovernmental organizations spearheaded the protest movement against the regime by innovative means, including street protests. By the fall of 2004, these organizations succeeded in getting several hundred thousand people into the streets throughout Ukraine. The nongovernmental organizations excelled at being peaceful, and they played a decisive role in the Orange Revolution. The Ukrainian events show how important a strong civil society can be.

Notes

1. Nadia M. Diuk, "Pervoe svobodnoe pokolenie: molodezh', politika i identichnost' v Rossii, Ukraine i Azerbaidzhane" [The First Free Generation: Youth, Politics, and Identity in Russia, Ukraine, and Azerbaijan], *Vestnik obshestvennogo mnenia*, Analytical Service of VTsIOM A, September–October 2003.

2. The first political journal to be published in Ukrainian by Drahomanov when he was exiled to Geneva in the 1880s bore the name *Hromada*.

3. For a good overview of nongovernmental organizations in Ukraine, see "Civil Society in Ukraine: Analytical Report," World Bank, 2003, prepared by Democratic Initiatives Foundation & SOCIS.

4. For a comprehensive overview, see "Nongovernmental Think Tanks in Ukraine: The Present State and Prospects (Razumkov Center analytical report)," *National Security and Defense* 10, 2003.

5. Ibid.

6. www.dif.org.ua/ep/en/pr.

7. www.irf.kiev.ua/old-site/eng/news/news.html.

8. www2.pravda.com.ua/en/archive/2005/february/4/tym.shtml.

9. Interview with Taras Stetskiv, March 11, 2005.

CHAPTER FIVE

Pora—"It's Time" for Democracy in Ukraine

PAVOL DEMES AND JOERG FORBRIG

THE ORANGE REVOLUTION was still in full swing when observers characterized developments in Ukraine as yet another example of an electoral revolution in post-communist Europe.[1] Similar to the experience in Slovakia, Serbia, and Georgia, Ukraine's presidential ballot was the moment when a broad-based democratic movement challenged a pseudodemocratic regime that was determined to prolong its rule through electoral falsification. No less surprising than in previous instances, this confrontation was eventually resolved peacefully and through free and fair elections that ousted a government with dubious democratic credentials. As a result, after the first attempt at democratization led to only thinly veiled authoritarianism, genuine democracy was given a second chance to take root in Ukraine.

This apparent pattern of electoral revolutions quickly drew the interest of analysts and policy makers alike. For policy makers, strategic questions posed themselves: Were they witnessing a new wave of democratization that could spill over to other countries in the post-Soviet world and beyond? How could democratic contagion be enhanced with Western assistance? Analysts swiftly identified prerequisites to make electoral revolutions successful, including semiauthoritarianism, modestly free media, political opposition, economic activity, and developed civil society.

Although comprehensive analyses and commensurate strategies have yet to develop, it is widely accepted that civil society was the central driving force behind the democratic breakthroughs. Evidence abounds that the scale, strength, and involvement of civic organizations relate directly to the success of electoral revolutions and to the quality of new democracies.[2] On this account, too, Ukraine's Orange Revolution paralleled earlier democratic openings in the region. Not only did numerous nongovernmental organizations (NGOs) play an active role before and during the 2004 presidential elections, their eventual success in pressing for democracy also hinged upon the concerted effort civil society undertook in general.[3]

A primary example of such coordinated and cooperative action across civil society organizations was the civic campaign of Pora. Inaugurated in March 2004, this campaign quickly grew into the largest countrywide network of NGOs, activities, and volunteers. By the time of its official closure in late January 2005, Pora had for many become as synonymous with the Orange Revolution as had Kmara with the Rose Revolution in Georgia, Otpor in Serbia's overcoming the Milosevic regime, and OK '98 for the ousting of the Meciar government in Slovakia.

Although only one of several concerted efforts, the scale and visibility achieved by Pora warrant a closer look at this particular campaign and its background and evolution, approach and activities, structure and resources, and accomplishments. Based on information provided by inside activists and outside observers, we show in this chapter how Pora crystallized several of the social and political factors that contributed to the success of the Orange Revolution.[4]

Razom nas bohato: Joining Forces in Ukrainian Civil Society

Pora's civic campaign and the broader contribution that NGOs made to the Orange Revolution are closely tied to the longer-term development and learning process of civil society in Ukraine. As noted elsewhere in this book, the years since Ukrainian independence in 1991 were characterized by developments in civil society in the country. In the 1990s, several organizations were formed to advocate for democratic development in Ukraine. Their activities included political and social analysis, public information, broad-based mobilization, citizen participation, and election monitoring. During successive parliamentary and presidential elections, these watchdogs and think tanks built their expertise and perfected their techniques. Gradually, and in response to the increasingly authoritarian tendencies of the Kuchma regime, civil society organizations began to form coalitions, cultivate relationships with democratic political actors, consult with their counterparts elsewhere in Central and Eastern Europe, and mobilize larger sectors of the public in Ukraine.

By early 2004, these developments had sufficiently prepared Ukrainian civil society to develop a comprehensive program of NGO activities in preparation for the fall 2004 presidential election. This program, entitled "Wave of Freedom," acknowledged the critical nature of the upcoming election for the further development of Ukraine. It also anticipated the Kuchma regime's widespread manipulation of the electoral process. Consequently, Wave of Freedom was designed as a nationwide civic effort, attracting an unprecedented number of civic organizations and addressing a complex set of election-related activities aimed to ensure a free and fair ballot.

Several NGO coalitions and numerous individual organizations underwrote the program, which combined elements of analysis, voter education and information, election monitoring, and preparation for social mobilization. Individual organizations committed their resources to projects to monitor the campaign finances of individual candidates, for the civic oversight of the drafting of voter lists, training for commissioners at polling stations, international observation of polling stations abroad, a hot line for election-related information, and a large-scale campaign of voter information and education.

On the national level, participating organizations included the Freedom of Choice coalition of Ukrainian NGOs, the Anticorruption Committee, and the Communication Development Center (all based in Kyiv). Regional partners of this program were, among others, the Fund of Local Democracy in Kharkiv, the Center for Supporting Private Initiatives—the Laboratory of Social Research in Lviv, the youth NGO Vsesvit in Simferopol, PR–Space in Dnipropetrovsk, and the Podlisky Center of Social Technologies in Vinnytsia.

Individual projects were to be coordinated to allow for maximum interaction. Think tanks that conducted analytical or monitoring projects, for example, supplied the results of their work to information and education efforts, while the entire network of the program's NGOs contributed to recording violations in the electoral process. Wave of Freedom represented a logical progression from hitherto looser forms of NGO cooperation.

Under the umbrella program, the central elements of voter information and social mobilization were Pora's responsibility. The basic idea behind Pora's campaign was that the absence of independent media was far-reaching and greatly assisted the incumbent regime in manipulating the public in the electoral process. Alternative mass media and sources of information were needed to guarantee free and fair elections and to give the Ukrainian public more accurate information about the electoral process, the contenders running for the presidency, the rights of citizens, the importance of voting, and possible state manipulation of the election. Alternative sources of information would be instrumental in mobilizing public protest against election fraud.

Given the governing regime's control over most state and commercial media, alternative sources of information were conceivable only in the realm of civil society. Specialized civic organizations—think tanks such as the Razumkov Center and the Democratic Initiatives Foundation, election-oriented groups, including the Committee of Ukrainian Voters, and media monitors like the Equal Access Committee—generated alternative, objective, and critical content on the electoral process. Civil society more broadly delivered this information directly to citizens nationwide.

For this purpose, the civic campaign Pora began early in 2004 as a joint effort of civic organizations. These included members of the five largest Ukrainian youth organizations: the Christian-Democratic Youth of Ukraine, the Union of Ukrainian Youth, Zarevo, Young Prosvita, and the Association of Law Students. Affiliates of the Freedom of Choice Coalition of Ukrainian NGOs joined in, as did several local NGOs and student organizations at universities and institutes of higher education. Altogether more than 150 different national, regional, and local NGOs eventually participated in Pora, which evolved into the largest civic movement hitherto seen in Central and Eastern Europe.

The Pora Campaign: Six Steps toward the Orange Revolution

Creating Pora was a formidable task. The sheer number of partner organizations posed a considerable managerial problem for building a concerted effort. In its ambition to be a nationwide campaign, the vast size of Ukraine was a challenge. Social, cultural, and administrative differences and regional diversity also had to be taken into account. The political climate in the country was oppressive and significantly in flux, thus requiring considerable flexibility. If, despite these challenges, Pora succeeded and contributed substantially to the Orange Revolution, it was not least the result of the systematic and skillful approach of its leaders, comprising six stages.

Step One: Framing the Campaign and Developing Pora's
Organizational Structure

Between January and March 2004, campaign partners set out to establish the main principles and tasks needed to guide Pora. The campaign drew on the experience of civic movements in Ukraine as well as other countries in the region. This inspiration was reflected in the principles that characterized Pora as a transparent, nonpartisan, and voluntary effort by civil society to strengthen democratic practices during the 2004 presidential elections. On that basis, campaign tasks included providing accurate information about the electoral process; increasing the voter turnout of democratically minded and Western-oriented social groups; making a democratic appeal to politically neutral or insufficiently informed voters; forming a volunteer network to cover the campaign; and rallying society in the event of electoral fraud. These principles and tasks were officially presented at the launch of Pora's civic campaign on March 9, 2004.

Next, a suitable organizational structure was needed. A campaign council was established in April 2004 at the initiative of Vladislav Kaskiv, a seasoned democratic activist and leader of the For Truth committee.[5] The council brought together prominent public figures, civic activists, representatives of the business community, parliament, the state administration, and international organizations. Members of the council included Markiyan Ivaschishin, a 1990 student-protest organizer; Taras Stetskiv, a member of parliament and the leader of the "Ukraine without Kuchma" action; Yuriy Pavlenko, a member of parliament and the head of the Youth Party of Ukraine; Oleksandr Yarema, the head of Christian-Democratic Youth of Ukraine; and Yevhen Zolotariov, an activist of the For Truth committee in Kharkiv.

The primary role of this council was to supervise and advise the campaign, make strategic decisions, and garner public and political support. Day-to-day management was handled by a coordination center, which was established in Kyiv and headed by Kaskiv. The center was to develop a national campaign network, formulate an information strategy and tactics, coordinate regional activities, publish and deliver campaign materials, and consult with political partners and allies.[6] On the regional level, Ukraine was subdivided into seventy-eight *kushches*, each corresponding to a territory of about half a million inhabitants, which made it possible to design campaign activities and address materials according to specific regional, cultural, and social information.

Kushchoviy's, or district leaders, were recruited to coordinate the campaign activities of mobile groups of ten to fifteen volunteers, or *riy's.*

With this structure, Pora devised an effective and flexible horizontal format, giving great organizational and financial autonomy to each regional partner. Regional offices were largely free to design activities provided that they respected the principles of the campaign and served its defined tasks. Autonomy also ensured the continuation of the campaign should any individual segment of the network cease to function. Various communication tools ensured that this structure could function as a coherent campaign. Pora was identified and recognizable through a symbol that, similar to its very name, conveyed the message "It's time!" A website was established at www.pora.org.ua that served as a source of information, communication, and coordination between campaign partners. Mobile phones were critical for Pora organizers for immediate messaging and information exchange. This phase of organizational development concluded with a meeting of seventy regional campaign coordinators in the western Ukrainian town of Uzhhorod from April 14 to 18, 2004.

Step Two: Developing a Campaign Strategy

The next phase in developing Pora consisted, between April and August of 2004, in elaborating a campaign methodology and information strategy. Since the mass media could not provide independent and accurate information about the upcoming election, the main idea was for Pora to build an alternative medium to address and inform citizens directly.

Accordingly, Pora leaders developed a strategy that envisaged several thematic components. A first one, "It's Time to Stand Up!" sought to attract and train a large number of volunteers to serve as communicators. Second, information was to be gathered from all available sources, including candidates, election authorities, analytic and research institutes, and those NGOs involved in monitoring the electoral process. This information was then to be prepared for dissemination directly to citizens nationwide under the slogan "It's Time to Think!" The focus of information was the electoral process, candidate programs, and voter rights. A third element, "It's Time to Vote," involved the mobilization of voters to take part in the elections. The fourth and final element of the strategy, "It's Time to Keep Watch!" was prepared to inform and mobilize the public in the event of manipulation of the electoral process and its results.

These themes provided the basis for more detailed planning. Each identified a specific target group and purpose. Accordingly, detailed messages for each bloc were formulated to be used during the preparation of the campaign, and a range of materials and activities was prepared to convey the messages. Materials included such printed matter as leaflets, booklets, posters, stickers, letters to individuals, audio and video tapes, bandanas, and banners. Activities envisaged ranged from personal contacts with citizens, the distribution of printed matter at universities, dormitories, public transport stations, and public places, to street activities, picketing, and demonstrations. These activities were to be accompanied by the maximum visibility of the campaign, its logo, and its purposes in the available mass media, on the Internet, and in the form of posters and even graffiti all over the country.

To test this strategy and measure the strength of the Pora organization before the 2004 presidential vote, Pora participated in a series of parliamentary and mayoral by-elections in several regions of Ukraine. A first demonstration of Pora activities took place during the mayoral elections in the Transcarpathian town of Mukachevo, followed by elections in the agrarian Poltava oblast in central Ukraine, the southern city of Odesa, and the industrial town of Vakhrushevo in eastern Ukraine. During these elections, Pora tried communicating between mobile group leaders, monitoring voter lists, accessing information, observing electoral commissions, controlling the use of administrative resources, monitoring the ballot, and organizing mass protests. No less important was trying out the various formats of informational and educational activities, such as "hand-to-hand" and door-to-door distribution. This made it possible for Pora to refine its techniques and improve their effectiveness. By the summer of 2004, Pora had developed a comprehensive and proven strategy and a detailed plan of action and time line for the big show in the fall: the presidential election.

These strategies were presented to the Pora network at an all-Ukrainian forum of activists on August 22, 2004. At that meeting, a division came to the fore within Pora. Strongly influenced by Serbia's Otpor and Georgia's Kmara, a significant group among Pora activists advocated a more spontaneous, less organized form of activities aimed at directly discrediting the Kuchma regime. Among well-known activists of this nonhierarchical group were Mykhailo Svystovych, Volodymyr Vyatrovych, Tatyana Boyko, Andriy Kohut, and Yaryna Yasynevych. These activists pressed for an "anticampaign" aimed at illuminating and condemning Kuchmism and the devastating effects of the regime on

Ukrainian society. This part of the network eventually labeled itself Black Pora. Its autonomy notwithstanding, Black Pora did not want to foster disunity. While autonomous, it followed the campaign's general principles and supplemented and contributed significantly to the "yellow" campaign we describe later.[7]

Step Three: Training Activists and Developing a Volunteer Network

In August and September of 2004, Pora moved on to develop and train its human resources. This was the first phase of Pora's campaign: "It's Time to Stand Up!" Broadening the volunteer network was, of course, the foremost task for a campaign that relied on people to carry its message directly to citizens all over the country. At the same time, the activists needed to become familiar with the goals and approach pursued by the campaign, and they had to be integrated into a general system of coordination and communication. Not least, they needed instruction in the techniques for interacting with the public, the media, and state authorities and for handling possible situations of conflict nonviolently.

For this purpose, Pora leaders organized a training camp for three hundred activists near the Crimean town of Yevpatoria in early August 2004. Addressing kushch and riy leaders, the program included a detailed presentation of the campaign, its work with volunteers, methods of voter mobilization and election monitoring, techniques for public action, contacts with the media, interaction with law enforcement bodies, and mechanisms of communication and coordination within Pora. For broader use among volunteers, these instructions and information were also prepared as manuals, such as "How to Inform the Public," "Rights during Arrest," "Violations of Electoral Law," and "Internal Communication and Coordination of Action." With its regional leadership thus formed and trained, Pora completed its organizational arrangements over the following weeks. The regional network of kushches and mobile groups for field operations was developed further, and necessary logistical and communication apparatus were put in place. These preparations were made final at a seminar for more than seventy regional NGOs supporting Pora volunteer groups, which took place in Kyiv on September 18, 2004.

At the same time, Pora entered its active phase by mobilizing volunteers on a broad scale. Timed to start with the end of summer vacations, the campaign went public and appealed to Ukrainians to join its ranks. Within a few weeks, Pora attracted more than thirty thousand volunteers and thus grew into a powerful movement, visibly covering the entire country. Although the majority of these volunteers were students and other young people, Pora also managed to reach gradually into society more broadly. Across the country, intellectuals, businesspeople, and civil servants became interested in the campaign, and their inclusion favorably changed and increased the resources available to Pora.

Step Four: Conducting the Information Campaign

September and October of 2004 came to be the core period for the public information and voter education components: phase two of the Pora campaign. In early September, "It's Time to Think!" was launched with the aim of providing voters with information about the elections, their rights as citizens, and the programs of individual candidates. Various forms of publications, leaflets, and stickers were distributed directly to Ukrainians at large: door to door, printed on sandwich boards, throughout the public transport system, through poster pickets, and in many other creative ways.

By the beginning of October, two more layers of the campaign had been put into action. "It's Time to Vote!" used classical get-out-the-vote techniques to encourage Ukrainians to participate in the election. A dozen concerts, various forms of public activities, and a range of printed products aimed to reach the more active segments of the population, especially young people, through youth organizations and universities. At the same time, "It's Time to Keep Watch" was launched, comprising activities aimed at the prevention of election fraud.

Personal letters were sent directly to the representatives of local governments, the heads of electoral commissions, and members of law enforcement to inform them of their personal legal liability should they breach electoral regulations. An important part of this phase was Pora's nationwide monitoring of the compiling of voter lists.

The information provided by Pora contrasted starkly with the coverage of the presidential election in the largely state-controlled mass media, which barely veiled its support of Prime Minister Viktor Yanukovych. In response, Pora began a special effort to discredit a range of state-controlled media outlets through the wide distribution of "They Lie!" stickers and through a series of protests near some of the most notorious broadcasters. These media-related activities became one of the most visible parts of the Pora campaign.

Pora also distributed thirty-seven different kinds of nationwide print products, with a total circulation of about forty million copies and many more at the regional level with messages of local interest. Pora leaders estimated that Pora activists had organized 750 regional pickets and public activities and seventeen rallies with more than three thousand participants. All told, Pora leaders estimated that they had reached about twenty-five million citizens of Ukraine, or more than half the country's population.

Step Five: Responding to Repression

The apparent effectiveness of Pora in the Ukrainian public led state authorities to initiate a wave of repression against the campaign and its activists. During the months of September and October alone, more than 350 Pora activists were arrested, fifteen students were expelled from universities, and more than thirty cases of physical violence against Pora volunteers were recorded, with attacks peaking shortly before the election. These assaults were evidence of the Kuchma regime's increasing nervousness.

On October 15, 2004, law enforcement agencies searched the Pora office in Kyiv. During the search, explosives were planted and subsequently discovered. A court case against Pora activists was opened for organizing illegal military units and terrorist acts. Searches followed in the offices of the Freedom of Choice coalition, one of Pora's main campaign partners, and in the private apartments of Pora leaders. Eventually more than 150 activists were detained and interrogated across the country. Fifteen criminal charges, ranging from counterfeiting and rape to the illegal possession of weapons and explosives, were brought. These criminal assaults were accompanied by a campaign through the state-controlled mass media to discredit Pora, including claims of Pora's terrorist and clandestine activities.

In response, Pora began to emphasize its youth base in its activities. Portraying itself strongly as a democratic student movement helped to dissociate Pora from the sinister images created by the state media. In the same vein, the campaign placed even greater emphasis on publicity and the transparency of its actions. Not only did Pora succeed in countering the false charges brought against it, it also managed to benefit from the state's defamatory campaign, which gave it a media presence, helping the Pora campaign increase its popularity at home and gain notoriety abroad.

Step Six: Mobilizing for a Free and Fair Election

The months leading up to the presidential election in Ukraine had made it increasingly clear that state authorities were not going to allow a free and fair ballot. Repression against the Pora campaign and other NGOs, election fraud earlier in the year, massive propaganda in the official media, and, not least, the mysterious illness that befell opposition candidate Viktor Yushchenko during the campaign combined to make clear to the democratic opposition that the incumbent regime was determined to use all means possible to stay in power.

The Pora campaign began to prepare actively for the mobilization of social protest. In mid-October, well before the first round of the presidential election, Pora transformed itself from a movement aimed at public information and education to one engaged in mobilizing citizens to protect their right to free and fair elections. Direct protest activities were planned, including mass demonstrations, tent camps, and student strike committees. To coordinate these activities, the coordination center of the campaign was transformed into an operative headquarters. Although still a national effort, Pora's protest activities now focused on the capital city, its main public spaces, Khreshchatyk road and Maidan, and its major political institutions.

The preparations for mass demonstrations also included greater coordination with other civil society organizations, Our Ukraine, and major organizations of the democratic opposition. The Freedom of Choice coalition of Ukrainian NGOs declared publicly its full support of the Pora campaign, and it subsequently hosted Pora headquarters on its premises. On October 15, 2004, Pora leaders began to coordinate mobilization and protest activities with the election headquarters of Viktor Yushchenko and the coalition of democratic forces *Syla narodu*.[8]

These preparations enabled Pora to respond immediately to the results of the first round of the presidential election on October 31, 2004. The next day, Pora issued a public statement questioning the preliminary results of the ballot, detailing a list of demands to the central election committee, the president, parliament, the prime minister, law enforcement agencies, and universities. It called upon the public to engage in protest. On November 6, 2004, Pora established a first tent camp on Kontraktova Plosha in Kyiv,[9] followed by others in Kharkiv, Donetsk, Cherkassy, Dnipropetrovsk, and Ternopil, which served as centers of social protest. At the same time, student strike committees emerged at more than seventy universities and institutes of higher education throughout the country. This expanding network of protest action provided the basis for a more detailed plan of action to take effect after the second round of the election.

The November 21, 2004, run-off between Yanukovych and Yushchenko was marked by government manipulation on an unprecedented scale, as was unanimously acknowledged by domestic and international observers alike. Pora responded instantly by staging mass protests on Maidan. On election day, Pora and the Yushchenko team had already turned Kyiv's main square into their center of public activities. Tents had been set up for each district to collect the protocols of regional election committees, a stage had been constructed for public announcements, and screens had been put in place to televise the results of the exit polls carried out by various institutions. Over the following days, this infrastructure became ground zero for the Orange Revolution.

In the early morning of November 22, 2004, Pora activists and students from strike committees at Kyiv's universities arrived at Maidan and were subsequently joined by thousands of protestors from all parts of Ukraine. Within the unfolding democratic revolution, Pora was primarily in charge of coordinating street protests, blockades of the presidential office and other sections of the state administration, and a tent camp near the Ukrainian parliament. Yet the most visible contribution of Pora was the tent city that sprang up in Kyiv's main boulevard of Khreshchatyk, which quickly grew to more than fifteen hundred tents and more than fifteen thousand inhabitants. Coordinating life in this camp, providing for the well-being and security of its residents, and distributing the generous help rendered by Kyiv locals in the form of clothes, food, and warm shelter were enormous tasks met well by Pora. Life in the makeshift city went on without harm to inhabitants, guests, or equipment until it was removed on December 13, 2004.

This visible presence of thousands of Pora activists and volunteers in the streets of Kyiv came to be the high point of this civic campaign. The initial Pora presence in downtown Kyiv helped to spark the mobilization of hundreds of thousands of Ukrainian citizens. Pora provided the nucleus for the unprecedented social mobilization that accompanied the Orange Revolution in Ukraine and ultimately led to its success.[10]

The Various Ingredients of Success

Several factors combined to make Pora a success. First was the emergence of a strong set of civic organizations and their eventual cooperation.

Distinct from previous elections in the country, the 2004 presidential ballot saw the emergence of a broad-based effort among civil society actors in Ukraine. Within Pora, this effort involved a joint campaign, a division of tasks, and close coordination across hundreds of NGOs nationwide. Within the broader Wave of Freedom program, an even larger number of civic organizations participated and contributed to informing, educating, and mobilizing the public. In part, this coordination and cooperation within civil society embodied a lesson from democratic breakthroughs in Central and Eastern Europe. Modified to fit Ukraine's circumstances, techniques from the Slovak, Serbian, and Georgian experiences gave Pora powerful tools with which to engage the public.

An important element of this process of learning and transferring experiences was a strong focus on young people and students. Indeed, Pora was considerably carried by what can be described as the first postindependence generation in Ukraine. Twenty- to thirty-year-olds, shaped by Western lifestyles, international experience, and global opportunity rather than the Soviet past, realized the discrepancy between democratic rhetoric and reality in the country and the personal disadvantages that that gap meant for them. The resulting resentment motivated them to pursue political change and provided a powerful reservoir that Pora could tap.

To reach its target group required modern communication techniques. Pora managed to build a quickly recognizable image that incorporated a clock at the eleventh hour and the Ukrainian word *pora*, which means "It's (high) time." Not only was this image appealing and widely present, it also conveyed a clear message that was further enhanced by a range of powerful campaign slogans: "My vote is my power!" "I vote, therefore I exist," "My vote is not for sale!" and many others similar in style. An image and tagline and slogans eventually evolved into a shorthand for the broader democratic message that Pora conveyed in its educational and informational activities. These slogans became forceful in mobilizing the public.

The resonance Pora achieved with the Ukrainian public was crucial, not only in fostering the cause of democracy in the country but also in securing the resources necessary to conduct its campaign. Distinct from its predecessors in the region, the Pora campaign was only sparsely supported by international donors. A mere $130,000 was contributed in foreign funding: by the Canadian International Development Agency, Freedom House, and the German Marshall Fund of the United States. By comparison, Pora's total financing was $1.56 million. In-kind contributions in the form of free publications, communications, and transportation exceeded an estimated $6.5 million. Domestic sources, particularly from Ukrainian entrepreneurs—many of whom had been involved in the student movement of the 1990s and could thus easily identify with Pora—provided the overwhelming majority of financial and material resources.[11]

Given its highly decentralized structure and national reach, information and communication technology constituted a further ingredient in the smooth and successful functioning of Pora. To span vast distances and coordinate hundreds of NGOs and thousands of volunteers, mobile phones, text messaging, email, and the Internet proved indispensable. They provided campaign participants with reliable channels of communication, and, more than once, instant contact put Pora a step ahead of state authorities aiming to prevent its activities.

Partnerships with democratic political actors also played a role. Although it was a nonpartisan campaign, Pora's basic demand to reinstall a genuine democracy in the country coincided with the program of the democratic opposition and its candidate, Viktor Yushchenko. As political tensions grew during the electoral campaign and as clashes with the government became more likely, close coordination with the democratic camp assumed central significance. It strengthened the sense among Pora leaders of potential sanctions by the authorities, provided information and political support, helped to attune social mobilization to political developments, and, not least, created links with those segments in the government loyal to democracy and the rule of law. Exemplary of the latter was the refusal by law enforcement agencies to use large-scale open violence against protestors or to counter the logistical support provided by the Ukrainian military to the tent camp set up by Pora.

Last, but not least, Pora's overwhelming and democratizing influence resulted from the strict adherence of its activists and volunteers to nonviolence. Faced with frequent open assaults and covert provocations by the state's administration and law enforcement agencies, Pora did not retaliate. This made Pora a powerful example of the effectiveness of peaceful civic disobedience and struggle for democratic rights. In so doing, the Pora campaign may well have positive reverberations for democratizing the political culture in Ukraine far beyond the Orange Revolution.

After the Orange Revolution: Transforming Pora

As we have described here, Pora derived its strength and eventual success from being able to build a broad-based coalition of civic actors and society. Across a wide spectrum of diverse organizations, social and economic status, regional identities, and political beliefs, this coalition was guided by the desire to again go down a path toward the democratic development of Ukraine. To be successful, the coalition had to set itself a clear-cut, short-term goal: free and fair presidential elections. Pora reinforced this central concern by committing all actors to the principle that the future of Pora—possible developments, organizational arrangements, and civic activities—was to be discussed only once the campaign had succeeded.

The Pora campaign officially closed at the end of January 2005, but the discussion of how to transform Pora and how to employ its enormous civic energy has continued.[12] A number of organizations have been established since those that evolved from the Pora campaign, with four organizations rooted in Yellow Pora and one succeeding Black Pora. Common to them all is a concern for the longer-term development of democracy in Ukraine, which, as many have acknowledged, was revitalized solely because of the Orange Revolution.

The first to emerge was the public organization the Pora Civic Campaign, whose creation was announced on December 9, 2004, immediately following the crucial phase of the Orange Revolution. For several leading activists, the central problem to be faced before democracy could take hold in Ukraine was corruption. The Pora Civic Campaign aims to address existing and emerging blatant deficits in this sphere. Evidence of corruption under the previous regime is being collected in order to hold the officials involved responsible. At the same time, public and political attention is to be drawn to the problem through the development of systematic anticorruption measures and watchdog activities.

A second spin-off from the Pora campaign is the nongovernmental organization Nova Pora. Central to this organization is the promotion of European values in Ukraine. As one of its first activities, Nova Pora organized a tent camp for visitors to the Eurovision song competition in May 2005. Longer-term plans include programs to develop new professional cadres for the new Ukraine, to strengthen knowledge of Europe and its core values in the country, to improve the situation of Ukrainians working and living abroad, and to develop knowledge and information about Ukraine in European countries.

The Pora political party is a third successor to the campaign. Conceived on January 12, 2005, it held its first party congress on March 24, 2005, and was officially registered on June 1, 2005. The party wishes to be a new political force that draws into political and public life young professionals who are committed to the spirit of the Orange Revolution but who are alienated from existing political parties. Its program advocates a system of strong public accountability by central and regional authorities; the development of society's self-organization and self-governance, anchoring the rule of law both in institutions and citizens; and the unity of Ukrainian society both politically and culturally.

As a fourth offspring of the campaign, the International Democracy Institute aims to build on the practical experience of Pora's civic campaign and of other democratic movements in Central and Eastern Europe and to offer this expertise to support democratization in the region. Civic activists, analysts, and experts will find in this institute a platform from which to promote democracy in post-Soviet republics. The institute responds to requests that Pora has received from other campaigns and is to be established with the support of the new government of Ukraine and several international organizations.

Last, the nongovernmental organization Pora derives from that part of the campaign that came to be known as Black Pora. Central to this wing of Pora was opposition to Kuchmism, or the pervasive effects that the previous regime had on society. Pora continues to address these effects as a central obstacle to democracy in Ukraine and works to overcome that legacy.

The outcome and effects of this continuing transformation of Pora are as yet unknown. Judging from previous examples of successful demobilizing and transforming movements, retaining the civic energy amassed, channeling it into new organizations and tasks, and adjusting relationships to changed politics and society are tasks no less daunting than those of building the original movement. These current and future challenges to Pora notwithstanding, the overwhelming significance of its campaign for the recent democratic breakthrough in Ukraine should be beyond doubt.

Notes

1. Vitali Silitski, "Has the Age of Revolutions Ended?" *Transitions Online*, January 13, 2005; Michael McFaul, "Transitions from Postcommunism," *Journal of Democracy*, 16(3) (July 2005).
2. *How Freedom Is Won: From Civic Resistance to Durable Democracy* (Washington, D.C.: Freedom House, 2005).
3. See chapter four, by Nadia Diuk, in this volume.
4. In addition to the information contained in this chapter, see also Vladyslav Kaskiv, Iryna Chupryna, and Anastasiya Bezverkha, *Pora: Vanguard of Democracy* (Kyiv: Pora, 2005), available at www.pora.org.ua.

5. The Committee "For Truth!" (*Za Pravdu!*) emerged in 2000 as a platform for several youth organizations, including the youth section of the Congress of Ukrainian Nationalists, the Association of Ukrainian Youth, and the Ukrainian Students' Union, as well as participants in the student protests of 1990.

6. At the coordination center, specialized departments were given the tasks of developing a national campaign network and coordinating regional activities (headed by Andriy Gusak); the formulation of an information strategy (Yevhen Zolotariov); publications and the distribution of campaign materials (Ostap Kryvdyk, Yaroslav Zen, Oleh Radiychuk); communication with the media (Anastasiya Bezverkha); contact with the international community (Nina Sorokopud); control and monitoring of the day-to-day functioning of the coordination center (Iryna Chupryna); and political consultation with partners and allies (Vladislav Kaskiv).

7. The distinction between Black and Yellow Pora is primarily based on the different symbolism used by the two segments. For detailed information on Black Pora, its distinct symbolism, philosophy, and activities, see the extensive web archives maintained at www.kuchmizm.info.

8. The coalition of democratic forces Syla narodu (Force of the People) was established on July 2, 2004, through an agreement between Viktor Yushchenko of the Our Ukraine bloc and Yulia Tymoshenko of the Tymoshenko bloc. The agreement stated that the two blocs "unite with the aim of ending the destructive process that has, as a result of the incumbent authorities, become characteristic for Ukraine. We unite to build a democratic Ukrainian state."

9. Kontraktova Plosha is one of the main squares in the historical center of Kyiv. It is the location of the National University "Kyiv Mohyla Academy," the most respected university of Ukraine. Students and professors of this university were among the first to join Pora and its protests. Kontraktova Plosha was also the venue of the *student viche* (grand assembly) of October 16, 2004, at which Viktor Yushchenko addressed more than ten thousand students from all over Ukraine.

10. A more detailed account of Pora activities and the broader role Ukrainian civil society played during the 2004 presidential elections can be found in *Ukraine's Orange Revolution: A Chronicle in Pora Newsletters*, which can be obtained at the Pora website at www.pora.org.ua.

11. See Vladyslav Kaskiv, Iryna Chupryna, and Anastasiya Bezverkha, *Pora: Vanguard of Democracy* (Kyiv: Pora, 2005).

12. Taras Kuzio, "Pora! Takes Two Different Paths," *Eurasia Daily Monitor,* 2(23) (February 2, 2005).

CHAPTER SIX

The Ukrainian Media Rebellion

OLENA PRYTULA

UKRAINIAN JOURNALISM HAS SOARED and tumbled, surviving periods of both revival and iron-fisted censorship. In the early 1990s, after the USSR collapsed, the Ukrainian media experienced euphoria brought on by its newly acquired freedom of speech, which was totally unrestrained at that time. Unfortunately, that euphoria did not last long.

In the early 1990s it became possible to launch a private newspaper, unlike an official *Pravda* or *Izvestiya*, and to launch a private radio station. From the mid-1990s, the number of television channels began to grow rapidly. A number of young journalists who had not worked under Soviet censorship surfaced and spread the standards of a new, liberal journalism at their workplaces. The surprisingly young age of nearly all the anchors on Ukrainian television likely springs from the difficulty older Soviet-era journalists had in adapting to work without Communist Party direction.

Only a few journalists noticed that the scope of their freedom was beginning to narrow. The 1994 presidential election campaign was run under strict state media control. Leonid Kuchma, the leading challenger, declared that Ukrainian television "had been turned into around-the-clock propaganda for [incumbent president] Leonid Kravchuk."[1] Kravchuk attempted to shut down Gravis TV—the only channel that had supported Kuchma. According to many analysts, this made Kuchma

look like a victim of censorship, which attracted the sympathy of journalists and contributed to the eventual defeat of Kravchuk.

The first reports of censorship under Kuchma appeared at the beginning of 1996, a year and a half after his inauguration. One analytical
evening show ran a story on the scandalous departure of several aides
from Kuchma's office and was then shut down at the request of the
presidential administration.[2] From that time on, journalists began expe-
riencing censorship and control. Calls from the presidential office, typically attributed to the heads of regional administrations, became the
rule. When a television station or newspaper dared to publish criticism
of the government or broadcast an interview with an "undesirable"
politician, officials would call in the owner or producer and dress him
down.

The heads of television stations soon anticipated the feedback from
Bankova Street (the location of the president's office) and started to apply different forms of censorship. Long before the presidential elections
of 1999, most television stations kept blacklists of politicians whom the
government "recommended" not receive publicity.[3]

Strict censorship soon led to flourishing self-censorship. Reporters
knew what would not survive the editor's scissors and deliberately refused to interview blacklisted politicians. Not only statements and interviews, but even events became subject to censorship. Sometimes it
was safer to ignore an event than to put it in a headline.

How did media oppression function in Ukraine? The difference between modern and Soviet censorship methods was that in the new system no one determined the Communist Party's preferences or labeled
materials undesirable. Even so, the modern system was quite effective.
Editors-in-chief, who were controlled by the authorities, discussed what
questions journalists were to pose when interviewing someone. The
general outline of prospective publications was also predetermined. Finally, all undesirable information could be excluded when the script
was edited merely because the "key viewer" (Kuchma's unofficial nick-
name among television managers) might not like it.

All journalists knew that if an undesirable piece of news aired, the
managers of the station would be called to the presidential administration. Such a summons might result in serious trouble for the station in
general, for its owners and managers, and for the journalist involved.
Like any other business in the country, television stations were directly
dependent on the final say of the president. Disgrace might result in the
exclusion of a journalist and his or her company from the president's

press pool. Far more serious actions might follow, such as tax inspections and lawsuits. So journalists abided by a set of simple rules, learning which material would pass the editor and which would not. This is how self-censorship developed, backed by the fear of being fired and getting the television station or the newspaper into trouble.

Representatives of President Kuchma denied the existence of censorship in the mass media. They called it editorial policy.[4] At the same time, there were at least two overt taboos. Journalists could not expose the financial or political partners of the owner of their media outlet and, most important, on television they could not criticize the president or his entourage in any way. Regional authorities kept local media under strict control in similar fashion.

Such control and censorship in the media reached a new peak in 1999, at the beginning of Kuchma's reelection campaign. At that time, Ukrainian journalists did not know that the situation could become even worse.

2001: The Gongadze Case

In 2000, tired of unemployment and censorship, Heorhiy Gongadze, an independent journalist, launched the online newspaper *Ukrainska pravda* and began sharply criticizing the government. Gongadze was last seen alive on September 16, 2000. His partially decayed and decapitated body was found two months later in a shallow grave seventy-five miles from Kyiv.

From the moment of Gongadze's disappearance, his fellow journalists asserted their right to cover the murder investigation, contrary to the objections of their managers and media owners. Obviously it was impossible to forbid journalists from covering an event that was crucially important to their profession.

On November 28, 2000, Oleksandr Moroz, the leader of the Socialist Party, delivered a speech in the Ukrainian parliament in which he accused President Kuchma of being involved in Gongadze's disappearance.[5] Moroz presented audiotapes as evidence;[6] they had been recorded in the presidential office by one of Kuchma's former bodyguards. The tapes made clear that Kuchma was irritated with Gongadze and asked his middlemen to get rid of him. The journalist's death turned out to be a politically motivated murder.

This news was a defining moment, marking a new stage of journalistic resistance, and it was the beginning of the Orange Revolution. The "Ukraine without Kuchma" campaign began against the president.

Thousands of people went into the streets demanding Kuchma's resignation and eager to learn the truth about Gongadze's death. At that
moment, it seemed that Kuchma's reign would collapse, if not today,
then tomorrow.

For the most part, Ukrainian television stations ignored the opposition rallies and the obvious political motives for the Gongadze murder,
although Ukrainian journalists were fighting for every single word in
their reports. Yet news about the investigation of the murder continued
to appear. At that point the authorities changed their tactics. Despite
their ban, they allowed the news to continue as written and manipulated it by providing false comments, which obfuscated the investigation. The interior minister, for example, gave various false versions of
Gongadze's murder.[7] In early 2001, the opposition campaigns came to
naught owing to disunity and weakness. Apathy and mistrust returned
to society.

2000–2003: *Temnyky*

In 2002, just a week before the parliamentary elections, *Ukrainska pravda*
wrote an article on so-called *temnyky:* guideline documents on how major
stories should be covered on television.[8] The word *temnyky* means
"themes" in Ukrainian (from *tema*—"theme" or "subject"), which is
media slang. Temnyky were unsigned, secret instructions that the presidential administration sent regularly to major state-controlled and private media outlets (primarily radio and television stations). One example
of such a *temnyk* was: "This week Viktor Yushchenko will make some
statements on his political bloc Our Ukraine. Please ignore them."[9]

Temnyky first appeared at the headquarters of the (United) Social
Democratic Party of Ukraine (SDPU[o]). The first instructions on the
coverage of events were sent during the 2002 parliamentary election
campaign to SDPU(o)-controlled media outlets. In late 2002, when Viktor
Medvedchuk, the head of the SDPU(o), became the head of Ukraine's
presidential administration, the number of coverage instructions grew
significantly, as did their persistence.

One could watch different television stations and find all too many
similarities in news coverage. At that time, all television channels and
politicians from the presidential camp denied the existence of temnyky.
Journalists had to keep silent about major opposition events. Sometimes
reporters would return from an event to their offices to find a prepared
report from the presidential administration.[10]

Only the television channel ICTV refused to carry out the instructions. The president's administration did not insist; it did not have to. Viktor Pinchuk, Kuchma's son-in-law (who controls the station), would never have dared to criticize his father-in-law or say something against his policies. But other channels had to comply with the temnyky. Disillusioned journalists began to resign because of the censorship. Others organized a strike committee and initiated parliamentary hearings testifying on freedom of the press and censorship.[11]

As a result of the parliamentary hearings, everyone in Ukraine soon knew what the word *temnyk* stood for. A resolution was adopted by parliament classifying instructions on coverage as a method of political censorship. Thus, the politicians officially admitted the existence of temnyky. This situation led to the establishment of the new Independent Media Trade Union.

Who Controls the Media in Ukraine?

Print Media

Unlike television stations in Ukraine, whose audience comprises many millions of people, print media has a less powerful influence. For this reason, the Ukrainian print media remained more independent. The authorities sent *temnyky* only to the newspapers under their control, which were not numerous.

Newspapers like *Den* (*The Day*) (circulation 50,000), *2000* (100,000), and *Kievskie vedomosty* (*Kyiv News*) (80,000) were under the influence of the (United) Social Democratic Party of Ukraine. Pinchuk's media holding included the tabloid *Fakty* (*The Facts*) (760,000). The leader of the Donetsk clan, Rinat Akhmetov, purchased a tabloid named *Segodnya* (*Today*) (750,000).

Nevertheless, opposition newspapers held very strong positions. In addition to the usual party-related bulletins, the Ukrainian opposition published newspapers of decent quality and quantity. The socialists had influence over one of the country's bestsellers, *Silsky visty* (*Village News*) (519,000), and the radical newspaper *Hrany+* (*The Sides*) (4,000). Yulia Tymoshenko and her followers published a popular newspaper called *Vechyrny visty* (*The Evening News*) (500,000). Viktor Yushchenko drew support from *Ukrayna moloda* (*Young Ukraine*) (150,000) and *Bez tsenzyry* (*Without Censorship*) (60,000).[12] Almost every region had a newspaper that spread the dissenting point of view. These newspapers also published articles on opposition websites.

Both pro-government and opposition newspapers criticized their owners' enemies and published only articles reflective of their own politics. The print media in general, however, reflected a broad spectrum of thought. People could find out what was inspiring the opposition and what the government wanted to say. But to find out what was really happening in the country, one had to read several newspapers.

Zerkalo nedeli (50,000) was a rare exception. It presented an independent point of view but definitely leaned toward the opposition. The commonly cited reasons for its independence were: (a) the owner was an American, although nationality was irrelevant since one of the owners of television channel 1+1, Ronald Lauder, was also American; (b) it had a strong team of independent and well-known journalists. The best Ukrainian journalists worked there, and their talents were recognized by several prestigious Ukrainian awards.[13]

Zerkalo nedeli allowed journalists from other print media and television stations to reprint their articles or comment on them. Given that such viewpoints were usually prohibited, *Zerkalo nedeli* was a unique platform. There, journalists who had quit their jobs because of censorship could work and earn a living.

The Internet

Unfortunately, Ukraine is not a high-tech country, but the political situation and violations of freedom of speech may explain the exceptional role of the Internet in the country. With an audience of 3 to 4 percent of the population, the Internet in Ukraine in 2000 and in 2004 reminded one of the "self-published" (*samizdat*) media of the 1960s, where one could read uncensored articles, get acquainted with different viewpoints, participate in discussions, and find out unofficial versions of events. Similarly, Internet sites became a platform for those journalists who could not publish their materials where they worked because of censorship.

People printed online articles and took them to their relatives, friends, and even to the rural regions where their parents lived. These articles were republished in regional presses, penetrating to even the most remote corners of Ukraine, where the Internet is still a novelty.

The number of Internet users in Ukraine is increasing very slowly owing to the lack of access to computers for the general public, rather expensive computers and Internet connections, and problems with old telephone networks. There are several hundred registered news sites in Ukraine today, but only about two hundred of these are active and updated regularly. Before the elections, there were more than two hundred informational websites, only twenty to thirty of which were being updated regularly. Like the print media, the Web presented both pro-government and opposition views, though the latter received much more traffic.

The SDPU(o) has long been present on the Ukrainian Internet. Since 2002 it has employed Russian political specialists who copied Russian website techniques during the Ukrainian election campaign. These specialists created a network of websites, each of which reprinted news from the others. When information appeared on one website, it was copied by another site, referencing the first site; then a third site copied it and referenced the second site, and so on. In this manner, the information was reproduced on several websites. Although it had an initial source, it was difficult to pinpoint. After that, other media (television or newspaper) could use the information (usually disinformation) as "laundered" by the Internet.

As happens so often with Russian political consultants, in this senseless transfer of political technology, they did not take into consideration one significant Ukrainian feature: there was less traffic on the Ukrainian Internet in 2002 than in Russia, and therefore less influence. After investing significant amounts of money in an Internet campaign in 2002, the SDPU(o) lost interest in the Internet in 2004. (This is understandable because Yanukovych was not really the SDPU(o)'s candidate.) As a result, the opposition and the Donetsk group dominated the Web.

Yushchenko and his allies made active use of the Internet. He and Tymoshenko held several Internet conferences. Yushchenko's site was updated to the level of the best Ukrainian news sites. It was a reliable, stable source of fresh information. The Yushchenko bloc had a site at www.razom.org.ua, and Yushchenko had a personal site at www.yushchenko.com.ua.

After the widely publicized and rather pompous opening of his website (www.ya2004.com.ua, the name of the site also means "Me2004"), Yanukovych used it to support his own reputation rather than provide useful information. The news was updated irregularly. The Internet team from Donetsk concentrated on provocation, which explains the titles of their sites (www.provokator.com.ua or www.bayki.com [*baika* means "rumor"]). The sites of the Donetsk clan are among the most popular: ForUm (http://for-ua.com), From UA (www.from-ua.com), Provokatsia (www.provokator.com.ua), Oligarch (www.oligarh.net), Politbaiky (http://bayki.com [*Politbaiky* means "political rumors"]), and KID (http://zadonbass.org).

Yanukovych

s. les

Thus far, the Internet has remained an unregulated space in Ukraine. Although laws mentioning the Internet have caused some anxiety for users, they have never been applied to the online mass media. The Internet can compete well with television in terms of the speed of its reaction to unfolding events. Under current conditions of censorship, the Internet proved an invaluable information resource, one that successfully broke through the censorship blockade.

In the months leading up to the revolution, the popularity of the antigovernment media rose sharply after the authorities forced one Internet provider to ban access to a website containing jokes about Yanukovych.[14] The intention of the authorities was thwarted. Many people had already downloaded the Internet jokes to their computers. In response to the ban, dozens of other sites appeared with similar information. Copies mushroomed; jokes were sent via email. At a certain point, it became impossible for the authorities to combat underground humor by filtering Internet content. Ukrainian Web surfers became sophisticated. They learned how to "see" the banned website using so-called anonymizers. Many news agencies then used this technology to prevent the filtering of their content.

During the revolution, the Internet helped to organize rallies. With the strict censorship of television, the Internet was the only medium through which one could find answers to basic questions: What is the date and location of the next meeting? What are the plans of the opposition? What is happening in the street? Sometimes events unfolded so rapidly that only Internet media provided people with up-to-date information.

The number of website hits increased as tension grew. In September, Ukrainian news websites attracted 6.3 million visitors; in October, 8.3 million; and in November, 19.3 million visitors.[15] The peak occurred in December, when Viktor Yushchenko won the third round of the elections. That month, the number of hits on Ukrainian news sites reached almost twenty million visitors.

During the revolution, *Ukrainska pravda* was the leading site on the Ukrainian Internet. On October 31, in the first round of elections, 130,000 readers visited *Ukrainska pravda* from all around the world (800,000 hits). In the second round, that number grew to 350,000 readers (almost one million hits a day). Finally, in the third round, the site drew 150,000 readers (1,800,000 hits).

While the Orange Revolution spread from Kyiv to the regions, the *Ukrainska pravda* site was writing a chapter on the modern history of Ukraine. The news feeds from the regions were vitally important.

Every ten to fifteen minutes another tent city appeared in some town or other, and that fact was soon reported on the air. News from the regions was read by opposition leaders on Maidan to millions of listeners in the streets throughout Ukraine.

Thousands of letters flooded the mailbox of *Ukrainska pravda.* Other news agencies were also working around the clock. Unian, the Ukrainian Independent Information Agency, provided its news free of charge. Interfax-Ukraine ignored the rule limiting the number of publications to ten news items an hour, as well as the rule demanding that the news be broadcast after a two-hour delay.

Television

Influential business groups had been getting ready for the presidential election for a long time. A multimillion-member audience had already been divided between competitive financial-political groups, which had to unite their efforts for the sake of the pro-authority candidate.

Information on who owned the television stations was not public, but it was an open secret often discussed by the mass media.[16] All the major Ukrainian television stations, with one exception, were controlled by pro-presidential forces and different financial-political groups dependent on the president and his administration.

There are six major national channels in Ukraine: the state-owned First National Channel (UT-1), plus privately owned Inter, 1+1, New Channel *(Novy Kanal)*, STB, and ICTV. Channel 5 and TRK Ukraina appeared just after the parliamentary elections in 2002, but their audiences were small.

Inter, 1+1, and the First National Channel were controlled by the (United) Social Democratic Party of Ukraine and its leader, Viktor Medvedchuk. The representatives of SDPU(o) officially owned only Inter. Channel 1+1 was under SDPU(o) control mainly because of its leader's personal influence on its Ukrainian owner, management, and editorial staff. The First National Channel came under Medvedchuk's control because of its old habit of blind obedience to authority. Inter and 1+1 are major popular channels in Ukraine. Together they cover 95 percent of the Ukrainian territory and their total audience is almost 48 percent of the market.[17] They effectively divide the advertisement market between them.

Viktor Pinchuk, Kuchma's son-in-law, tried to shatter the monopoly. Originally he owned ICTV; later he purchased New Channel and STB.

Pinchuk joined his major network stations into a holding company, resulting in a total audience of 35 percent, with network coverage of about 70 percent.[18]

Other stations did not play a significant role in the media market except for one phenomenon among small cable channels: Channel 5.

Channel 5 — єдина альтернатива

Just after the parliamentary elections, the opposition started working on a plan to break through the information blockade. To buy an already popular station with a multimillion-viewer audience was impossible for the following reasons: (a) the media was already divided between major players; (b) to buy a station required large amounts of money, which the opposition could not afford, considering the expensive campaign ahead; and (c) Kuchma's total state control would never allow the opposition to realize such a plan. The president's administration kept a watchful eye on any change in the stockholders of a major mass media outlet.

In 2003, the opposition ventured to buy a small broadcasting company called NBM. It was little known at that time, but it possessed its own network in Ukraine. Since 2002 it had been broadcasting to twelve Ukrainian regions (including south and east Ukraine) and Kyiv. At the time of the purchase, the station had a maximum audience of 8 million (the population of Ukraine is 48 million), and it covered only 30 percent of Ukrainian territory.[19]

One of the new owners of Channel 5 was Petro Poroshenko, who also owns the Leninska Kuznia shipyard, the Roshen chocolate factory, and the *Pravda ukrayiny* (*Truth of Ukraine*) newspaper (circulation 35,000).

What caused the enormous success of Channel 5? First, there had been no alternative viewpoint on television in Ukraine whatsoever. Viewers knew what to expect from Channel 5: undistorted facts and the latest news from the opposition. Second, some talented journalists were unemployed because they had been censored by their former employers in the media. Consequently, Channel 5 had a number of popular anchors whom the viewer knew could be trusted.

In addition, the staff and the owners of the station had signed an agreement according to which management guaranteed noninterference in the creative process.[20] The agreement was signed in public, which increased the responsibility of the parties and drew attention to the channel. This became a contributing factor in gaining the trust of Ukrainians in the channel.

Official censorship and the government's fear of the opposition had resulted in a complete blackout of any live political talk shows. Channel 5 was also the only one inviting guests without restriction. As Andriy Shevchenko, a Channel 5 journalist, put it: "The people have almost forgotten what it is like to hear the news live, on the air. The country wants to talk on both sides of the screen."[21]

It is also relevant that the channel refused to show the so-called parquet events (meetings of high government officials). All the other channels began their news programs with an enumeration of the president's meetings, showing handshakes accompanied by monotonous comments.

Despite these advantages, the station's studio was poorly equipped. At times its news programs looked amateurish, and it had many problems with live reporting. These difficulties were because of a lack of financing and the inexperience of the people involved in setting up the channel.

The form, however, did not matter. Content was far more important for viewers. They craved different news, truthful news. Despite all its faults and difficulties, the channel gained popularity. In just five months, Channel 5's news program "Rush Hour" showed a record rating of 0.7, which is good considering that network coverage was just 30 percent.[22]

Radio

Of all media, radio played the most modest role during the Orange Revolution. Long before the elections, the authorities did their best to block radio channels from providing independent views. They had considerable success. Among the news-based Ukrainian radio stations, the following warrant mention:

Radio ERA. This station belongs to the son of a former head of the Security Service of Ukraine (the SBU), Andriy Derkach, who made his choice in favor of Yushchenko just before the election. This decision saved the station. At that time the station broadcast in thirteen regions on the FM band.

International radio stations, the so-called Western voices: Voice of America, Radio Liberty, Deutsche Welle, and the BBC. These radio stations continued broadcasting on the short waves, as during the Cold War. Some regional FM stations, however, also rebroadcast them.

Radio Continent. This was the only radio station that broadcast Western voices in Kyiv. In late 1998, Heorhiy Gongadze hosted programs on this station. In March 2004 the authorities shut it down. Its owner, Serhiy Sholokh, received political asylum in the United States.

Public Radio. This station, which was sponsored by international radio organizations, was refused a broadcasting license by the National Television and Broadcasting Council of Ukraine. This forced the station to broadcast on the Internet, resulting in a very limited audience of fifteen hundred to two thousand a day. Popular journalists from other media hosted its programs. Public Radio declared that it would follow the international nonaffiliation standards while presenting information and inviting guests into the studio. Closer to the revolution, this station's programs began appearing on the other stations in Kyiv and the regions; print and Internet media published its most interesting interviews.

Public Radio gave free reports and programs to the regional radio stations, and program transcripts to the printed media. Since September 2004, ERA had been broadcasting Public Radio's most prominent programs. ERA, like many others, also rebroadcast BBC news. Even without a broadcasting license, the mere existence of the station irritated the authorities and demonstrated the possibility of an information breakthrough on the Internet.

Radio Liberty, the Voice of America, and Radio Continent. Radio Dovira stopped rebroadcasting Radio Liberty on February 17, 2004. Dovira attributed the decision to inconsistency between the news product of Radio Liberty and its own concept. Afterward Radio Liberty could be heard on Radio Continent. Yet in early March 2004, the authorities closed down the station. The statements of official U.S. representatives of Radio Liberty, Voice of America, and Radio Continent fell on deaf ears. Their meetings with the Ukrainian government proved fruitless.

In April 2004 the chairs of Radio Liberty, Voice of America, and Radio Continent visited Ukraine. The representative of Radio Liberty announced that the rating analysis for the station put its audience at nearly 8.4 percent of the population. He emphasized that even for a commercial radio station, 5 percent was a significant rating.[23]

In June 2004 a member of the board of directors of Radio Liberty, Geoffrey Girshberg, met with the speaker of the Ukrainian parliament, Volodymyr Lytvyn. The speaker sent a letter to the government summarizing the results of that meeting and requesting help to get Radio Liberty back on the air.[24] But broadcasting was controlled by the president or the government, not parliament.

Radio Liberty started signing rebroadcasting agreements with regional stations, such as Radio Takt in Vinnytsia. It was not easy. The death of the head of the Poltava regional radio company, Yuriy Chechyk, remained suspicious. He had died in a car accident on his way to the capital, where he was to sign a rebroadcasting agreement with Radio Liberty. In September 2004, Radio NART (Honest Signal), bought on the eve of the elections by Yushchenko supporters, began rebroadcasting Radio Liberty.

Although general data on the radio audience in Ukraine are not readily available, research by the SIREX Marketing Service shows that the audience of the most popular news radio in November and December 2004 in the capital (during the heat of revolutionary events), Radio ERA, was rather small: about fifty thousand people.[25] This was an insignificant change from August and September 2004, when about 47.5 thousand Kyiv residents listened to Radio ERA.[26]

Like Internet websites, radio stations used humor as a weapon against the regime. On the eve of the election, many FM stations broadcast comic advertisements that ridiculed pro-regime candidate Viktor Yanukovych, who fainted when someone threw an egg at him. Political jokes and rhymes were also popular.

In November, Radio Kyiv decided to broadcast around the clock. The programs of this and other radio stations were broadcast right in the campus of freedom on Maidan and Khreshchatyk, which were filled with the tents of demonstrators. Gala Radio opened its news office right in the campus to broadcast news and music to the inhabitants of the tent city.

Unfair Actions against Ukrainian Mass Media

The following is a list of examples of the most unfair actions of the authorities against the mass media in Ukraine in 2004:

1. In February 2004, Radio Liberty was denied the opportunity to broadcast on FM frequencies. As a result, people could listen to it

only on short wave, as in Soviet times. People close to the SDPU(o) bought the frequencies on which Radio Liberty had previously broadcast.

2. Radio Liberty started broadcasting on a different FM station, Radio Continent, which also broadcast the news of the Ukrainian BBC, Voice of America, Deutsche Welle, Polish Radio, and Public Radio. In early March 2004, Radio Continent was cut off, purportedly because of a licensing problem.

3. In July 2004, the general prosecutor's office (GPO) accused the Volia cable company of distributing pornography, unlicensed broadcasting, and money laundering. One of the reasons for the GPO's interest in the station was the rebroadcasting of Channel 5 programs by its cable network.[27] Volia, which belongs to the international investment company Ukrainian Growth Fund and is managed by the international company SigmaBleyzer, had been broadcasting to more than five hundred thousand subscribers in Kyiv.

4. On fourteen occasions, various printing offices refused to print an edition of the Donetsk regional opposition newspaper *Ostrov* (*Island*).

5. In March 2004, eight months before the election, the court withdrew Channel 5's broadcasting rights, declaring its license illegal. The Kyiv television company TV-Tabachuk, owned by Donetsk representatives, brought suit against Channel 5 for the right to broadcast on the same frequency. They planned to broadcast for the Kyiv region beginning in September 2004. On October 14, Channel 5 was prohibited from broadcasting in Kyiv because it lacked a license there. Then, on October 18, the court decided to seize Channel 5's accounts. The company's accounts were frozen as a result of a court claim brought by member of parliament Volodymyr Syvkovych,[28] who headed the parliamentary commission responsible for the investigation of Viktor Yushchenko's poisoning. Because of the licensing problem, the channel survived under uncertain conditions until the election. Its accounts were unfrozen only three days before. The authorities did not dare to close the channel down. Instead, in the fall of 2004, the authorities took a different route, closing down Channel 5 in specific regions of Ukraine. According to the separate decisions of different regional authorities, the channel was closed down in Transcarpathia, Kharkiv, Donetsk, Kirovohrad,

Dnipropetrovsk, and Mykolaiv.[29] Some cable operators voluntarily closed down the channel, while others made it part of a more expensive package.

Media Trends before the Election

2004: The Year of the Election

The main trends in the Ukrainian mass media before the election were:

- Reinforcement of the propaganda element and reduction of information content
- Constraints on the freedom of speech
- More widespread distribution of temnyky to instruct journalists on what issues they were to report during a particular week and in what manner; as a result, the news reports given on different channels became strikingly similar (which was mind-numbing for the viewers)
- A lack of competition in news broadcasting; smears against the professionalism of journalists. "Real" journalists simply had no need to chase after news and sensational stories
- A lack of immediate reaction to events; a lack of live discussion on current topics
- A rise in Internet readership to 8 percent

According to a television viewers' survey conducted by the Academy of Ukrainian Press and the Institute of Sociology of the National Academy of Sciences of Ukraine, "On the main TV stations, the news was increasingly limited to a single viewpoint in comparison with June. Such coverage reached 90 percent and higher."[30]

In the summer, four months before the election, 98 percent of the evening news content on the First National Channel represented one point of view. For the channels Ukraina, 1+1, Inter, ICTV, STB, and the New Channel, the percentages were 96, 92, 91, 90, 89, and 88, respectively. Meanwhile, the First National Channel, 1+1, and Inter did not broadcast any statements at all by Viktor Yushchenko and Oleksandr Moroz. Channel UT–1 would not broadcast any statements by any opposition politician whatsoever. This situation persisted throughout the course of the whole election campaign, until the beginning of the "journalistic rebellion."

In September and October, a month before the election, a single viewpoint on the unfolding events continued to dominate the news coverage, from more than 90 percent on the First National Channel to 66 percent on Channel 5.[31] If statements by Viktor Yanukovych received three
times more news time than those of Viktor Yushchenko in the first week
of October (1,514 seconds against 445 seconds for Yushchenko), the proportion grew to fourfold in the first week of November (1,884 against
447 seconds). The Inter and Ukraina channels gave six and nineteen times
more news time to Viktor Yanukovych, respectively.

The D-Day of the Ukrainian media resistance movement was October 28, 2004. Three days before the election, forty journalists, representing five television stations, publicly declared that they would not obey
temnyky, or secret instructions.[32] One day after that, representatives of
eighteen television stations and media companies joined the journalists
in refusing to follow the government's temnyky.

Unfortunately, this event did not influence viewers or voters to the
extent hoped. The failure was the result of powerful media indoctrina-
tion during the previous several months. Moreover, despite the refusal
of a number of journalists to work under censorship, the general trend
on the major television channels was unaffected. Experts noticed general changes in broadcasting, but the main analytical programs were
still biased and full of propaganda.[33]

The initiative shifted to the Internet, where on October 25 the civic
initiative "The Orange Ribbon" evolved.[34] As a result, hundreds and
thousands of orange ribbons appeared on cars, ladies' handbags, back-
packs, bicycles, suits, hats, Internet banners, and the title pages of
websites. Initial support for this campaign came from the population of
Kyiv. People demonstrated their unity with the orange ribbon and in
other ways, not only to support Yushchenko as a presidential candidate, but also to express disagreement with the biased media and with
the falsification of election results. People with orange ribbons smiled
involuntarily as they passed by one another, and unfamiliar people
greeted one another as though they were family. The gesture became
an open protest against the authorities and against those who chose to
support them. At that point, some television anchors frequently appeared in orange pullovers even when the news they reported showed
no trace of journalistic ethics. No one could prohibit them from wearing
orange.

Yushchenko's staff managed to install a mobile television unit on
Maidan and rented a satellite channel. Live broadcasts were freely

available around the clock to any television company in the world and to any viewer with a satellite aerial. During the election campaign the opposition used huge mobile television screens. When a rally was announced in this or that city, a mobile workstation with a large screen was set up, and people were shown a documentary or the main events on Maidan. On September 18, on European Square in Kyiv Yushchenko delivered his first public speech after his poisoning. The speech was broadcast live by satellite to the largest squares of almost all regional centers, where half a million people watched it.[35] Bypassing official television channels, most Ukrainians could watch and hear Yushchenko speak.[36]

In discussing the role of Ukrainian journalists in the revolution, one cannot ignore the fact that journalists and the police were the last professions to join the revolution. The revolution began on November 22. That was the moment when the first tents appeared on Maidan. Channel 5 was the only one to broadcast the first signs of unrest and public civil disobedience.

The pivotal moment for the Ukrainian mass media was November 25, when the censorship system so aptly constructed by the regime collapsed like a house of cards. That was the day when the commitment to cover the events fully and without prejudice was broadcast on television. Everything began in a very symbolic manner: the deaf people of Ukraine were the first to hear the truth. On Thursday, November 25, Natalia Dmytruk, a sign-language interpreter on the state television channel, ignored the anchorwoman's text about the election results. Instead, she told her viewers: "The official results from the Central Election Commission have been falsified. Do not trust them. Yushchenko is our president. I'm really sorry that I had to translate lies before. I will not do this again. I'm not sure if I will see you again."[37]

The statement by Dmytruk was followed by declarations by the state television channel and channel 1+1.[38] The television station owned by Viktor Pinchuk, ICTV, decided to broadcast news about Ukraine in the style of the leading foreign media. This technique allowed it to broaden media coverage and counter the biased reporting style of Russian television stations, which were deliberately distorting information coming from Ukraine. For the first time during the election, the opposition appeared on national television, and government-controlled television stations presented Yushchenko in a positive light.

From this point, Maidan protests became the main subject of Ukrainian television. Forgotten talk shows were back on air, animated by guests representing opposing sides of the political spectrum and the barricades. Unbiased news was back too. Channel 5 and the Kyiv Community Channel broadcast directly from Maidan.

Channel 5 was now ranked third in popularity among nationwide television stations, with an audience of 11 percent.[39] The most popular station in Ukraine was Inter, with 22.6 percent. In second place was channel 1+1 with 16.1 percent. Then came New Channel and ICTV (7.0 percent and 6.4 percent, respectively). The government channel UT–1 was in sixth place (6.3 percent), and TRK Ukraina was seventh, with 4.7 percent.[40]

The same happened with Internet readers. The Internet audience rose 50 percent during the election. According to a December 2004 summary, Ukrainian Internet users numbered 5,905,465, or 12 percent of the population; in October that number had been around four million, or 8 percent.[41]

All this caused unprecedented openness by Kuchma and his administration during their last days in power. The television stations were broadcasting direct feeds from Koncha Zaspa, a small village where the cottages of the former Ukrainian elite were located. There, Kuchma conducted anticrisis think-tank meetings with Yanukovych and Medvedchuk. Later the stations broadcast the press conferences following roundtable negotiations between the authorities and the opposition under the aegis of international observers and mediators.

Conclusions

The Orange Revolution opened a path for a Ukrainian media revolution, and journalists were at the root of that revolution. Several factors contributed to the change and require further development.

1. This is a story of a media underground resisting the regime, finally resulting in a readiness to fight for one's rights. The tragedy of Gongadze and strict censorship demonstrated that journalists faced common problems and threats. This awakening led to professional unions, the formation of local free-speech groups, and parliamentary hearings on freedom of speech and censorship.
2. The existence of an independent media, such as Channel 5, *Zerkalo tyzhnia,* and the Internet was important. The launch of Channel 5, which broadcast in the capital and in key regions, was crucial. It was particularly important, given the regime's strict censorship policy, that the Internet provide new opportunities for independent media. Its main advantage is that it does not require a

large investment. Usually, independent media platforms are created by well-known journalists who are well aware of professional ethics and capable of defending their professional rights. These journalists must have good management skills. Ukraine needs more than numerous foreign trips, exchanges, and training seminars; it needs training for media managers.

3. Certain personal examples and instances of collective resistance contributed to the victory: for example, the public confrontation between the Channel 5 journalists and the authorities. Channel 5's victorious public protest proved that journalists can protect their right to broadcast uncensored information even under near-total media control.

4. Corporate and public control over media activities was essential. Ukraine needs a highly developed civil society and influential public organizations that will be able to change media behavior should journalists violate professional ethics. Anchors and reporters who lied on the air had difficulties when facing their relatives and those critical colleagues who had the privilege of working in the free media. Such journalists had to handle the cynical statements of politicians who brazenly claimed that no censorship existed. Social control and ethical standards were vital. The place for social debate in Ukraine was the Telekritika website (www.telekritika.kiev.ua), which featured genuine discussions of professional ethics. Several civic institutions monitored the television broadcasts and the press, issuing monthly reports and publicizing the results of their research.

5. Without the capitulation of media management, the media revolution might have proved far less effective. Media manipulation technologies failed because of the presence of alternative sources of information, which made managers understand that they had to change their news coverage. It became evident to media managers that the authorities would not be able to hang on to power. Eventually they either let their journalists act freely or even joined them in their struggle for freedom of speech.

6. The Orange Revolution was the first revolution to use modern technology and the Internet to full advantage. Funny stories, jokes, and symbols of the revolution were sent from one friend to another using email, blogs, and even short message services. Websites that provided free access to revolutionary songs and jokes about the government-backed candidate became extremely popular.

While preparing this chapter, I repeated in my memory the whole story of the Orange Revolution. You can find it—day by day, minute by minute—on the websites that covered those revolutionary days. Anybody on the Ukrainian Internet can find this record of contemporary history.

Hundreds of years ago one needed several years to put history on paper, to write a book. Now we can watch a revolution in another country on television and the Internet. The Orange Revolution was the first to happen mostly as a result of globalization and the development of new media technologies.

Notes

1. From a statement made in parliament by Kuchma. *Golos ukrayiny*, June 1994.
2. Yulia Mostova, "Tak kto zhe prikryl liubimuiu programmu prezidenta?" [Who Closed the President's Favorite Program?], *Zerkalo tyzhnia*, January 6–12, 1996, available at www.zerkalo-nedeli.com/nn/show/66/5003/.
3. Vakhtang Kipani, interview with ICTV director Dmitry Kiselev, *Kievskie vedomosti*, available at http://kipiani.org/samizdat/index.cgi?378.
4. Interfax-Ukraine, December 17, 2002.
5. Moroz's statement in parliament, Interfax-Ukraine, November 28, 2000.
6. "Transcript: What Do Melnychenko's Tapes Say about Gongadze Case?" Radio Free Europe/Radio Liberty, March 3, 2005, available at www.rferl.org/featuresarticle/2005/03/9f32ac57-9d6d-45f7-bcbf-b93c8e7fb263.html.
7. Deputy Interior Minister Mykola Dzhiga's statement, RIA Novosti, May 16, 2001, available at www.korrespondent.net/main/19478/.
8. The first article in the Ukrainian press on *temnyky*. "Medvedchuk wants to be the third president," *Ukrainska pravda*, March 25, 2002, available at www.pravda.com.ua/news/2002/3/25/21983.htm.
9. For a few examples, see: Vakhtang Kipani, "*Temnyky*: The Best," *Ukrainska pravda*, October 27, 2004, available at www.pravda.com.ua/news/2004/10/27/13093.htm.
10. Andriy Shevchenko, parliamentary statement, *Ukrainska pravda*, December 4, 2002, available at www.pravda.com.ua/archive/2002/december/4/3.shtml.
11. "Ukrainska presa gotuetsia do straiuku" [The Ukrainian Press Prepares to Strike], *Ukrainska pravda*, October 5, 2002, available at www.pravda.com.ua/archive/2002/october/5/1.shtml.
12. "The Press in Ukraine," *BBC News*, February 7, 2005, available at http://news.bbc.co.uk/1/hi/world/europe/4073375.stm. See also Nathalia Gabor and Zoya Skoropadenko, "The Ukrainian Media Landscape," European Journalism Centre, October 2002, available at www.ejc.nl/jr/emland/ukraine.html. See also website of *Kievskie vedomosty* at www.kv.com.ua/?m=about.
13. Ibid.
14. Viktor Chivokunia, "Sait anekdotiv pro Yanukovycha zablokovanii" [Yanukovych Joke Site Blocked], *Ukrainska pravda*, October 12, 2004, available at www.pravda.com.ua/archive/2004/october/12/5.shtml.
15. Globalnaia statistika interneta (Global Internet Statistics), Sputnik Media, available at http://index.bigmir.net.

16. *Telekritika*, June 18, 2004, available at www.telekritika.kiev.ua/tvweek/?id=15965.
17. "'1+1' podlezhit privitizatsii" ['1+1' Subject to Privatization], *Kommersant*, July 18, 2005, available at www.kommersant.ua/doc.html?DocID=591713&IssueId=29697.
18. TV ratings, available at www.prioritet.tv/pages/reiting.php.
19. Mikhailo Kramarenko, interview with the heads of Channel 5, *Telekritika*, May 26, 2003, available at www.telekritika.kiev.ua/interview/?id=8873.
20. An agreement signed by Channel 5 staff and the owners of the station *Telekritika*, June 11, 2003, available at www.telekritika.kiev.ua/comments/?id=9111.
21. Aleksandr Mikhelson, interview with Andriy Shevchenko, *Telekritika*, October 13, 2003, available at www.telekritika.kiev.ua/interview/?id=11231.
22. Natalia Ligachova, interview with Andriy Shevchenko, *Telekriticism*, March 5, 2004, available at http://telekritika.kiev.ua/interview/?id=14110.
23. "Kakije novosti slushat', dolzhna reshat auditorija, a ne president i oligarhi" [People Should Decide What to Watch, Not the President or Oligarchs], *Tovarishch*, 26 (April 2004), available at www.tovarish.com.ua/archive/611/Kakye_novosty_s.html.
24. "'Svoboda' ta 'Golos Ameryky' majut' povernutysia v ukrajinskyj efir" [Radio Liberty and the Voice of America Must Return to the Ukrainian Airwaves], *Telekritika*, June 12, 2004, available at www.telekritika.kiev.ua/news/?id=15869.
25. SIREX Marketing Service Research, November–December 2004, available at http://ofm.net.ua/index.php?option=com_content&task=view&id=23&Itemid=46.
26. Ibid., August–September, 2004, available at http://ofm.net.ua/index.php?option=com_content&task=view&id=24&Itemid=46a.
27. Sergei Leshchenko, interview with Petro Poroshenko, *Ukrainska pravda*, July 30, 2004, available at www2.pravda.com.ua/ru/archive/2004/july/30/1.shtml.
28. Ibid.
29. "Natsionalna rada z pitan telebachennia i radiomovlennia zakrila ochi na problemu nezakonnikh vimknen po Ukraini teleperedach '5 kanalu'" [The National Committee on Television and Radio Closed Its Eyes to the Problem of the Illegal Cutoff of Channel 5's Programs in Ukraine], *Telekritika*, October 13, 2004, available at www.telekritika.kiev.ua/news/?id=17842.
30. "Povidomlen iz sinkhronom V. Yanukovycha u serpnevikh vipuskakh novin zalishaetsia vdvichi bilshe, nizh u V. Yushchenka" [There Is Two Times More News on Yanukovych in August than News on Yushchenko], *Telekritika*, August 9, 2004, available at www.telekritika.kiev.ua/news/?id=17275.
31. "Monitoring politicheskikh novostei" [Monitoring of the Political News], *Telekritika*, October 19, 2004, available at www.telekritika.kiev.ua/mon_tvnews/?id=18777.
32. "No to censorship!" Journalist's statement, *Ukrainska pravda*, October 28, 2004, available at www.pravda.com.ua/news/2004/10/28/13127.htm.
33. "Publichno zadeklarirovannaia redaktsionnaia politika" [Editorial Politics Publicly Declared], *Telekritika*, October 29, 2004, available at www.telekritika.kiev.ua/mon_tvnews/?id=18583.
34. "Kievskoie metro poviazano oranzhevymi lentami" [Kyiv Metro Tied with Orange Ribbons], *Syla narodu*, October 28, 2004, available at www.silanaroda.com/index.php?itemid=337&mode=full.
35. "Viktora Yushchenka pochula i pobachila vsia Ukraina" [All Ukraine Heard and Saw Viktor Yushchenko], on the website of Yushchenko's political bloc, available at www.razom.org.ua/ua/news/2181/.
36. Igor Zhdanov and Yuriy Yakimenko, "Formula oranzhevoi pobedy: zametki nepostoronnikh nabliudatelei" [The Formula for Orange Victory: Notes from Direct Observers], *Zerkalo tyzhnia*, January 22–28, 2005, available at www.zerkalo-nedeli.com/nn/show/530/49002/.

37. Unian, November 25, 2004, available at www.pravda.com.ua/news/2004/11/25/14162.htm.

38. Ibid., available at www.pravda.com.ua/news/2004/11/25/14167.htm "1+1" Statement. www.1plus1.net/about/news.phtml?637.

39. According to a survey conducted by GfK–USM.

40. Interfax-Ukraine, "'5 kanal' vyshel na tret'e mesto po reitingu telekanalov v Ukraine" [Channel 5 Moves into Third Place among Ukrainian TV Stations], December 6, 2004, available at www.telekritika.kiev.ua/news/?id=19715

41. Globalnaia statistika interneta (Global Internet Statistics), Sputnik Media, available at http://index.bigmir.net.

CHAPTER SEVEN

Western Influence

OLEKSANDR SUSHKO AND OLENA PRYSTAYKO

WESTERN ENGAGEMENT IN THE 2004 Ukrainian presidential election began long before the vote took place and remains a hotly debated issue. Viktor Yanukovych's former campaign director Vyacheslav Chornovil, for example, argued in a July 25, 2005, interview that the United States had been trying to bring Viktor Yushchenko into power since the early 1990s.[1]

To assess the role of the West realistically, we must distinguish myth from reality, which is the objective of this chapter. Yet perceptions, even mythical ones, of the role of the West and various individual Western actors were an integral part of the 2004 Ukrainian political campaign and had a real impact.

———————————

Since the Orange Revolution, several comprehensive analyses of the 2004 political changes have been published in Ukraine and abroad. The external impact on the 2004 election has been the focus of several papers, including a special issue of *National Security and Defense* magazine from the Razumkov Center (no. 5, 2004). The comprehensive book *Presidential Elections and [the] Orange Revolution: Implications for Ukraine's Transition,* from the Friedrich Ebert Foundation (Helmut Kurth and Iris Kempe, editors, Kyiv, 2005), also contains a chapter by Kempe and Iryna Solonenko on foreign support. In this chapter, we use statistical data and quotations first published in those publications. Note that Oleksandr Sushko contributed to the report on Ukraine in Freedom House's *Nations in Transit 2005.* Some of the assessments in this chapter are based on that book.

"Western Interference" and Domestic Policy Debates

Debates on the role of the West in Ukraine's 2004 presidential campaign began a year before the elections, inspired by Georgia's Rose Revolution. The Georgian case shocked Ukraine's post-Soviet elite, which had been elaborating its strategy for the succession of power. President Leonid Kuchma and his entourage wanted to prevent such a scenario in Ukraine. They accused Georgia's new leaders of massive use of Western support. Such charges were supported by a series of interviews on the role of the United States, and of George Soros personally, given by former Georgian president Eduard Shevardnadze to the Russian mass media. The official line stressed that the mass movements were inspired from the outside and were connected with Shevardnadze's former transoceanic patrons' dissatisfaction with his policies.

Ukrainian leaders just repeated that viewpoint: "The process of power transfer can take place only by the will of the nation. Without manipulations and external interventions. According to Shevardnadze such interventions took place in Georgia," President Kuchma told the *Fakty i kommentarii* (Facts and Comments) newspaper in December 2003.[2] Ukrainian complaints about the Western impact focused on "foreign interference." Various "examples" of involvement were given: official statements of Western governments and parliaments, declarations of international organizations and their representatives, technical assistance, and support for nongovernmental organizations.

In January 2004, President Kuchma answered a question about the initiative by Viktor Yushchenko, the leader of the Our Ukraine bloc, to set up a special commission of the Parliamentary Assembly of the Council of Europe (PACE) monitoring committee in the country. The proposed commission would have monitored the problems related to the constitutional and political reforms and the actions of different political forces. Kuchma replied:

> We needn't be solicited in favor of democracy. We in Ukraine need democracy more than someone in Western Europe where not everybody knows that such a country exists . . . We are grateful to accept the advice of representatives of more experienced democracies than ours. But we also know well where advice ends and interference into our internal affairs begins. I am not confident that all those who visit us with the mandates from the Council of Europe feel that borderline . . . We are aware that the Council of Europe needs Ukraine no less than we [need] the Council of Europe.

This makes ultimatums irrelevant. You shouldn't behave like our opposition. Our opposition is just some ten years old, and you are much older, so, behave like adults.[3]

In a January 2004 statement, the Ministry for Foreign Affairs "hailed" the world's interest in Ukraine's internal reforms. But it stressed that "biased statements" from PACE coreporters Hanne Severinsen and Renatha Wolwend, on the progress of constitutional reform, constituted acts of "interference into the internal affairs of the country, which does not encourage the establishment of the standards of the Council of Europe in the Ukrainian state."[4]

The debate about Western support for nongovernmental organizations (NGOs) mattered because NGOs and independent think tanks monitored the election at several levels. In 2004, at the initiative of communists supported by pro-Kuchma factions, the Verkhovna Rada (parliament) introduced a temporary investigative commission to establish the facts of external interference in the Ukrainian election campaign by NGOs funded by foreign states. It was chaired by Communist Party of Ukraine (CPU) member Valeriy Mishura, known for his strong anti-Western attitudes. The commission's objective was to investigate the impact of foreign financial assistance to Ukrainian NGOs as well as the activity of Western NGOs in Ukraine. In May 2004, the chair of the commission published a report (which was not approved by the whole commission), in which Ukrainian NGOs and foreign donors were accused of lobbying for foreign (Western) interests. According to Adam Martyniuk, communist first deputy chair of the Verkhovna Rada, "Ninety percent or more of the foundations existing in Ukraine engage not in what is written in their official documents but are established to influence the internal situation in our country." Martyniuk wanted such foundations to lobby for Ukrainian interests, "Not as we see it today, when they lobby for the interests of those states and those services that fund them." He noted that the problem concerned some media as well. Martyniuk claimed, "Some funds have been spent to support [the] mass media, while the lion's share has been used to lobby for foreign interests."[5]

As the election approached, more and more publications and segments of the pro-Kuchma media (such as the newspapers *2000* and *Ponedelnik*, and the television channels Inter and 1+1) propounded the view that the opposition, led by Yushchenko, represented the interests of Western (mostly American) circles, while the Kuchma-Yanukovych camp represented national and patriotic interests.

This situation in the media affected the whole campaign and led to a polarization of public opinion with regard to foreign policy. Massive anti-Western propaganda during the 2004 presidential campaign decreased public support for Ukraine's membership in the North Atlantic Treaty Organization (NATO) (which stood at 15 percent in early 2005, a decline of 12 percent compared with early 2004) and the European Union (which declined to about 50 percent).[6]

Western Interests

The West had a real interest in Ukraine in 2004 because Ukraine is a borderland country between democratic Europe and authoritarian, corrupt, post-Soviet Eurasia. Pluralistic and autocratic trends coexisted in its "defective democracy." In 2004 those trends clashed. It was a real chance to get the country back on the democratic path after several years of degradation. The Ukrainian political stage was occupied by the unpopular, stagnating Kuchma regime and a growing reformist opposition led by Viktor Yushchenko. As their resources were approximately equal (the opposition had wider public support, but the government had administrative resources), external factors could be vital.

The interests of the external players sprang primarily from their systems of values. Their main objective was to spread their own practices to neighboring territories and beyond. For both Western and Eastern external players, the idea was "be like us." The difference was the substance of the proposed "us"—the particular principles of an actor.

True Western interests were guided by common values, which were to be embedded in a stable and democratic Ukraine as an object of Western influence. According to a report from the Razumkov Center:

> The EU, USA, OSCE, NATO and other Western states and international organizations are interested in Ukraine being a stable, predictable country with legitimate authorities. Only the free election of representative bodies of power is an indicator of their true support by society, and, therefore, a sign of the absence of fundamental contradictions between the interests of the state and citizens, which are constantly fraught with the threat of conflict. Hence, the West is interested in the introduction of democratic principles and standards into Ukraine's political practice and their strengthening.[7]

At the same time, most Western actors preferred a victory by Yushchenko, who was committed to democratic values, to a victory by Yanukovych, who was associated with authoritarianism and corruption.

This affected the behavior of many Westerners involved: politicians, journalists, and even election observers.

From the first preparations for the 2004 presidential election, Western actors and institutions saw it as an important test case for political transformation.[8] Ukraine's domestic agenda concerned the separation of powers based on democratic principles and a demonstration of national independence from Russia. The real democratic choice between two candidates was the positive difference between Ukraine and other states of the Commonwealth of Independent States, where the population either does not have a real political choice, and power is concentrated in one person, or the choice is between a democratic candidate and a communist. To reinforce its resistance to interest groups, the political system had to become more transparent and align itself more strongly with democratic and formal processes. To further its interests in Ukraine, the West was first and foremost concerned with democratic standards in the election campaign and beyond.

Therefore, Brussels, Berlin, and Washington were preoccupied with the election being conducted according to international democratic standards rather than with the identity of the victor, pretending that both candidates were committed to democracy and a market economy. The election was perceived not only as a litmus test for democratic reform, but also as a step to guarantee stability and security.[9]

Western actors had a clear idea of what procedures, if not what outcome, the election should follow. Madeleine Albright,[10] George H. W. Bush, Richard Holbrooke, Zbigniew Brzezinski, and Wesley Clark, all of whom visited Ukraine in 2004, stressed the international relevance of the Ukrainian elections by highlighting the importance of a free and fair election process.[11]

The Council of Europe expressed its concerns about the internal situation in Ukraine based on an information mission to Kyiv, March 16–19, 2004.[12] The mission's main recommendations pointed out restrictions on democracy, lack of judicial independence, widespread corruption, and violations of media freedom.

All these statements contributed to the consolidation of Western activity during the campaign, the vote, and the counting of the vote.

Major Western Actors: Common Interests, Different Tactics

The United States and the European Union, international observation missions to the election campaign, and supporters of the Ukrainian NGO sector were active in democracy promotion in Ukraine long before the presidential election campaign of autumn and winter 2004. They appealed to Ukrainian authorities in the name of international democratic standards and became major Western actors during the campaign,[13] but their tactics differed significantly.

Western involvement in the presidential election took different forms. Several methods used were typical of Western participation in election campaigns in countries on the border of the democratic world. They ranged from political declarations and financing Ukrainian NGOs to international observation missions and mediation during the November political crisis (see "International Observation Missions and Their Efficiency" and "Western Support to the Ukrainian NGO Sector" below). Besides governmental and NGO actors, Western public relation firms also contributed to the 2004 Ukrainian campaign. Their approach was value neutral, so anybody who paid could use such services. Several Western public relations companies worked for Yanukovych's campaign.

The European Union

One of the purposes of European Union policy toward Ukraine is to establish and strengthen its democracy. The basic bilateral agreements between the European Union and Ukraine include it as a purpose of their development of relations. Ukraine is also one of the target states of the European Commission's European Neighbourhood Policy, which aims at creating "a ring of friends" across European Union borders that will share common European Union values.[14] This purpose determined European Union policy toward the Ukrainian election campaign.

Though they shared the same goal, new and old European Union member states chose different approaches. The recent velvet revolutions of the new European Union members helped them to understand Ukraine's internal political processes, and they made full use of that understanding during the settlement of the Ukrainian political crisis. Some new European Union member states demonstrated the deepest involvement in the historic change of the Ukrainian election. In those states, Ukraine's movement toward democracy was seen as a way to resist the neoauthoritarian influence of Putin's Russia over Ukraine and to spread stability and prosperity, not only in Ukraine, but also in Central and Eastern Europe.

These states, some of which border Ukraine, made political declarations that made clear their interests in the Ukrainian election. For

instance, when the *Sejm*, Poland's parliament, adopted a resolution calling for a free and transparent election in Ukraine, 330 members of parliament voted in favor, with only twelve against and twenty-two not
voting.[15] The Polish statement was much more positive than the declarations of the U.S. Congress, the German *Bundestag*, the Council of Europe, or the European Commission. Instead of criticizing the lack of
media freedom or fairness in the election campaign, Poland expressed
support for Ukraine's future in the European Union and in NATO. This
declaration was of the same tenor as comments made by President
Alexander Kwasniewski in a September 2 article in the *International Herald Tribune:* "The EU has fallen short of offering any incentives to the
opposition in Ukraine."[16] He indicated that the European Union should
not stop its enlargement with Turkey, which meant offering Ukraine an
opportunity for accession. During an official visit to Kyiv on November
12 between the first and the second rounds of the election, Wlodzimierz
Cimoszewicz, Poland's foreign minister and new chair-in-office of the
Council of Europe, called for a free and fair vote. His clear position influenced the schedule of his visit. Instead of meeting with Prime Minister Yanukovych and President Kuchma, as originally planned, the Polish minister met only with the speaker of parliament, the head of the
Ukrainian Central Election Commission, and opposition presidential
candidate Yushchenko.[17] Slovak prime minister Mikulas Dzurinda emphasized on several occasions that "Slovakia wants to act as Ukraine's
voice at the European table."[18] The Slovak government did not miss a
chance to declare that the elections should be conducted in a free and
fair manner.[19] Of course, neighboring states also sent election observers.
In addition to observers deployed by international organizations, the
Slovak government sent sixty observers, and Poland sent twenty-four
observers for the first round.[20]

The new European Union members' active involvement in the election campaign, through mediation (by presidents Alexander
Kwasniewski of Poland and Valdas Adamkus of Lithuania), the sending of observers, and numerous statements by Polish officials and institutions, encouraged the Ukrainian opposition.

Initially, the old European Union member states were cautious and
practiced their traditional Russia-first policy. In autumn 2004, it appeared
difficult for the European Union to formulate a unified policy backed
by both new and old member states. One dilemma was the conflict between a desire to have a democratic neighbor and their energy dependence on Russia. Finally, pressure from the United States and the new

European Union member states, combined with concern over the danger of a bloody Ukrainian political crisis after the second vote of November 21, tipped the European Union's position in favor of active involvement to buttress democracy in Ukraine.

Despite the differing positions of the old and new member states, the European Union sent a strong and consistent message during the culmination of the Ukrainian campaign and the Orange Revolution. Reacting to the first-round election, European Union leaders regretted that it did not meet a number of requirements to be considered democratic and noted that the conditions were not fair for all candidates during the preelection period.[21] The Presidency of the European Union expressed serious doubt that the official results of the election reflected the will of the Ukrainian people.[22] In contrast to President Putin, European Union leaders demanded reconsideration of the election outcome, thus rejecting Yanukovych as the legitimate president of Ukraine.[23]

Similarly, European decision makers did not accept the outcome of the second tour because of the lack of democratic standards, and they supported a peaceful solution of the crisis on a legal basis. European Union High Representative for Foreign and Security Policy Javier Solana, Polish president Kwasniewski and Lithuanian president Adamkus became important in the negotiations between conflicting parties.

The European Union used carrots rather than sticks in its strategy for enhancing democracy in Ukraine: future European Union policy toward the state depended on Ukraine's adherence to democratic principles during the election campaign. The danger of a bloody political crisis after the second vote forced the European Union to change to a stick approach with political means: "The November 21 run-off's preliminary returns must be thoroughly checked. If Ukrainian authorities fail to do so this will have very serious consequences for relations between the EU and Ukraine, in particular, in implementing the European Neighborhood Policy."[24]

The United States

The position of the United States was straighter from the beginning. It had long seen Ukraine at the forefront of democracy in the post-Soviet space. On October 7, 2004, U.S. ambassador to Ukraine John E. Herbst reiterated the readiness of the U.S. government to cooperate with the future president, be he Yanukovych or Yushchenko, and said that "what matters is the election process's honesty and transparency."[25]

The United States' goal coincided with that of the European Union: an election campaign under democratic principles and the further democratic development of Ukraine. At the same time, the United States preferred the stick: nonadherence to democratic principles would lead to negative political and economic consequences for the state. In addition to numerous statements by acting and former U.S. leaders to encourage Ukrainian adherence to democracy,[26] the United States chose to exert direct individual influence on Ukrainian authorities.

In 2004, several famous U.S. political and social leaders (Madeleine Albright, Zbigniew Brzezinski, George H. W. Bush, Richard Holbrooke, George Soros, Wesley Clark, Richard Armitage, and others) visited Ukraine with only one mission: to prevent Kuchma and his entourage from adopting an authoritarian, illegitimate solution to the probable political crisis.

In addition to putting political pressure on Ukrainian authorities, the United States used the threat of sanctions. On September 15, Congressman Dana Rohrabacher submitted a bill entitled "Ukraine Democracy and the Election Act of 2004." The bill called on President Kuchma and Prime Minister Yanukovych to "stop overt, flagrant and inadmissible violations of Ukraine's human rights commitments to the OSCE, and guarantee respect for fundamental democratic liberties." It proposed sanctions should violations of the standards listed in the bill continue. These included barring top officials of the Ukrainian government and their family members from entering U.S. territory, confiscating their property in the United States, freezing their bank accounts, seizing the funds in those accounts, and banning loans to them.[27]

United States deputy state department spokesperson Adam Ereli said on November 1 that the second round of the election on November 21 presented "an opportunity for Ukraine to affirm its commitments to democratic principles, and we urge the Ukrainian authorities to allow the people of Ukraine to choose freely."[28] In a letter to President Kuchma, President George W. Bush noted that "a tarnished election will lead us to review our relations with Ukraine."[29] The letter was given to Kuchma during the five-day mission of Senator Richard G. Lugar, chair of the U.S. Senate Foreign Relations Committee, as a personal representative of President Bush, to observe the second round of the Ukrainian presidential election.

On November 22, immediately after the falsified vote, Lugar issued the first strong Western message on Ukraine (at about 3 p.m.). He stated that Kuchma held personal responsibility for the peaceful and lawful settlement of the political crisis after the second round of voting.[30] The statement by Secretary of State Colin Powell on November 24 proved that the United States was serious about nonrecognition of the second vote. Powell stated that the United States "cannot accept the Ukraine election result as legitimate" and called for an investigation. He warned that if there were no investigation, there could be implications for U.S. relations with Ukraine.[31]

Comparing the impact of the European Union versus that of the United States, we conclude that the United States was clearly the more active Western contributor to international efforts in Ukraine during the 2004 presidential election. Both official and nongovernmental U.S. representatives demonstrated the will to take the stronger action to prevent fraud and ensure a fair election result. The United States also contributed more financial and technical support.

The European Union was divided into two blocs: a Western European bloc with a more moderate approach, which became truly active only during voting and the Orange Revolution, and a Central European bloc (the four Visegrad states and the Baltic states), which was proactive from the very beginning, strongly committed to helping Ukraine to return to the democratic path. Central Europeans convinced the old member states to adopt a firm common position during the Orange Revolution. As a result, the West as a whole took consistent and effective action to prevent the use of force in Ukraine and to ensure a peaceful, ultimately democratic solution to the November–December 2004 political crisis.

The strong common, consolidated message that the West delivered to Ukraine (and also to Russia) was important for Ukraine's 2004 democratic success. Still, that success would not have been possible through Western efforts alone: the active part of Ukrainian society played a crucial role in the democratic explosion of the Orange Revolution.

Western Support to the Ukrainian NGO Sector

Western donors focused their activities on the election process and often found NGOs to implement their ideas. Their activities included supporting independent public opinion polls, carrying out independent exit polls, producing television spots, encouraging people to vote, publishing and distributing literature explaining people's rights, and supporting human rights organizations in monitoring violations and prosecuting violators. By doing this, Ukrainian civil society protested against the obvious election fraud of the second round of elections and became a decisive part of the Orange Revolution.

International donors provided special support for NGOs involved in the election-monitoring process. In particular, a consortium of Western donors supplied funds for an election exit poll. The national exit poll, led by the Democratic Initiatives Foundation, proved to be a success despite tensions that appeared among polling organizations within the project. Special election-oriented donor programs were offered by the International Renaissance Foundation (IRF, which is the Soros Foundation in Ukraine) and the National Endowment for Democracy (a U.S. donor organization).[32] In particular, beginning in the fall of 2003, the IRF provided almost $1.3 million to Ukrainian NGOs to carry out election-related projects.[33]

The European Commission's National Indicative Program 2004–2006 set aside some ten million euros out of a total of 212 million euros to support civil society, the media, and democracy.[34] Further, the European Commission allocated one million euros to the Central Election Committee of Ukraine. It also supported Ukraine's civic life and its ability to conduct a free and fair election through a variety of technical assistance projects.[35] The U.S. Agency for International Development (USAID) gave $1.475 million for election-related activities.[36]

In 2004, USAID extended grants to Development Associates, Inc., and Freedom House to assist in administering and monitoring the election process. It initiated a new program, "Monitoring of Elections in Ukraine," which was intended to help the public ensure more transparent, competitive, and fair elections. Monthly roundtables on election problems brought public figures and government officials together. Election commission members and observers received training.

This training was fully compliant with USAID obligations and bilateral documents. In particular, in 2004, USAID signed a memorandum of understanding with the Central Election Commission on the main directions and goals of cooperation in elections. Pursuant to this document, the main objectives of the program were "to increase the level of professionalism, competence, and independence of election commission members; the effectiveness of Ukrainian civic organizations in monitoring the electoral process; and citizens' awareness of their rights and responsibilities as election participants."[37] Accusations that such activity interferes in domestic affairs therefore do not correspond to the true state of affairs.

Western Public Relations Assistance to Yanukovych's Camp

The amount of Western public relations assistance used by the pro-government camp during the campaign remains a mystery. Contracts and relations in this area remain mostly nontransparent.

136   OLEKSANDR SUSHKO AND OLENA PRYSTAYKO

During a visit to the United States in October 2004, a Yanukovych advisor, Eduard Prutnik, the man responsible for the prime minister's contacts with the West, arranged a press conference, "The Position of Ukraine between East and West." At that conference Prutnik spoke together with Aleksei Kiselov, a U.S. citizen born in Odesa and affiliated with the company North Atlantic Securities. According to *Ukrainska pravda,* Kiselov admitted his involvement in brokering a contract between Yanukovych and Washington, D.C.-based DCS Co. but denied that his client paid $750,000 for public relations services. Prutnik and Kiselov tried to convince an audience that Yanukovych was a new leader for Ukraine, one who had proved that his efficient internal policy would lead Ukraine to a prosperity based on stability.

Kiselov was a key person in the provision of American public relations services for Yanukovych. Because of his efforts several American firms were involved in the promotion of the Ukrainian prime minister in the United States. The U.S. justice department provided *Ukrainska pravda* with a list of organizations involved in cooperation with Yanukovych's government in 2003–2004 and registered in accordance with the U.S. Foreign Agents Registration Act of 1938: Venable, LLP, registration no. 5435; Potomac Communications Strategies, Inc., registration no. 5588; Creative Response Concepts (no registration file); DB Communications, LLC, registration no. 5634; JWI, LLC, registration no. 4990; and Aleksei Kiselov, registration no. 5572.[38]

Western sources also reported contacts between former Yanukovych chief of staff Serhiy Tyhipko and political consultant Douglas Schoen.[39] According to *Zerkalo tyzhnia,* the Greenberg, Carville, and Shrum agency conducting the campaign of U.S. presidential candidate John Kerry also consulted for Yanukovych.[40]

The public relations strategy offered by Kiselov was too similar to those often used by discredited third world politicians to improve their image in the West. Ultimately, those efforts failed to represent Yanukovych as a representative of a "New Ukraine" that would boast of rapid economic growth, stability, and good governance.

International Observation Missions and Their Efficacy

Election observers were the most significant product of joint efforts by international institutions and Western governments. Generally speaking, election observation is one of the most powerful instruments of Western influence. The OSCE mission to Ukraine was one of the largest

Table 7.1. Foreign Observers at the 2004 Ukrainian Presidential Election

	International Election Observation Mission (OSCE/ODIHR, NATO PA, PACE, OSCE PA, EP)	Official Observers from Foreign States	Official Observers from International Organizations	Total
First round (October 31, 2004)	650	214	1,591	2,455
Revote of the second round (December 26, 2004)	1,367	3,281	8,996	13,644

Sources: Helmut Kurth and Iris Kempe, eds., *Presidential Elections and Orange Revolution: Implications for Ukraine's Transition* (Kyiv: The Friedrich Ebert Foundation, 2005), 116. Data based on OSCE/ODIHR (www.osce.org/odihr/documents.html) and Central Election Commission of Ukraine (www.cvk.gov.ua) websites.

Note: EP: European Parliament; NATO PA: North Atlantic Treaty Organization Parliamentary Assembly; OSCE/ODIHR: Organization for Security and Cooperation in Europe/ Office for Democratic Institutions and Human Rights; OSCE PA: Organization for Security and Cooperation in Europe Parliamentary Assembly; PACE: Parliamentary Assembly of the Council of Europe.

to date. Ukraine hosted a record number of international observers for the December 26 rerun. Despite the Christmas holidays, the total number of foreign observers, more than thirteen thousand, was the highest in the history of international election observation.

According to Kempe and Solonenko, national and international election observation is an increasingly effective tool whenever democracy is under pressure, as in Belarus or in Serbia under President Slobodan Milosevic. In Ukraine, election observers pointed out how unfair the elections had been. The OSCE/ODIHR, together with the parliamentary assemblies of the OSCE, the Council of Europe, NATO, and the European Parliament, conducted both short- and long-term monitoring of the Ukrainian elections (through the International Election Observation Mission [IEOM]). In terms of the number of participants (428 for the first round, 650 for the second round, and 1,367 for the revote), this was one of the largest election observation missions to date.[41] For instance, 511 OSCE observers were deployed to the 2004 presidential elections in Georgia, and 258 observed the Serbian presidential elections in

2002.[42] In addition to the observers from international organizations, a huge number of observers were also sent to Ukraine by national governments and nongovernmental organizations.

According to the preliminary statement of the International Election Observation Mission, published on November 1, 2004, "The 31 October presidential election in Ukraine did not meet a considerable number of OSCE, Council of Europe and other European standards for democratic elections. This election process constitutes a step backward from the 2002 elections." The election process was characterized by significant shortcomings (although there were some positive aspects worthy of note). The most important shortcomings were:

- The lack of separation between resources owned or managed by incumbent political forces and the state resources of Yanukovych's team
- The overwhelming bias in favor of Yanukovych in the state media
- Interference by the state administration
- The use of media guidelines from the government to homogenize media policy
- The dissemination of inflammatory campaign material of anonymous or unclear origin
- Inaccurate voter lists and confusion in the formation of polling station commissions, which impeded the ability of voters to check their entries
- A large number of errors and omissions in the voter lists, which jeopardized the principle of universality of the vote
- The inefficiency of the Central Election Commission to ensure the uniform application of the law[43]

The democratic shortcomings and lack of international standards for free and fair elections increased the West's attention before the second election round. When evidence suggested that Yanukovych had violated democratic standards to win the closely contested election, IEOM issued a statement heavily criticizing Ukraine for not meeting international standards for democratic elections.[44] According to the preliminary statement, state authorities and the Central Election Commission displayed a lack of will in conducting a genuinely democratic election.[45] That statement drew countless official reactions from Washington, Brussels, Berlin, Warsaw, and other European capitals and made headlines worldwide. Later, the IEOM assessment of the second round, in addition to the results of the exit polls conducted by various Ukrainian institutions, provided the most important support for the opposition demand to nullify the result and to conduct a free and fair vote.

During the rerun of the second round, the OSCE increased the number of international observers to guarantee a democratic process. According to the statement of the IEOM on the December 26 rerun, "The process brought Ukraine substantially closer to meeting OSCE election commitments and Council of Europe and other European standards." Democratic progress was reported regarding the balanced media coverage and equal campaign conditions in general.[46] As the Razumkov Center's report concluded, the "social demand for monitoring of the election campaign by foreign observers may be testimony not so much to the understanding of the role and possibilities of Western structures as the extreme mistrust of Ukraine's society in the Ukrainian authorities."[47]

International observation missions in Ukraine in 2004, taken together, were the largest in election-monitoring history. They contributed greatly to ensuring free and fair elections, especially during the rerun on December 26. Yet Ukrainian success proved only that international observation missions may be successful if national observers professionally assist foreigners. The Orange Revolution proved that international observation works as an efficient instrument only in combination with political and judicial procedures and domestic civil activity.

Crisis Mediation during the Orange Revolution

The fraudulent second vote on November 21, which was followed by mass rallies in Kyiv and other Ukrainian cities, created the need for international mediation. Protestors blocked government buildings in Kyiv, and the threat of bloody clashes with police became real. The leaders of several states and international organizations decided to come to Kyiv to launch negotiations under an international umbrella.

Polish president Alexander Kwasniewski, Lithuanian president Valdas Adamkus, OSCE secretary general Jan Kubis, European Union High Representative for the Common Foreign and Security Policy Javier Solana, and Speaker of the Russian State Duma Boris Gryzlov arrived in Kyiv on November 26 to resolve the political crisis. After a two-hour discussion at the Mariinskyi Palace in Kyiv, the participants, including Kuchma, Yushchenko, Yanukovych, and the speaker of Ukraine's supreme council, Volodymyr Lytvyn, reached an agreement and issued a statement on the resolution of the political crisis in Ukraine.

The statement said that both sides opposed the use of force, which could result in escalation and bloodshed. The two major sides (Yushchenko and Yanukovych) agreed to set up working groups for negotiations. The two sides thanked the representatives of the European Union, the OSCE, the presidents of Poland and Lithuania, and the speaker of the Duma for their readiness to continue facilitating the negotiations aimed at resolving the crisis.[48]

Commenting on the results of these joint efforts, Solana said a day later: "The most important point is that both parties to the conflict have pledged to refrain from resorting to force under any circumstances. They have also decided to immediately form working groups to regulate the conflict." Solana said the only obligation of the protestors was to refrain from blocking administrative buildings.[49] The opposition did not fulfill that obligation.

The mediated talks between Yushchenko and Yanukovych prevented the escalation of hostility and opened a path toward a political solution based on the December 3 decision by the Ukrainian supreme council to conduct a rerun of the second round of elections on December 26. Mediation played an important role in preventing the use of force during the Orange Revolution. It was an efficient tool for achieving a peaceful solution in Ukraine during the most crucial days of the revolution, when radicals in the government camp tried to convince Kuchma to use the police and the army against protestors in the street. The international mediation mission did not yield a final political decision, but it did provide a basis for one. It reassured Ukrainian society that the democratic world was carefully observing the political drama in Ukraine.

Conclusions

The "values-driven" approach represented by most of the Western actors during the 2004 presidential campaign in Ukraine did not entirely exclude the sympathies and preferences of the West. On the one hand, the West was reluctant to offer Ukraine the prospect of integration into the Euro-Atlantic structures. While demanding transition toward a market economy and democracy, the West focused on supporting a free and fair election. From the Western perspective, it was more important to assess the election process than to decide who would be the future president of Ukraine. Consequently, Western decision makers did not openly support either candidate.

On the other hand, a fair evaluation of Western motives and actions proved that "it is obvious that Europe and America would prefer Viktor Yushchenko to win, rather than Viktor Yanukovych," as retired U.S. member of Congress John Conlan recognized before the elections.[50] That preference played a role in Western actions.

Among the Western actors the United States was the most active contributor to international efforts in Ukraine in terms of consistency, allocated assistance, and readiness to implement radical measures if democracy had failed. The European Union had two different faces: a Western European bloc, with a more moderate approach, which became truly active only during the election and the Orange Revolution; and a Central European bloc, which was proactive from the very beginning, strongly committed to helping Ukraine to return to democracy. The Central Europeans brought Europe to a common position during the Orange Revolution. They enabled the consistent, effective action of the West as a whole to prevent the use of force in Ukraine and to ensure an ultimately democratic solution to the November–December 2004 political crisis.

To a great extent, the common Western strategy came about because the European Union overcame its typical Russia-first policy approach toward Ukraine and followed a united, more aggressive strategy of defending Ukrainian freedom against Russia. This turnabout became possible as a result of the efforts of its new member states, which saw their active role as mediators of the Ukrainian political crisis as an excellent way to share their experience on human rights and dignity with Ukraine, and to position themselves as the main internal European Union forces shaping Eastern policy. The main Western actors, pursuing the same goal with different instruments, found a common strategy that coincided with internal demands and the courage of Ukrainians.

The 2004 Ukrainian crisis and the Orange Revolution contributed substantially to the unity of the West. The strong common, consolidated message, delivered from the West to Ukraine (and, importantly, to Russia) demonstrated real Euro-Atlantic political integrity, which is increasingly rare because of the frequent disputes between the European Union and the United States, as well as between old and new Europe. But success would not have been possible through Western efforts alone. It was the active part of Ukrainian society that made Ukraine the world's biggest democratic success story in 2004.

Notes

1. "Interv'iu Tarasa Chornilova" [Interview with Taras Chornilov], *Korrespondent*, July 25, 2005, available at www.korrespondent.net/main/126716.
2. *Fakty i kommentarii* [Facts and Comments], November 29, 2003.
3. Interfax-Ukraine, January 22, 2004.
4. Razumkov Center, *National Security and Defense*, no. 5/2004, Kyiv, 10.
5. Ibid.
6. Data from the Democratic Initiatives Foundation, February 2005, and the Razumkov Center, January–March 2005.
7. *National Security and Defense*, 21.
8. Anders Åslund. "Left Behind: Ukraine's Uncertain Transformation," *The National Interest*, 73 (fall 2003), 107 16.
9. Helmut Kurth and Iris Kempe, eds., *Presidential Elections and [the] Orange Revolution: Implications for Ukraine's Transition* (Kyiv: Friedrich Ebert Foundation, 2005), 111–12.
10. Madeleine Albright, "How to Help Ukraine Vote," *New York Times*, March 8, 2004, A19.
11. Kurth and Kempe, *Presidential Elections*, 113.
12. Council of Europe, "Compliance with Commitments and Obligations: The Situation in Ukraine," SG/Inf(2004)12, April 8, 2004, available at www.coe.int/t/e/sg/Secretary-General/Information/Documents/Numerical/2004/SGInf(2004)12E.asp.
13. For more details, see *National Security and Defense*, 21.
14. Benita Ferrero-Waldner, "The European Neighbourhood Policy," available at http://europa.eu.int/comm/world/enp/index_en.htm.
15. "Seym Polshtche zaklinayv ukrainsky vlady provesti tchesni vibori" [The Polish Sejm Urges the Ukrainian Government to Carry out Honest Elections], Pro Europe, October 22, 2004, available at www.proeuropa.info/news/?id=843&PHPSESSID=4e1dcd730b379cc1d0b1e58cd2e31eeb.
16. Judy Dempsey, "Poland's Vision of the European Union," *International Herald Tribune*, September 2, 2004.
17. "Poland Urges Ukraine to Hold Fair Presidential Vote," *RFE/RL [Radio Free Europe/Radio Liberty] Newsline*, 8 (215, part 2) (November 15, 2004), available at www.rferl.org/newsline/2004/11/151104.asp#archive.
18. Dzurinda said this during a joint press conference with his Ukrainian counterpart Viktor Yanukovych, on June 21, 2004, in Kyiv. In European Union Business, available at www.eubusiness.com/Slovakia/040621174553.lg4nkpec.
19. Daniel Forgacs, "Slovensko Vyvá_a demokraciu na Ukrajin" [Slovakia Calls for Democracy in Ukraine], *Narodna obroda*, October 20, 2004, 2; "Prezidentské vol'by na Ukrajine bude monitorova_ 108 slovenských pozorovatel'ov" [108 Slovak Observers Will Monitor Ukrainian Presidential Elections], Press Agency of the Slovak Republic, October 19, 2004.
20. Official website of the Central Election Commission of Ukraine, available at www.cvk.gov.ua/wp0011.
21. "Declaration by the Presidency of the European Union on the Presidential Elections of October 31, 2004, in Ukraine," November 1, 2004, available at www.eu2004.nl/default.asp?CMS_ITEM=987B8A310E8C4173BC1BC45E72D9A412X1X66772X44.
22. "Declaration by the Presidency of the European Union on Ukraine," November 22, 2004, available at www.eu2004.nl/default.asp?CMS_ITEM=B2C459EC419347E59AA019D53CAE787EX1X60623X25.
23. Among many statements see: "Bundesaußenminister Fischer besorgt über gravierende Mängel bei zweiter Runde der Präsidentschaftswahlen in der Ukraine" [Federal Foreign

Minister Fischer Is Concerned over Disturbing Shortcomings in the Second Round of the Presidential Elections in Ukraine], Pressemitteilungen, November 23, 2004; and "Powell Rejects Ukraine Election, Threatens Action," Reuters, November 24, 2004, available at www.reuters.com/newsArticle.jhtml?type=worldNews&storyID=6910773.

24. "Eurocommission President José Manuel Barroso Urges Thorough Check into November 21 Run-off Returns," Ukrinform, November 24, 2004, available at www.elections.ukrinform.com.ua/article.php?a=0637&lang=en.

25. For factual information on the participation of international actors, see the website of the Informational Center of the Working Group for Supporting Official Observers from Foreign States and International Organizations. Ukrinform, available at www.elections.ukrinform.com.ua:8101/?lang=en.

26. Ibid.

27. "America's Final Warning," Zerkalo tyzhnia, 37 (512) (September 18–24, 2004) , available at www.mirror-weekly.com/nn/index/512/.

28. "U.S. Agrees with OSCE That Ukraine Vote Was 'Step Backward,'" November 21, 2004, available at http://usinfo.state.gov/eur/Archive/2004/Nov/01-993156 .html.

29. "Remarks by U.S. Senator Richard Lugar on the Ukrainian Presidential Elections," November 22, 2004, available at www.globalsecurity.org/wmd/library/news/ukraine/ukraine-041122-lugar.htm.

30. Ibid.

31. Michelle Kelemen, "U.S. Calls for Probe in Ukraine Election," November 24, 2004, available at www.npr.org/templates/story/story.php?storyId=4186197.

32. Oleksandr Sushko et al., Nations in Transit 2005 (New York: Freedom House, 2005).

33. International Renaissance Foundation, "Promotion of the Fair and Open Election of 2004," October 2004, available at www.irf.kiev.ua/files/eng/news_381_en_pdf.pdf.

34. European Commission, "National Indicative Programme Ukraine," August 4, 2003, available at http://europa.eu.int/comm/external_relations/ukraine/csp/ip03_04_08.pdf.

35. The European Commission's Delegation to Ukraine, Moldova, and Belarus, "European Union Funded Projects in Support of the Presidential Elections in Ukraine," available at www.delukr.cec.eu.int/site/page31321.html.

36. USAID Mission to Ukraine Data Sheet, FY 2004 Program, available at www.usaid.gov/our_work/democracy_and_governance/regions/ee/ukraine1.pdf.

37. USAID website, available at www.usaid.kiev.ua/news_full.shtml?p=172.

38. "Osobova Sprava" (personal file) website, available at http://sprava.civicua.org/yanukovich/ya029usa_image.html.

39. National Security and Defense, 23.

40. Yulia Mostovaya, "When the Process Is More Important than the Result," Zerkalo tyzhnia, 7 (April 30, 2004) , available at www.mirror-weekly.com/nn/index/492.

41. Website of the Central Election Commission of Ukraine, available at www.cvk.gov.ua/pls/vp2004/wp0011.

42. Kurth and Kempe, Presidential Elections, 116.

43. International Election Observation Mission (IEOM), "Statement of Preliminary Findings and Conclusions," November 1, 2004, available at www.osce.org/documents/odihr/2004/11/3771_en.pdf.

44. IEOM. The mission was jointly organized by OSCE Office for Democratic Institutions and Human Rights (OSCE/ODIHR), the OSCE Parliamentary Assembly (OSCE PA), the Parliamentary Assembly of the Council of Europe (PACE), the European Parliament (EP), and the NATO Parliamentary Assembly (NATO PA).

45. IEOM, "Statement of Preliminary Findings and Conclusions," November 22, 2004, available at www.osce.org/documents/odihr/2004/11/3811_en.pdf.

46. IEOM, "Preliminary Statement on the Repeat Second Round of the Presidential Election in Ukraine," December 27, 2004, available at www.osce.org./documents/odihr/2004/12/4007_en.pdf.

47. *National Security and Defense*, 24.

48. "Statement on Resolution of the Political Crisis in Ukraine Adopted after Roundtable at Mariinskyi Palace," Ukrinform, November 26, 2004, available at www.elections.ukrinform.com.ua/article.php?a=0737&lang=en.

49. "Javier Solana Comments on Multipartite Meeting in Mariinskyi Palace as Early Important Step toward Stabilizing Situation in Ukraine," Ukrinform, November 27, 2004, available at www.elections.ukrinform.com.ua/article.php?a=0785&lang=en.

50. John Conlan, "The Illusory Influence of Europe, America, and Russia on Ukraine's Presidential Elections," in *National Security and Defense*, 57.

CHAPTER EIGHT

Russia's Role in the
Orange Revolution

NIKOLAI PETROV AND ANDREI RYABOV

RUSSIA'S INVOLVEMENT IN THE Ukrainian presidential election in October and November 2004 is widely viewed as the Kremlin's greatest foreign relations blunder since 1991.[1] The problem is not that the Kremlin gambled on a candidate who lost, but that the Kremlin's involvement was so conspicuous and crude. The Kremlin seemed not only to want to win, but also to demonstrate that Ukraine remains a part of Russia's vital sphere of influence, where the Russian government has a right to act as it would within its own borders. As the election progressed, the Kremlin's clumsy intrusion drove Russia ever further into a dead end, while raising the stakes. The result was not simply a defeat, but a scandalous humiliation. The Ukrainian presidential election has already bred numerous myths. In this chapter we analyze the forms of Russia's involvement in the Ukrainian presidential election, how Russia made its decisions, and the reasons for the failure of its strategy.

The Significance of the Ukrainian Election for Russia

Over the past several years, Russian foreign policy has sought gradually to restore and increase Russia's international influence in the post-Soviet space. The Russian political elite wanted to take the lead role in

We are grateful to Marina Barnett for translating this chapter from Russian into English.

economics, politics, and, in time, possibly the military on CIS territory. Through such dominance, the Kremlin hoped to increase its political weight vis-à-vis other global powers: the European Union, China, and the United States. Moscow was painfully aware that without Ukraine's participation in such regional unions, the unions would be flawed. Ukraine, however, had refused to join the Eurasian Economic Community (EEC), which aimed at establishing a common policy in external economic activities, prices, and tariffs, limiting its cooperation with EEC to observer status in May 2002.

This circumstance prompted Moscow to initiate a new integration project, the Common Economic Space (CES). After long deliberations and internal political discussions, President Leonid Kuchma's administration agreed to Ukraine's participation. Nevertheless, officially, Kyiv would sign only a framework agreement with the CES and not an agreement on a customs union or on the creation of supranational institutions. The Ukrainian government explained this position by stating that it was trying to combine cooperation with the CES with gradual adaptation to the European Union's requirements for countries seeking membership.

The Ukrainian presidential election campaign of 2004 was considered a crossroads by the Russian elite since choosing the country's future direction was on the agenda. Ukraine faced integration with the Euro-Atlantic structures or close economic cooperation with Russia as well as political and military-political maneuvering between Russia and the West. This understanding defined Russia's political course in the Ukrainian election. Russia set only one goal: to keep Ukraine in the sphere of Russian influence, and, at a minimum, to maintain their existing relationship. Any other option was ruled out.

This fundamental decision to support a candidate chosen by Leonid Kuchma was made in the summer of 2003, long before the official election campaign began. The Kremlin concluded that close cooperation with the president of Ukraine would be the optimal Russian foreign policy. The chief of the Russian presidential administration at the time, Aleksandr Voloshin, played the key role in formulating this policy. As Vyacheslav Nikonov, a highly influential Russian political consultant who worked for Viktor Yanukovych's election campaign, admitted, "Our Ukrainian policy was locked on Kuchma, and therefore, on the candidate he chose. It was not Putin who chose Yanukovych."[2] In the summer of 2003, Voloshin rejected all attempts by Russian political experts associated with the Kremlin to suggest Ukrainian politicians worthy of Moscow's support.[3]

The Kremlin refused to interact with opposition leader Viktor Yushchenko. His repeated efforts to initiate a constructive dialogue on bilateral relations with the Russian leadership were unsuccessful. Considering that Yushchenko was one of most probable presidential candidates, high-ranking Russian envoys tried in unofficial contacts to understand his position on issues considered important by Moscow. In particular, Moscow was interested in Yushchenko's views on the status of the Russian language in Ukraine; on the position of the Russian Orthodox Church and its relationship with the Ukrainian Autocephalic Orthodox Church; on cooperation between the two countries' military-industrial complexes in building and exporting armaments; on Ukraine's participation in CES; and on its future relationship with NATO. According to the Kremlin, Yushchenko did not provide a definite answer to any of those questions. That led Russian leaders to conclude that he was a pro-Western politician and that his victory would have severe repercussions for Russian policy in the post-Soviet space.

How Yanukovych Became the Kremlin's Hope

The Russian leadership reached its final decision to support Yanukovych in July 2004, soon after Kuchma designated him as his successor.[4] Moscow's support of the Ukrainian president was first made public during the July 26, 2004, meeting of the two countries' leading businessmen, organized in Crimea under the patronage of the presidents of Russia and Ukraine.[5]

As subsequent events showed, this one-sided approach limited Russia's maneuvers during the election, making its policy a hostage of the interests of President Kuchma and his associates. Yet, as became known later, Kuchma was not particularly interested in Yanukovych's victory. The weakening of both candidates opened certain opportunities for him to stay in power, leaving Russia in jeopardy. Remaining loyal to Kuchma, Moscow had no influence on the Ukrainian president's domestic politics and unambiguously demonstrated its support of Yanukovych.[6]

Still, after the decision to support Yanukovych had been made, rumors circulated in Moscow that certain *siloviki* (military and security service personnel) suspected that it would be easier to agree on Russian investments in Ukraine with the pragmatic Yushchenko than with Yanukovych, who represented the interests of the mighty Donetsk clan, a serious competitor to Russia's metallurgical corporations. If these

concerns did exist, they did not influence official Russian policy on the
Ukrainian election.

The Kremlin Strategy

The Kremlin's strategy for the Ukrainian election campaign took form
gradually during 2004. It was based on the premise that the centerpiece
of the upcoming election would be a struggle between proponents of a
pro-Western and pro-Russian orientation for Ukraine. This would be a
confrontation between eastern Ukraine, drawn toward friendship with
Russia, and the nationalistic western part of Ukraine. The Kremlin sought
to emphasize this confrontation and to secure Yanukovych's victory by
expanding the friendly eastern region's influence over central Ukraine,
while blocking any influence from the western region.

Russia pursued this strategy in two main directions. The first was the
active participation of Russian public relations experts and image makers in Yanukovych's election campaign. The second element comprised
economic and political concessions to convince Ukrainian public opinion of the importance of cooperation with Russia.

Gleb Pavlovsky, Vyacheslav Nikonov, and other Russian public relations experts assured the Kremlin that the success of the election campaign depended on three issues.

First, the economic successes of the eastern regions should be publicized across Ukraine by explaining that they provide 70 percent of
Ukraine's gross domestic product and are the locomotive of rapid economic growth. To a large extent, it is true that the eastern region owes
these results to its close economic cooperation with Russia.

Second, an aggressive and straightforward public relations campaign
should force Yanukovych on Ukrainian voters. This approach was based
on a principle, tested in Russian election campaigns, that concentrating
all media on a particular subject for a limited period brings the results
desired.

Third, the campaign should exploit eastern Ukrainian phobias about
western Ukrainians and paint Yushchenko and his coalition as evil. That
evil would be connected to the darkest side of Ukrainian history, namely,
Nazi oppression. This picture, crudely and directly imposed on the public, was supposed to force voters into a hard choice between good and
evil.

Moreover, the Yanukovych faction drew extensively on administrative resources during the campaign, as well as on election day and

RUSSIA'S ROLE IN THE ORANGE REVOLUTION 149

during the vote count. The use of administrative resources meant mounting massive pressure on state employees, pensioners, and other people dependent on the state to vote for Yanukovych. The Yanukovych campaign also intended to use such other methods as early voting, voting from home, "carousels" (repeat voting), and, finally, the falsification of the vote count.

The grave mistake in this strategy was that it amounted to an attempt to transfer Russian election strategies automatically to a country with a different political environment. The Russian public relations experts and image makers did not even want to consider the specifics of the Ukrainian political public conscience. Their strategies had worked in Russia amid growing political indifference, which facilitated voter manipulation. But Ukraine was going through a rapid politicization of the population and the rise of a national movement with a pronounced anti-oligarchic character. As revolutionary processes in other countries have shown, an acceleration of economic growth combined with strong social conflicts contribute to sharply rising public expectations. Under such conditions, the conservative principle "just don't make it worse," which dominated the post-Soviet space in the 1990s fails to satisfy. A wide public begins to rally around new political goals that quickly gain popularity. Under Ukrainian conditions, the aggressive mass media promotion of one candidate, combined with the blatant slander of another, could only produce a result completely different from what Russian political experts had repeatedly achieved at home.

Because anti-oligarchic moods and hopes for a European future for Ukraine came to dominate public opinion, propaganda about the economic successes of Yanukovych's government and power structures, which helped only the rich, could not tip the scale in favor of the prime minister.

A critical campaign against westernization did not have the desired effect either, as Yushchenko's election campaign did not appeal to traditional Ukrainian nationalism but instead called for the building of a new democratic Ukraine as an inseparable part of Europe. Modern Russia had lost its status as an attractive political example for the majority of Ukrainians, in spite of the large number of Ukrainian migrant workers there.

Some well-known Russian political consultants believed that Yanukovych had a chance to win the election without resorting to large-scale fraud. They wanted to rely on the support of the population of the Crimea, Donbas, Slobodskaya Ukraine, and South Podneproviye and use flexible election techniques to persuade voters in the central regions (Malorossia) and on the Dnepr's right bank to vote for Yanukovych. Yet this approach required Russian public relations experts to transform their usual techniques entirely, which they were not prepared to do, being completely confident in the effectiveness of their own methods. This was probably not only a result of inertia, but the general mood in Moscow as well. Many victories in election campaigns at different levels led the Russian political elite to believe that any goal could be achieved with their standard methods and administrative resources anywhere in the post-Soviet space.

Nonetheless, serious differences existed among the Russian political consultants. Marat Gelman, who left Ukraine before the official start of the election campaign, recommended emphasizing Yanukovych's most attractive features. Pavlovsky suggested mobilizing pensioners by raising pensions. Nikonov wanted to concentrate all attention on criticizing Yushchenko.[7]

Russia's policy on Ukraine during the entire post-Soviet period sought to keep Ukraine within Russia's sphere of influence by granting it concessions, mostly economic. Russia reduced Ukraine's gas debt from $2.2 or $2.6 billion to $1.4 billion. In the fall of 2003, Russia abolished quotas for Ukrainian steel pipes because Ukraine's pipe production was largely controlled by Viktor Pinchuk. On September 15, 2004, at a summit of heads of states participating in the Common Economic Space, the presidents of Russia and Ukraine signed an agreement to transfer the collection of value-added taxes on oil and gas to the country of destination. This agreement meant that $800 million was transferred from the Russian to the Ukrainian treasury, which provoked wide criticism in Russia, as Russia received nothing in return. Meanwhile, the agreement on an international gas-transport consortium between Russia, Ukraine, and Germany was blocked because Ukraine insisted on securing 51 percent of the shares of the consortium. Nor was the issue of reversing the Odesa-Brody oil pipeline for the transportation of Russian oil solved.

During the election campaign the issues of dual citizenship and simplified registration procedures for Ukrainians working in Russia arose. The Russian government supported these ideas in order to persuade Ukrainians to vote for Yanukovych. Yet tax breaks could hardly make Yanukovych attractive to most people; they perceived such breaks as benefiting only the Ukrainian elite. Such measures had most effect among the Ukrainian diaspora in Russia and in eastern Ukraine.

The head of Russia's presidential administration, Dmitri Medvedev, was in charge of official Russian strategy in the Ukrainian election. Pavlovsky, the president of the Foundation for Effective Policy and an advisor to the presidential administration, was responsible for intellectual support. Neither the Ministry of Foreign Affairs nor the presidential administration's Department of Foreign Affairs was involved. Only branches dealing with domestic politics took part, as was usual for important missions in the post-Soviet space. A peculiarity of the Ukrainian presidential campaign was that it was headed by the chief of the Kremlin administration. This underlined the importance President Putin attached to the Ukrainian election, but it also showed that other influential people with experience in post-Soviet politics had chosen to avoid responsibility for the election, fearing failure. The prevalent view was that the deputy head of the presidential administration, Vladislav Surkov, who was an election expert, had successfully distanced himself from participation.

Siloviki

The role of siloviki in the Ukrainian election is rather obscure. According to some sources, Putin deliberately kept siloviki out of the campaign. In the fall of 2004, it was rumored in Moscow that Putin had strictly prohibited any state bodies from getting involved in Russian policy in Ukraine without coordinating their positions with those who were officially responsible. Reportedly, siloviki were supposed to get involved in the campaign only in extraordinary situations, for example, if it became necessary to use force to suppress opposition rallies. Even so, siloviki appeared to comment on Russian policy on the Ukrainian election. Notably, Russian political consultant Stanislav Belkovsky made statements in the Ukrainian media clearly aimed at discrediting other Russian public relations experts working for Yanukovych.

Soon after the second round of the elections, Maidan–INFORM published a piece on the arrival of a Russian special forces unit called *Vympel*, which supposedly arrived in Kyiv to evacuate Kuchma and his closest associates, as well as secret documents, if necessary.[8] However, after the victory of the Orange Revolution, Oleksandr Turchinov, the new head of the Security Service of Ukraine, rebutted this claim, indicating that troops from Donetsk and the Crimean OMON (riot police) had been mistaken for Russian special forces.

Business

Russian big business found itself in a rather complicated situation. At the July 26 summit in Crimea, representatives of Russian business circles, including the heads of leading industrial and financial corporations like Alfa-Bank, Basic Element, Gazprom, LUKOIL, the National Reserve Bank, Sistema, Tatneft, Vneshtorgbank, and others, were able to give financial assistance to Yanukovych.[9] Some industrial-financial groups, including influential Gazprom, Basic Element, and Interros, were interested in supporting the existing Ukrainian regime and shared completely the Kremlin's policy of providing comprehensive assistance to official Kyiv. Gazprom and Interros became the main sponsors of Russian involvement in the Ukrainian election. Although other corporations (including Alfa-Group, the National Reserve Bank, Severstal, and UGMK) whose interests clashed with those of Kuchma's clan and the Donetsk group were prepared to support Yushchenko, their attempts were blocked by the Kremlin.

Nevertheless, some Russian corporations contributed clandestinely to Yushchenko's campaign and provided Russian political consultants for the Ukrainian opposition. Russian medium-sized businesses tended to support Yushchenko, but that assistance was not significant.

Financing

It is hard to estimate the true scale of Russian financial support in the Ukrainian presidential election campaign. Different sources have provided radically different assessments. According to the Russian political consultants working for Yanukovych, the financing was insignificant, only $5–$10 million.[10] In their opinion, the Yanukovych campaign was financed mostly by Ukrainian sources. According to some foreign experts, Russian spending ran to $600 million, with $100–$200 million donated by Gazprom alone.

The $600 million figure seems to be a myth, as is the statement by Nikolai Kovalev, the former director of the Federal Security Service (FSB) and now a deputy in the Russian Duma, that the United States spent $1 billion in Ukraine. There is another opinion: "According to expert estimates, the Ukrainian presidential election budget exceeded $1.5 billion, with Yanukovych's campaign costing up to $900 million." These numbers would mean an expenditure of up to $50 for each voter (there are 30 million eligible voters in Ukraine) and of up to $100 for each vote cast. Citing Russian publications, professors Timothy Garton Ash and Timothy Snyder put the Russian contribution to the Yanukovych campaign at a more modest $300 million.[11] An estimate of $50 million for the "Russian project" is more probable, with the cost of Yanukovych's billboards alone estimated at $10–$15 million. In a televised debate with Pavlovsky, Belkovsky claimed that "the amount of money the Donetsk group spent on Yanukovych exceeded the total budget of Yushchenko and Yulia Tymoshenko by approximately fifteen times." Pavlovsky did not dispute the claim.

The financial debate could go on forever. In any event, Yanukovych did not lack funds and could afford any projects or proposals he wanted to pursue.

Channels of Influence

Regarding management, Russia influenced the election campaign's daily operations through several channels, including two Yanukovych campaign headquarters—the official one and the one in Donetsk—as well as the "Russian Club," established in Kyiv by Pavlovsky on August 31, 2004. The Donetsk headquarters, which employed people especially trusted by Yanukovych, was the most significant channel of influence. In Donetsk, it was possible to bypass all infighting among the presidential candidate's associates and have direct access to Yanukovych. Vyacheslav Nikonov oversaw the work of Russian political consultants in the Donetsk headquarters.[12] The Russian Club organized various events to promote friendship and cooperation with Russia among Ukrainian voters. It was responsible for organizing a widely publicized meeting between the governors of the border regions of the two countries. According to experts, including Russians working for Yanukovych, however, the club was largely ineffective. Pavlovsky preferred to exert influence through personal consultations with key figures in Yanukovych's campaign.

The attempt to maintain a strategic alliance with Kuchma, who was trying to weaken both leading candidates and simultaneously to support Yanukovych, caused obvious disarray among the Russian actors in Ukraine. Those who were traditionally closely associated with Kuchma, notably Russian ambassador to Ukraine Viktor Chernomyrdin, remained fairly passive during the election. In one interview, Chernomyrdin sharply criticized the activities of Russian political consultants working for Yanukovych.[13] The situation was further complicated by President

Kuchma's administration, led by Viktor Medvedchuk, who meddled in Yanukovych's election campaign. His primary objective was to serve Kuchma's interests. In all this, Russian political consultants often found it hard to persuade the leaders of Kuchma's administration to undertake various actions. Before the mass opposition protests following the second round of the election, Russian political consultants warned Medvedchuk that heightened political tensions could be dangerous for Kuchma. Confident of the efficacy of his vast administrative power, however, Medvedchuk chose to ignore those warnings. This is what Pavlovsky said about his mandate:

> If we had had the power to consult with our Ukrainian partners on preventing counterrevolution, and not on the elections, then this misfortune would never have happened. But we didn't have such powers. Unfortunately, our Ukrainian partners didn't want to examine this theme either. To be honest, official circles in Russia also failed to face up to this, in my view. The Foundation for Effective Policy is a private organization and works only on contract. In Ukraine I had no contract. I see no reason to hide a contract with a Ukrainian candidate, for example, with Yanukovych. I would have been proud of such a contract but had none. In Kyiv many Russian specialists did profitable business, working for the headquarters of candidates and local oligarchs. Pick whichever famous name you like, and he was in Kyiv: Marat Gelman, Stas [Stanislav] Belkovsky, Igor Mintusov, Sergei Dorenko . . . "How many are they? Where are they being driven?"[14] At the request of my Moscow clients, I worked, naturally, with the government political coalition, which ran Viktor Yanukovych. This group of politicians was broader than [that of] Yanukovych headquarters, and broader than the coalition of the former centrist parliamentary majority. It was a group that coalesced around President Kuchma, connected by complicated agreements, a peculiar consensus—temporary and very unstable, as we have seen. Its main problem was Kuchma himself, who did not want any stability beyond himself. That's his philosophy. If Yeltsin had behaved like Kuchma in '99, then Moscow would have boiled over somewhere in October, and Putin would never have become president. On the other hand, Moscow would have witnessed the impressive picture [of] "The People's Fury" under the leadership of the Moscow mayor's office, the television moguls, and goodwill ambassadors from

every European insect. But in the given case I worked with the Kyiv governmental coalition, and outside those boundaries I had no power to act, unfortunately.[15]

The Russian Card and Putin's Visit before the First Round

By the beginning of October 2004, the campaign appeared to take a favorable turn for Russia, as Yanukovych started playing the Russian card vigorously. He made strong promises: to make Russian an official language, to allow dual citizenship, and to simplify voter-registration procedures for Ukrainian citizens in Russia. Yanukovych presented some of these proposals in an address on October 6.

On October 8, a congress of representatives of the Ukrainian diaspora in the Russian Federation took place in Moscow's Colonnade Hall, one of the most prestigious conference halls in the Russian capital. On the eve of the congress, the Russian mass media circulated the results of public opinion polls, according to which 90 percent of Ukrainians living in Russia supported Yanukovych. The central streets of Moscow were adorned with "Yanukovych Is Our President" banners that surprised most Muscovites. The congress, attended by the head of the Russian presidential administration, Dmitri Medvedev, adopted an appeal to all Ukrainians to support Yanukovych.[16] In the perception of Russian political consultants, the election campaign was taking a straightforward and aggressive character, with which they were familiar. But among the Ukrainian electorate such obtrusive efforts, as well as Pavlovsky's categorical statements in the local press calling Ukrainian voters to "resign themselves to the inevitable," produced only antagonistic feelings. Moscow tried to force the idea of friendship with Russia, which was possible only under a Yanukovych presidency, upon the Ukrainian population. It did not work.

The early September attempt to poison Yushchenko diminished the impact of the Russian political consultants. Although no official evidence was presented to identify the culprit, the public suspected forces supporting Kuchma and Yanukovych. Slanderous Internet articles claiming that Yushchenko's disfigured face symbolized the appearance of the Antichrist in Ukraine only reinforced that assumption. The Ukrainian population's negative reaction to such blunt insinuations further damaged the Russian position.

According to various opinion polls, the two leading candidates' chances for victory were about equal at the beginning of October.

The well-known Ukrainian service SOCIS (the Center for Social and Political Investigations) showed Yushchenko leading with 35 percent over Yanukovych with 30 percent. The Russian Public Opinion Foundation, however, registered a small advantage for Yanukovych, 33 percent versus 31 percent for Yushchenko. In any case, Yanukovych did not have a persuasive lead. After the election, Pavlovsky complained that for the first time in his career as a political consultant he did not have a good sociological base.

Not long before election day, Russian political consultants, aware of the instability of Yanukovych's position, suggested taking decisive measures, fundamentally transforming the election struggle. President Putin's visit to the Ukrainian capital was organized on their initiative. According to public opinion polls, Putin was the most popular politician in Ukraine. The official pretense was that his appearance could create a turning point in the campaign just before the election. By design, during a televised press conference, a Ukrainian viewer asked Putin whether he had any plans to run for the Ukrainian presidency after his term in Russia expired. Some have claimed that the real motivation for the Russian political consultants' actions was different. By the end of October, it became apparent that the vast funds allocated by Russia to the Ukrainian election campaign had been spent inefficiently, and some had been stolen. President Putin's authority was required to justify these wasteful expenditures, even if he failed to change the course of the election campaign. If Yanukovych had won the first round, political consultants would have had a strong argument that it had happened because of Putin's direct involvement in the campaign. Yet neither Putin's visit to Ukraine, nor his televised communication with Ukrainian voters, radically changed the preelection mood.

Apart from political and ideological influence on the campaign, the Russian authorities planned to use administrative resources, first of all, in the vote count at polling stations on the territory of Russia. Originally their plans focused on the one to one and a half million Ukrainian voters in Russia, most of whom, it was expected, would vote for Yanukovych. Pavlovsky, together with the Moscow Congress of Russian Ukrainians and the group Yanukovych, Our President, produced the campaign newspaper *Ukraine's Hour* especially for these voters. Thanks to countermeasures by Yushchenko's team and Kuchma's indecisiveness, this plan did not work. On October 24, the Central Election Committee of Ukraine made the decision to open forty-one additional polling stations on the territory of the Russian Federation. Remarkably, the Russian authorities denied the requests of Yushchenko representatives to be observers at most of those stations. Then, prompted by the protests of opposition leaders, the Supreme Court of Ukraine decided to allow the opening of only four polling stations: in Moscow, Rostov-on-Don (where only a few thousand Ukrainians voted), St. Petersburg, and Tyumen.

The Emphasis on Administrative Interference in the Second Round

When the first round of the election proved unsuccessful for Moscow, the Russian strategy changed. On November 12–13, Vladimir Putin visited Crimea, where he met with Kuchma and Yanukovych. During this visit, Yanukovych was reportedly advised to rely mostly on administrative interference: to maximize the voter turnout in the regions that supported Yanukovych in the first round, while replacing disloyal local officials with more industrious bureaucrats in other regions. Putin's meeting with Kuchma was rather restrained because, in the Kremlin's opinion, Kuchma had acted indecisively after the first round and tried to negotiate with the opposition. He had lost Moscow's trust.

All these recommendations, however, came too late. Although administrative resources improved the voter turnout in the East, mainly in the Donetsk and Luhansk regions and in Crimea, the state bureaucracy did not consolidate around Yanukovych. After the first-round victory of the opposition candidate, many bureaucrats wished to secure guarantees that they would not be punished if they carried out illegal actions.

The Russian side undertook another important political maneuver between the first and second rounds. Since the second-round outcome depended to a large extent on the votes that had gone to candidates defeated in the first round, the Yanukovych campaign began the energetic cultivation of those candidates. Most important were Oleksandr Moroz, the leader of the Socialist Party, and Petro Symonenko, the leader of the Communist Party, who came in third and fourth, respectively, in the first round. But since Moroz had a long-standing agreement to support Yushchenko in the second round, the Kremlin could fight only for the support of the communists.

Apparently, the Kremlin had asked Gennady Zyuganov, the leader of the Russian Communists, to persuade Symonenko to urge his electorate to vote for Yanukovych. After a talk with Putin, Zyuganov agreed to do what he could in exchange for Kremlin financing of the Communist Party of the Russian Federation (CPRF) and the cessation of negative coverage of his party in the state-controlled media. The Kremlin overestimated the influence of CPRF over their Ukrainian counterparts. Symonenko was extremely annoyed, having had more than fifty thousand votes stolen from him and assigned to Yanukovych in the Donetsk region alone in the first round. Moreover, the Communist Party of Ukraine (CPU) leader was afraid that if he supported a candidate from the party of power at a time when an anti-oligarchic mood dominated in the electorate, the Communist Party might lose influence even among its strongest supporters. As a result, CPU decided to urge its supporters to cast their votes for neither of the two candidates in the second round.

The Russian Orthodox Church, which had initially supported Yanukovych, albeit with some reservations, started to distance itself from the Ukrainian election campaign, trying to maintain constructive relations with both leading candidates. This reportedly irritated the Kremlin.

Moscow's Confusion at the Start of the Orange Revolution

Moscow was completely shocked that Ukrainian voters responded to the falsification of the second-round vote with massive protests, which paralyzed the state authorities. This became obvious when Putin, prompted by Kremlin bureaucrats, congratulated Yanukovych upon his victory three times, although the political crisis was already evident.

Putin believed that he had agreed to the scenario of a Ukrainian power transfer with the main players, including Kuchma and the U.S. president, and he never expected a "game not by the rules" with such independent factors as people in the streets and changes in the agreed positions of the players. Putin's psychological state can to some extent be described by the following statement by Belkovsky at a press conference at the Russian news and information agency RIA Novosti on May 17, 2005.

> As someone, involved to a fair degree in the revolutionary events in Ukraine, I can say that in June 2004 America assumed a number of obligations to Russia, one being not to impede Viktor Yanukovych's victory, and it met its commitments until the end of November 2004. All American financing of the Ukrainian opposition had been discontinued since June 2004. On November 23 and 30 of 2004, the U.S. ambassador to Ukraine [John Herbst] did all he

could to prevent rebellious people from occupying administrative buildings, the building of the Ukrainian presidential administration, and [the building] of the Ukrainian cabinet of ministers, which would have been very easy to do at that time. Forces guarding those buildings were completely unprepared for resistance. They were ready to disperse and even to run away. Only when it became clear that these revolutionary processes were irreversible, and that power did not actually belong to the acting president, Leonid Kuchma, and that Viktor Yanukovych will not be president, only then did America legitimize the new power. In that sense, America's tactics were much more skilled and competent than Russia's, which counted on the completely baseless illusions of Viktor Yanukovych's victory until the very last moment.[17]

To excuse the Kremlin's defeat in the Ukrainian election, the Russian media suggested that the United States, the European Union, and Poland had organized a conspiracy against the regime in Kyiv. The purpose of this conspiracy was allegedly to remove the legitimate authorities through massive demonstrations by Yushchenko supporters. Later, Pavlovsky explained the Russian political consultants' fiasco in Ukraine using the same accusation: "If we had the mandate to advise our Ukrainian partners not on the election, but on preventing a counterrevolution, this disaster would not have happened."[18]

The most hotly debated issues regarding Russia's policy in the Ukrainian election were whether Moscow had seriously considered assisting Ukraine in using force to suppress Yushchenko supporters, and to what extent it advocated the separatism of the eastern regions—namely, initial autonomy to be followed by a merger with Russia. Apparently some members of the Russian leadership, especially among the siloviki, advocated such radical measures. Moreover, some believe that the siloviki had specific plans to assist Ukrainian security forces, including bringing in troops mustered by several Russian corporations. Nevertheless, even if these plans did exist, they could be realized only if the Ukrainian authorities, starting with President Kuchma, had consented and if the Kremlin had made a firm political decision. Kuchma, however, clearly wanted to preserve room to maneuver in his domestic political games.

When Putin was confronted with the consolidated Western position, insisting on a revision of second-round results, he chose not to exacerbate the situation any further. In a last-ditch attempt to claim victory, Russia tried to rally Yanukovych supporters in the eastern parts of

Ukraine at the Summit of Councils of Eastern Regions, held on November 28 in Severodonetsk. The summit supported Ukraine's federalization and the creation of an eastern autonomous republic. Moscow mayor Yury Luzhkov attended the summit and made a statement in support of that initiative. The summit, however, could not exert any serious influence. Further, in order to preserve some freedom to maneuver, Yanukovych was forced to distance himself from the radical resolutions of the summit.

By the time a conciliatory commission, including representatives from the European Union, the United States, and Russia, started to work, the Kremlin had no clear strategy. A common problem of current Russian politics resurfaced. In a system of overcentralized power, no one wanted to take responsibility for decisions in a crisis. As a result, at the critical moment, no able person could be found to represent Russia's interests in the negotiations. The chair of the State Duma, Boris Gryzlov, famous for his complete inability to make any independent decision, was sent to Kyiv, but he managed only to repeat the Kremlin's obsolete position, which had been formulated immediately after the second round. He demanded the unconditional recognition of Yanukovych's victory and an immediate halt to widespread street protests by Yushchenko supporters. In the new situation, that position had no chance of success. Consequently, Russia lost its ability to affect the results of the conciliatory commission's activity.

As a result, the Kremlin lost its opportunity to manipulate the election campaign before the third round. Perceiving Moscow's moral and political fiasco, Yanukovych began actively to emphasize his detachment from Russia, sharply criticizing the eastern separatists. Although other Russian political consultants, including Sergei Zerev, the head of the Krosna company and the former deputy head of the presidential administration, reportedly replaced those who failed, this shuffle had no noticeable affect on the campaign. The Kremlin, realizing the inevitability of Yanukovych's defeat, was forced to abandon its former stake in the validity of the second-round results and to consider principles for new relations with Ukraine, which would have to be built after Yushchenko's victory.

Conclusion

The Kremlin was not managing its own political project in Ukraine as much as it was deeply, but somewhat blindly, involved in Kuchma's political project. Putin himself gave a paradoxical admission or explanation at his first meeting with Yushchenko on January 24, 2005: "You knew before and know now that Russia never works behind the curtains in post-Soviet space. We never bypass the acting leadership of that or another country, even [when] working with an opposition faction. This fully applies to Ukraine as well. Lately, we have been doing what the acting Ukrainian leadership asked us to do."[19]

The Kremlin's involvement consisted largely of money that was officially transferred to the Ukrainian budget, making a couple of important populist gestures—including the twofold increase in pensions—possible for Yanukovych. It included the "big gun" of President Putin's personal visit to Kyiv. It included the loud and somewhat incoherent involvement of an army of Russian political consultants, including "Kremlinites" Nikonov of the Politika Foundation and Pavlovsky of the Foundation for Effective Policy (who are, by the way, more famous for their propaganda than for election successes). It included support for Yanukovych vis-à-vis Yushchenko by the Russian mass media and even the general prosecutor's office. The Kremlin's goal was to recreate a regime in Ukraine that would not be acceptable in the West. It would therefore be more dependent on Russia, similar to Kuchma's regime after the scandals of his second term. In such a scenario, Ukraine would have formed the key link in the Common Economic Space, the Kremlin's (and Putin's) most important integrative project, into which a great deal of money and strength has already been poured.

Although almost all the components of the Kremlin's project in Ukraine (except the mobilization of the votes of more than a million "Ukrainians in Russia") were realized more or less successfully, the Ukrainian version of the "successor project" failed. It is hard to say definitively whether Russia's involvement helped or hurt Yanukovych. As often happens in politics, the responsibility for failure fell not on the head of the presidential administration in charge of the Ukrainian election, nor on its direct executors, the political consultants, but on the "dark forces of a Polish-American conspiracy" and on Kuchma, a servant of many masters who outwitted himself.

The Ukrainian Orange Revolution had a strong destabilizing effect on post-Soviet authoritarian and semi-authoritarian oligarchic regimes, most of which have enjoyed Russia's active support. It became obvious that if Russia continues to base its policies on conservative principles and to support these regimes, it will find it hard to maintain its leading position in the post-Soviet space.

Unfortunately, Russian official circles did not learn from the events in Ukraine. Instead of realizing the mature nature of the changes taking place in the post-Soviet space, they reacted by making the prevention of another Orange Revolution in Russia and other CIS countries the cornerstone of their domestic and foreign policies. Nonetheless, in 2005 the president of Kyrgyzstan, Askar Akaev, also a leader of an oligarchic political regime, was ousted as the result of public protests. Moreover, the final result of the presidential election in Ukraine led to a revival of the Russian democratic political opposition, which, within its limited scope, supported Yushchenko during the campaign.

Notes

1. See the many newspapers and magazines from the end of 2004 and the beginning of 2005 that were nearly identical in their assessments. See also the opinions given by experts of disparate political stripes collected by Yanukovych's chief political consultant Mikhail Pogrebinsky and published in *Orange Revolution: The Ukrainian Version* (Moscow: Yevropa Publishers, 2005).
2. Vyacheslav Nikonov, "Maidan nezalezhnosti," *Politicheskiy zhurnal*, 2005, 1:69–70.
3. Stanislav Belkovsky testified to the Kremlin's change of position, related to Aleksandr Voloshin leaving his post as well as to the lack of unity on October 29, 2004. "It was in January 2004 that analytical structures, close to the Kremlin, prepared a list of potential candidates that could successfully run against the leader of 'Our Ukraine.' The list contained the names of six people, including Vladimir Radchenko, Secretary of the National Security and Defense Council of Ukraine, Serhiy Tyhypko, governor of the National Bank of Ukraine, and Sergey Grinevetskiy, the governor of the Odesa region. Their political merits and myth-creating abilities combined, these politicians might have constituted decent competition for Yushchenko. Moreover, a victory of any of these candidates, unlike the formally fixed success of Yanukovych, would have been perceived by the Ukrainian people as legitimate and would not have resulted in a revolutionary uprising."
4. According to available accounts, Pavlovsky was already working on the "Yanukovych as successor" project at the beginning of summer. It is also well known that during a meeting in Crimea, March 21–22, 2004, Putin could not find the time to meet with Yanukovych, who was to have been presented as his successor. But on May 15, during Yanukovych's visit to Moscow, Putin not only appeared with him publicly and congratulated him on his economic successes, he also approved the idea of redistributing tax receipts to the advantage of Ukraine.
5. Andrei M. Kolesnikov, *Pervyi ukrainisky: Zapiski s peredovoi* (Moscow: Vagrius, 2005), 123 24, 126–33.
6. On October 29, 2004, Stanislav Belkovsky said, "Viktor Yanukovych is certainly no Russian protégé. He is an experimental creature that was supposed to prove the omnipotence of the Russian 'politico-technological' machine. That machine did not work. Moreover, it largely contributed to the success of Viktor Yushchenko."
7. Ukrainian political scientist Dmytro Vydrin, the director of the European Institute of Integration and Development, on December 2, 2004, said: "There came Muscovites, my colleagues, whom I love and respect, and offered considerably easier ways. Marat Gelman came and said, 'There are "[bill]boards" that turn people into zombies. If we

have negative boards, we will incite people against Yushchenko, and positive boards will push people toward Yanukovych. Give me some money, and I will cover the whole Ukraine with these boards, and nothing else will need to be done.' They were plastering Ukraine with those boards, but . . . nothing was happening. Then Pavlovsky would show up and say, 'Don't listen to this Gelman, and don't listen to anybody. Let's count how many voters there are in Ukraine. Is it about thirty million? Fourteen million of them are pensioners, that's 50 percent. You raise their pensions, and I will tell you how to better advertise it.' Pensions were raised, but that didn't work either. Then Slava Nikonov came and said, 'Everything you have been told before was wrong. Let's do as Dorenko does. Dorenko killed Primakov with only one hip. As for you, you have Yushchenko's liver, and kidneys, and face, and all his medical records.' The plan was as follows, 'We will be broadcasting Yushchenko's medical records on TV for twenty hours a day, and Dima Kislev will point and illustrate in detail all [the] physiological processes in Yushchenko's body. We have to do it so that people will be wanting to throw up at their first glance at Yushchenko because they will associate him with his decaying liver, failing kidneys and with his urine and feces tests that will constantly be on their TV screens.' This is what those Moscow guys are all about."

8. "Vityaz"—tol'ko prikrytie? available at http://maidan.org.ua /static/news/ 1101331214. html.

9. Kolesnikov, *Peryi ukrainisky*, 133.

10. According to a leading Kremlin political consultant, the financing for all their work came from Ukrainian sources—from Yanukovych headquarters and directly from Russian-Ukrainian businesses. "Russia wanted to take part in the elections using Donetsk money. That was the problem. We were supposed to advance Russia's interests on Yanukovych's money" (interview with the author, August 1, 2005).

11. Timothy Garton Ash and Timothy Snyder, "The Orange Revolution," *New York Review of Books*, April 28, 2005.

12. Nikonov, the president of the Politika Foundation, who had become known as an assistant to Vadim Bakatin, the last chair of the Soviet KGB, earned a solid position within the Kremlin's political "consultant" pool during the presidential election of 1996. He took part in several regional campaigns (in Leningrad, Pskov, Bashkiria, and Ulyanov), none of which was particularly successful. Since 1998 he has been actively participating in Yury Luzhkov's "Otechestvo" (Fatherland) party. On the threshold of the 2003 election, Nikonov became the head of "Yedinstvo vo imya Rossii" [Unity in the Name of Russia], the Moscow bureau of "Yedinstvo's" think tank.

13. Interview with Viktor Chernomyrdin in *Moskovsky komsomolets*, January 14, 2004. Chernomyrdin: "You shouldn't get Russia's position mixed up with the actions of some Russian political 'consultants' working here. These are two absolutely different things. The political 'consultants' work for money. They are for hire in Russia, they are for hire here, and they can be for hire in any other country. I always say—if you have the money, hire. Our, Russian, as well as Western political 'consultants' worked for Yanukovych, as well as for Yushchenko. So, let's not get Russia mixed up with this." The interview continued:

"So, you never supported our PR experts, who were running around here, stuffing their pockets with money at the election. On some days they were screaming out loud, 'Where is that Chernomyrdin? What kind of an ambassador is he? Why isn't he doing something while we're working here?'"

"If it were up to me, those workers . . . They had no relation to the embassy. I have never been to their headquarters, have never gone there. They are mercenaries."

"And they have never come to see you?"

"I met them at various press conferences and roundtables, where I participated."

14. From Pushkin's famous poem "Demons," which describes mysterious spirits swirling about a sled during a blizzard. Most Soviet schoolchildren learned it by heart.

15. *Nezavisimaya gazeta*, December 7, 2004.

16. *Na fone "oranzhevoi revolyutsii." Ukraina mejdu Vostokom i Zapadom. Vchera. Segodnya. Zavtra* [Against the Background of the Orange Revolution. Ukraine between East and West. Yesterday. Today.] (Moscow: Institute of CIS Countries), 10.

17. Press conference with political scientist Stanislav Belkovsky, Federal News Service, May 17, 2005.

18. *Nezavisimaya gazeta*, December 7, 2004.

19. "Nachalo vstrechi s Prezidentom Ukrainy Viktorom Yushchenko" (The Beginning of the Meeting with Ukrainian President Viktor Yushchenko), January 24, 2005, available at www.president.kremlin.ru/appears/2005/01/24/2005_type63377type82634_82944.shtml.

Conclusion:
The Orange Revolution
in a Comparative Perspective

MICHAEL MCFAUL

Patterns of Electoral Breakthrough in the Postcommunist World

IN THIS BOOK, we have explained an extraordinary moment of popular mobilization against the illegitimate actions of an incumbent government in Ukraine in the fall of 2004. The Orange Revolution will be remembered as one of the pivotal moments in Ukrainian history, an observation that by definition makes the event remarkable. Still, the Orange Revolution was not the first such case, but the third, following Serbia in 2000 and Georgia in 2003. Perhaps Ukraine helped to inspire a fourth: Kyrgyzstan in 2005.[1] These cases of democratic breakthrough are similar to one another or different from other conventional democratic transitions or revolutions in four critical respects.

First, in all four cases, the spark for a regime change was a fraudulent national election, not a war, an economic crisis, a coup, or the death of a dictator. The trigger was an event scheduled and organized by those in power, not those challenging power. Second, in all four cases, the challengers to incumbents deployed extraconstitutional means to ensure that the formal rules of politics embodied in the constitution would be followed. Revolutionary means are usually deployed to achieve revolutionary ends; there is a fundamental transformation of the regime and a rewriting of the political rules (and often the economic rules) of the game. In addition, many successful transitions from authoritarian rule involve negotiations in establishing new democratic institutions.[2] In each of these cases, however, the challengers to the existing regime were not seeking new rules or a different kind of regime. Instead, they were defending the political rights of citizens and the democratic practices already codified in existing constitutions. Negotiation was only one of several means used to achieve that end in one case, Ukraine. In the three other cases, roundtables or negotiations between the ancien régime and its challengers did not play a central role. Third, during different periods, all four cases experienced dual sovereignty, in which incumbents and challengers both claimed to be the sovereign authority of the same territory. Fourth, all these revolutionary situations ended without a massive use of violence by either the state or the opposition. To varying extents, the opposition groups in these countries used extraconstitutional tactics, but violence was not a tool in the arsenal deployed. Those who eventually fell from power did consider using coercive methods to stay in power, but each incumbent leader, when push came to shove, refrained from calling out the troops to repress popular protests.

Given the similarity of outcomes in the four cases, are there certain necessary conditions that produced them? In this chapter I seek to identify those factors present in the three cases of democratic breakthrough: Serbia, Georgia, and Ukraine, as well as to make comparative judgments about Kyrgyzstan, which shares some but not all the features of the three other cases.[3] When observed in isolation, each case of breakthrough seems distinct, unprecedented, and unlikely to be repeated. When compared, however, several of the conditions that have been identified in this book as crucial for breakthrough did play a central role in other transitions from postcommunism. The list of conditions for democratic breakthrough include (1) a semiautocratic regime, (2) an unpopular leader of the ancien régime, (3) a strong and well-organized opposition, (4) an ability to create the perception quickly that election results were falsified; (5) enough independent media to inform citizens about the falsified vote, (6) a political opposition capable of setting in motion tens of thousands of demonstrators to protest electoral fraud, and (7) a division between intelligence forces, the military, and the police. In addition, external actors can facilitate the development of many of these domestic factors.

In focusing only on those factors present in all cases, I hope in this chapter to highlight those commonly assumed to be central to democratization but that were not instrumental in these cases.

Competitive Authoritarianism

All autocratic regimes are vulnerable to collapse at some point. But which kinds of autocracies are more vulnerable than others? To date, the debate has not been resolved. Some posit that semiautocratic or competitive authoritarian regimes better facilitate democratization than do full-blown dictatorships, while others argue that semiautocracies or partial democracies in fact impede genuine democratization to a far greater extent than do more rigid autocracies. Liberalized autocracies can partially diffuse social pressures for change and thereby avoid regime collapse more effectively than full-blown dictatorships.[4]

In the second wave of democratization in the postcommunist world, none of the regimes was a full-blown dictatorship. Instead, they were various shades of competitive autocracy or partial democracy in which the formal rules of democracy, and especially elections, were never suspended and competition still mattered.[5] As the chapter by Anders Åslund demonstrates clearly, divisions between oligarchs associated with the ancien régime can also play a critical role in exposing a regime. The particular regime type allowed pockets of pluralism and opposition within the state, which proved critical to a democratic breakthrough.

In Ukraine, President Leonid Kuchma sat atop a similar semiautocratic, semidemocratic regime. Kuchma aspired to construct a system of managed democracy that included formal democratic practices but the informal control of all political institutions, similar to Putin's regime in Russia. Kuchma's regime never achieved as much success as did his Russian counterpart. Because Kuchma never enjoyed the overwhelming public support that Putin garnered in the first years of his rule in Russia, the Ukrainian president was more constrained when trying to limit political autonomy and opposition. In addition, Kuchma's inept and crude attempts to squelch opposition voices—be they his alleged collusion in ordering the murder of journalist Heorhiy Gongadze (the founder of the Internet publication *Ukrainska pravda*), his jailing of former energy minister Yulia Tymoshenko, or his dismissing his successful and popular prime minister, Viktor Yushchenko—served to garner even greater opposition. This social response to bad and autocratic government is what most distinguishes Ukraine from its Slavic neighbors. The Ukraine without Kuchma campaign from December 2000 to March 2001 and the results of the March 2002 parliamentary elections demonstrated that Ukrainian society was active and politically sophisticated. Especially after the electoral success of Our Ukraine in the 2002 parliamentary vote, Ukraine's opposition also had a foothold in the institutions of state power. Finally, Ukraine's business tycoons, or oligarchs, were not completely united by the ancien régime. Ukraine's three largest oligarchic groups did back Kuchma, and they wielded their media and financial resources on behalf of Kuchma's candidate in the 2004 presidential election, but significant if lesser oligarchs decided to back Yushchenko, as did tens of thousands of smaller businesspeople, meaning that Ukraine's economic elites were divided, not united, in the fall of 2004.

This kind of regime, holding on to power in the fall of 2004, was not unique to Ukraine. On the contrary, semiautocratic regimes are common in the postcommunist world and were necessary features of the revolutionary breakthroughs in Georgia, Kyrgyzstan, and Serbia.

Milosevic and his regime in Federal Republic of Yugoslavia is probably the most poorly understood. During the tragic years of interstate war, ethnic cleansing, and economic decline in the federal republic, Milosevic placed greater limits on political autonomy and individual freedoms. Yet he never erected a full-blown dictatorship. He harassed the opposition movements but never outlawed them. He occasionally shut down independent media outlets and ordered the assassination of outspoken journalists, but he also allowed such critical outlets as the B–92 radio station to reopen. He allowed human rights organizations to continue their work, and although he wielded the power of the state to influence and falsify the outcome of elections, he never banned elections altogether. The continued practice of elections allowed pockets of political autonomy to remain even within Serbian state structures. Parliamentary elections helped to sustain opposition leaders and parties, even if they enjoyed no real decision-making power during the heyday of Milosevic's autocracy in late 1999 and 2000. More important, the practice of elections for local government allowed the democratic movement to gain a foothold in more than a dozen regional parliaments in 1996–1997 (though only after the *Zajedno* opposition movement demonstrated publicly for one hundred days to pressure Milosevic to allow the real winners to take power). Perhaps most critically, democratic opposition leader Zoran Djindjic became the mayor of Beograd in 1997. With control of these regional governments also came control over regional media outlets, a vital resource in Milosevic's ouster in 2000.

Had Milosevic succeeded in constructing a full-fledged dictatorship, it is unlikely that the regime would have collapsed in 2000. Key is the central event that triggered the regime's collapse: the 2000 presidential election in which the opposition was allowed to compete, which would not have occurred in a fully realized autocracy.

In Georgia, Eduard Shevardnadze allowed for a more pluralist regime than Milosevic's. In fact, the former Soviet foreign minister came to power to reverse the autocratic tendencies of Georgia's first post-Soviet president, Zviad Gamsakhurdia. Shevardnadze also had to purge the young Georgian state of criminal elements, preserve the country's territorial integrity, and end civil strife by arresting and disbanding paramilitary organizations tied to Gamsakhurdia. In the first years of his presidency, Shevardnadze created the permissive conditions for democratic institutions and actors to emerge, such as independent political parties, civic organizations, and private media, including Georgia's most popular television station, Rustavi 2. Shevardnadze's critical role in ending the Cold War also cast him as a democrat in the West. In the last years of his rule, however, Shevardnadze tried to limit the democratic process as well as the autonomy of political actors.[6] Western and local observers concluded that the parliamentary elections of 1995 and 1999, which delivered majorities to Shevardnadze's Citizen's Union of Georgia (CUG), and the 2000 presidential election that returned Shevardnadze to power in a landslide victory, were neither free nor fair, continuing a trajectory in which "the fairness of the political process [was] in decline for several years."[7]

Yet Shevardnadze's ambition to construct a managed democracy greatly exceeded actual achievements. The Georgian government's heavy-handed attempt to mute Rustavi 2 in October 2001 failed and instead sparked popular protest in defense of the television station. Attempts at monitoring and curtailing the activities of civil society activity also had little effect. Shevardnadze's state lacked the resources to be more authoritarian. Moreover, Shevardnadze remained reluctant to crack down on his opponents since the leaders of Georgia's opposition came from Shevardnadze's own government. Before the political crisis surrounding the state's assault on Rustavi 2, Mikheil Saakashvili, Zurab Zhvania, and Nino Burjanadze—ultimately the three leaders of the Rose Revolution—were all members of Shevardnadze's CUG. Saakashvili served as Shevardnadze's justice minister, while Zhvania had been the parliamentary chair and the one many also considered to be the president's chosen heir.

Kyrgystan's Askar Akaev started out as the most democratically minded president in Central Asia, one who had constructed the most democratic regime in the region. Over time, however, Akaev gravitated toward the autocratic ways of his fellow Central Asian leaders, although he never constructed a regime as autocratic as those of Uzbekistan and Turkmenistan. Opposition groups were weak but not completely squashed; a few independent media outlets remained active, and competing clans placed limits on Akaev's ability to control all the political and economic resources of his country.

Unpopular Leaders

As detailed by Taras Kuzio in chapter three, a second necessary condition for a democratic breakthrough in the three countries was the decline in popularity of the leader of the ancien régime. This factor may seem obvious, but it also a feature that distinguishes these cases from countries such as Russia, where President Putin is still popular, or countries like Mexico during the heyday of semiauthoritarian rule when the Institutional Revolutionary Party (PRI) could manufacture electoral victories without major voter fraud. In Serbia, by the summer of 2000, polls conducted by the Institute of Social Sciences showed support for Milosevic to be less than 30 percent.[8] In Georgia, as early as 2001, 82 percent of respondents reported that Georgia was going in the wrong direction, up from 51 percent the year before.[9] Approval ratings for Kuchma in Ukraine and Akaev in Kyrgyzstan also declined considerably in the final year of their reigns.

If the levels of popular support were weak in all four cases, the causes of unpopularity were both different from case to case and difficult to trace within cases. In Serbia, Milosevic was at one time a popular leader who had won free and fair elections in the 1990s and persistently sought electoral mandates. Milosevic obviously believed in his own ability to win yet another election in the fall of 2000. He himself had changed the constitution to allow for the direct election of the president of the Federal Republic of Yugoslavia (FRI) and then scheduled the date of the first direct election well before his term was to expire. By 2000, however, several military defeats (the capitulation to NATO in 1999 being only the last in a series of losses), combined with years of economic decline, severely undermined Milosevic's electoral support. By the fall of 1999, his approval rating had dropped to less than a quarter of the population.[10]

Like Milosevic, Shevardnadze initially enjoyed several years of popular support. Over time, however, Shevardnadze failed to produce a sound economic policy or sustained economic growth. At the same time, his government grew increasingly corrupt. In 1999, Transparency International concluded that Georgia was one of the most corrupt countries in the world, ranking it eighty-fourth of ninety-nine countries.[11] As the result of investigative journalism by Rustavi 2, the level of corruption in Shevardnadze's government became a central political issue in Georgia on the eve of the 2003 parliamentary elections. Similar to Milosevic, Shevardnadze's failure to win wars (especially in Abkhazia in 1993) or settle territorial disputes with Abkhazia, South Ossetia, and Adjaria also contributed to the decline of his status.

Leonid Kuchma won presidential elections in 1994 and 1999 that were judged to be free and fair by the standards of the region. Moreover, during Kuchma's second term in office, Ukraine showed record economic growth numbers, reaching a 12 percent increase in the gross domestic product between 2003 and 2004. Like Georgia, however, high levels of corruption in Ukraine denied Kuchma the popular support that 12 percent growth should have generated for him. But the most important factor in his low public approval ratings had little to do with the economy and everything to do with the murder of Gongadze. Tapes of conversations between Kuchma and subordinates leaked to the press strongly suggested that the Ukrainian president had played a role in ordering Gongadze's execution. More than any other event, Gongadze's murder exposed the illegitimacy of Kuchma and his allies.

Akaev did not lose wars or order the murder of a popular journalist. After more than a decade in power, however, Akaev's corruption and nepotism were notorious. The Kyrgyz president did succeed in implementing modest economic reforms and in generating modest economic growth but not nearly enough to offset the pent-up demand for a change in government.

Organized Oppositions

As discussed by Adrian Karatnycky in chapter two, a strong and well-organized opposition faction—or the perception of a united front—is a third factor crucial for a democratic breakthrough, although the extent of unity varies across the four cases discussed here, calling into question its necessity as a factor. In Serbia and Ukraine, unity before the election was critical to success; in Georgia and Kyrgyzstan, less so. This difference, however, may be a function of the kind of election in question. In Serbia and Ukraine, the election that provoked a breakthrough was a presidential contest, while in Georgia and Kyrgyzstan, the triggering vote was a parliamentary election. In all four cases, however, a feasible alternative to the incumbent leader seemed critical.

Throughout the 1990s, personality clashes had plagued the Serbian democratic movement. Zoran Djindjic, the leader of the Democratic Party before his murder in 2003 and one of Serbia's first democratic leaders with a national following, also headed the most organized democratically oriented political party. Over the decade, however, his popular support waned. Vuk Draskovic, a poet-turned-opposition-leader, was another charismatic figure from the early years whose popularity ebbed and flowed. Other human rights leaders played instrumental roles in challenging the Milosevic regime, but they also bickered among themselves, which tarnished the image of these "democrats."

In January 2000, building on the success of the Alliance for Change created in 1998, Serbia's democrats agreed to set aside their differences to create a united front, the Democratic Opposition of Serbia (DOS). What was most important, DOS settled behind one presidential candidate, Vojislav Kostunica, for the September 2000 presidential election. At the time, Kostunica headed the small Democratic Party of Serbia (DSS), which enjoyed only a small part of the organizational muscle of Djindjic's Democratic Party. In addition, Kostunica did not enjoy the name recognition that both Djindjic and Draskovic had. Yet polls showed that Kostunica's newness, coupled with his brand of moderate nationalism, made him the ideal opposition candidate. Once DOS decided to participate in the presidential vote and the accompanying parliamentary and local elections, Djindjic made a major sacrifice in stepping aside rather than running for president in 2000. Instead he worked behind the scenes in forging a new coalition. Draskovic and his Democratic Renewal Party eventually decided not to join DOS, but the perception of unity created by the formation of DOS and its single candidate, Kostunica, cast Draskovic as a spoiler at a time when the Serbian electorate of a democratic orientation wanted unity and victory.

Ukrainian democrats also created the perception of unity in the run-up to the 2004 presidential election. In the previous decade, Ukraine's democratic forces had remained divided and disorganized. In Ukraine, opposition unity was complicated by the presence of the strong and legitimate Socialist Party, which made cooperation with Ukrainian liberals difficult. Nor, for many years, had there been a single, charismatic opposition leader who stood out as an obvious first among equals. Ironically, Kuchma helped to create such a leader when he dismissed Viktor

Yushchenko as his prime minister in 2001. At the time Yushchenko cut an image of a technocratic economist, not a stump politician.

Nonetheless, he was a popular prime minister with a record of achievement while in office, making him a dangerous opponent to the party in power. Yushchenko succeeded in creating a new electoral bloc, Our Ukraine, which captured a quarter of the popular vote in the 2002 parliamentary elections. Our Ukraine's success in 2002 made Yushchenko the focal point of a united front for the presidential election in 2004. Most important, Tymoshenko—an opposition leader with more charisma than Yushchenko but also more baggage—agreed not to run independently for president but instead backed Yushchenko, in effect playing the same unifying role in Ukraine that Djindjic had played in Serbia.

Because the election that eventually triggered a democratic breakthrough in Georgia had a parliamentary context and was not a presidential vote, the democratic opposition had not united beforehand. In a parliamentary vote with proportional representation, Georgian parties did not have compelling incentives to unite.

Instead, the opposition ran in three separate blocs: the National Movement, headed by former justice minister Mikheil Saakashvili; the Labor Party, headed by Shalva Natelashvili; and the Burjanadze Democrats, headed by former speakers Nino Burjanadze and Zurab Zhvania. Even according to the exit poll and the parallel vote count, the leading opposition party, the National Movement, won only 20 percent of the popular vote. How surprising, therefore, that Saakashvili became Georgia's president just one month later.

In Georgia, unity came after the election and not before. The revolutionary moment demanded a revolutionary leader, and Saakashvili was that leader. He gave fiery speeches, evoked popular protest, and took bold decisions, which quickly established him as the obvious leader of the Rose Revolution. Of Georgia's opposition leaders, Saakashvili also had the weakest connections to the ancien régime, a fact that played in his favor during this period of polarization. Zhvania and Burjanadze therefore made the decision to stand with and behind Saakashvili. Had either defected, the final phase of the Rose Revolution might have ended much differently. Saakashvili's decision to storm the parliament and press for the president's ouster after a parliamentary vote were actions more radical and more unconstitutional than any taken by Serbian or Ukrainian democrats. Had part of the Georgian democratic opposition refused to endorse Saakashvili's moves, Shevardnadze might have been tempted to fight harder to stay in power. After Shevardnadze resigned and a new presidential election was scheduled for January 2004, Georgia's democratic leaders remained united by Saakashvili. Amazingly, the young hero of the Rose Revolution won 96 percent of the vote. Two months later, in March 2004, the democrats stayed together in one electoral bloc and captured a solid majority of the seats in parliament.

Kyrgyzstan is strikingly different from the other cases in that the opposition had not united before the spring 2005 parliamentary elections. As demonstrated in Georgia as well, unity before a parliamentary election is harder to achieve. Similar again to Georgia, however, the opposition did unite into a single electoral bloc behind one leader, Kurmanbek Bakiev, to compete in the hastily scheduled presidential vote in July 2005. The only other serious opposition leader, Sergei Kulov, accepted the role played by Djindjic, Zhvania, and Tymoshenko and agreed to back Bakiev in return for becoming prime minister. Bakiev won the July 2005 vote handily.

Independent Electoral Monitoring Capabilities

As discussed by Nadia Diuk in chapter four, a robust civil society that matured over decades was critical to fomenting the Orange Revolution. Civil society provided several key precipitants to democratic breakthrough, including a fourth condition critical to success: the ability of nongovernmental organizations to provide an accurate and independent account of the true vote quickly after the polls close. This component was also present and important in Serbia and Georgia. In Kyrgyzstan, the role of independent actors in providing the perception of a falsified vote may have been less important. The perception of a falsified vote was widely shared even without data to actually document it.

In Serbia, the Center for Free Elections and Democracy (CeSID) provided the critical data that exposed voter fraud in the first round of the presidential election in September 2000. Exit polls were illegal in 2000, so CeSID conducted a parallel vote tabulation (PVT), a common technique now used in many transitional democracies. CeSID founders originally employed the technique in Bulgaria.[12] They posted their representatives at seven thousand polling sites, which allowed them to produce a remarkably sophisticated estimate of the actual vote. On election night, a DOS official announced the results of their "party monitoring," and that statement provided the basis for Kostunica to call for mass protests. The reality was that the parties did not have the capacity to conduct a parallel vote tabulation. Instead, the DOS official who had made the announcement did so because he was aware of the general trends that CeSID was tracking at the time.[13] CeSID, in other words, made the claim of falsification legitimate. CeSID's figures also supported Kostunica's claim that he had won more than 50 percent in the first round of the election and therefore did not need to stand for a second round.

In Georgia, independent electoral monitoring also played a critical role in the Rose Revolution. Because international assistance for election monitoring spiked considerably before the 2003 parliamentary vote, NGOs, in cooperation with polling firms, carried out an exit poll and a PVT, the first time that either had been executed in Georgia. The International Society for Fair Elections and Democracy (ISFED) carried out a comprehensive PVT, while a consortium of polling agencies, in cooperation with an American firm, surveyed more than twenty thousand voters in five hundred election precincts.[14] In addition, ISFED and the Georgian Young Lawyers' Association (GYLA) fielded 2,300 and five hundred election observers, respectively, accompanied by international delegations from the Parliamentary Assembly of the Council of Europe, the International Election Observation Mission of OSCE, and a mission from the Commonwealth of Independent States. The results from the PVT and exit poll were remarkably similar and strikingly at odds with official tallies. Observation teams from ISFED and GYLA bolstered the claims from the PVT and exit poll by documenting instances of voter fraud.

In Ukraine, the Committee of Ukrainian Voters (CVU) played the central role in monitoring all rounds of the 2004 presidential vote. The committee also conducted a parallel vote tabulation. A consortium of polling firms, coordinated by the Ukrainian NGO Democratic Initiatives Foundation, executed exit polls, though so too did firms associated closely with the Kuchma regime. Compared with the novel Georgian efforts at exposing fraud, the Ukrainian organizations had years of experience. At the same time, they also faced a much more sophisticated voter manipulator. Kuchma and his allies executed successfully two novel methods for obscuring the actual tally, which frustrated attempts by independent actors to expose fraud. First, Kuchma's regime falsified the vote at the level of precincts, and not between the precinct level and higher levels of counting, where fraud traditionally occurs.[15] A parallel vote tabulation attempts to expose fraud by sampling the genuine vote count at the precinct level. But if the precinct numbers are already fraudulent, then a PVT will also reflect the result of the falsified vote, an outcome that CVU had to face. Second, Kuchma's government muddied the results of the exit polls by compelling two of the consortium partners to use a method in the second round different from the method used by the other two polling firms more closely tied to the opposition.[16] After the second round of the presidential vote, therefore, two different exit poll numbers were released, each with a different result.

When these quantitative, or macro, methods for exposing fraud yielded ambiguous results, qualitative, micro methods came to the rescue. Individual election monitors, fielded by CVU and other NGOs, reported hundreds and hundreds of instances of irregular procedures. So too did international monitors. At the same time, turnout levels in some regions in the east were so outrageously high that election analysts knew they could not be true. This combination gave a few members of the Central Election Commission the courage to refuse to certify the final count, eventually sending the issue on to Rada.[17] The supreme council then used the evidence of fraud collected by CVU and the other NGOs to overturn the official results and call for a replay of the second round of the presidential election, which Yushchenko won decisively. Of course, it is unlikely that either CEC or Rada would have acted as it did if hundreds of thousands of protestors were not on the streets.

In Kyrgyzstan, a coalition of 170 NGOs called Democracy and Civil Society placed 1,735 observers throughout the country to monitor the election and release qualitative reports about cases of falsification. Democracy and Civil Society, however, did not complete a parallel vote tabulation or an exit poll. Instead, claims of falsification in just a handful of electoral districts sparked the Kyrgyz uprising.

A Modicum of Independent Media

As discussed by Olena Prytula in chapter six, the creation of a foothold for independent media was critical in creating momentum for the Orange Revolution years before the 2004 presidential vote. During the events of political confrontation, independent media played a positive and significant role in communicating news about falsified votes and in helping in turn to set in motion popular opposition to the regime after the vote, not only in Ukraine, but also in Serbia, Georgia, and to some extent, Kyrgyzstan. Years before these pivotal elections, independent media outlets also played a central role in developing other factors discussed here, including weakening the popularity of incumbents and strengthening support for the opposition. At the moment of a break-through, media that were autonomous from the state played an independent and necessary role in triggering regime change.

In Serbia, several important independent media outlets contributed to the second factor, the decline of Milosevic's popularity. The B–92 radio station led the charge, providing critical yet professional coverage of Milosevic and his regime since the station first went on the air in 1989.[18] Veran Matic, B–92's cofounder, also played an instrumental role in establishing the ANEM network, a network of regional radio and, later, television stations that distributed independent news broadcasts. The BETA news agency, Radio Index, the independent dailies *Blic, Glas Javnosti, Pobjeda, Vijesti,* and *Danas;* the weeklies *NIN, Vreme, Argument, Svedok,* and *Monitor;* and eventually the television station Studio B were also key in providing Serbians with alternative sources of news to the state-controlled or state-loyal stations. Critical coverage of Milosevic's wars, his economic policies, and his government's violent arrests and abuses of young Otpor protestors helped to undermine his support among the population. Immediately after the 2000 election, independent media played a direct and central role in broadcasting the news of a falsified vote, which in turn helped to bring people into the streets. At the time, Milosevic had taken B–92 off the air, so the ANEM network, along with Radio Index in Beograd, proved especially pivotal during this crisis. Without these media, popular mobilization would have been much more difficult to achieve.

Independent media also played a critical role in Georgia. In the last years of Shevardnadze's rule, independent media considerably shook Shevardnadze's popularity. Among them one of the most popular and influential, the independent channel Rustavi 2, played the most active role against Shevardnadze. Two programs on Rustavi 2—*60 Minutes* (a show exposing corruption modeled after the CBS program in the United States) and *Dardubala,* a satirical animated cartoon—were the most popular and the most damaging. Rustavi 2, together with several smaller media outlets, was also extremely important during the Rose Revolution itself. Immediately after the results of the exit poll and PVT became available, they were broadcast on Rustavi 2 endlessly, right next to the official results released by the Central Electoral Commission of Georgia. Unlike opposition media in Serbia, Ukraine, and Kyrgyzstan, Rustavi 2 had already become the most widely watched television network in Georgia before the revolution, giving the opposition a valuable tool for mobilization. Once people took to the streets to protest the falsified election, Rustavi 2 maintained continuous coverage of the demonstrations, which helped to bring more people into the streets, especially after it became clear that the state was not going to use violence to suppress protestors. Other networks formerly loyal to Shevardnadze soon followed Rustavi 2's lead in providing coverage of the protests, which added to the groundswell of opposition.

In contrast to Serbia and especially Georgia, Ukraine's democratic opposition had access to fewer traditional sources of independent media. There was nothing akin to B–92, the ANEM network, or Rustavi 2 in Ukraine. By 2004, Ukraine boasted several independent television networks, but all the major channels were owned or controlled by oligarchs loyal to Kuchma and Yanukovych. Some important print newspapers provided independent sources of news, but all had limited circulations. Compared with Serbia and Georgia, however, Ukraine's opposition had one advantage: the Internet. Coming just a little bit later than the other two revolutions and in a country a little bit richer and therefore with a little more connectivity, the Orange Revolution benefited tremendously from the Web. In fact, the Orange Revolution may have been the first in world history organized in large measure on the Web. The Internet publication *Ukrainska pravda* most certainly ranked as one of Ukraine's essential outlets of news and analysis in the last years before the collapse of the Kuchma regime. By the end of the Orange Revolution, it was not only the most popular Internet site, but also the most widely read publication of any kind in Ukraine. During the critical hours and days after the second-round vote, *Ukrainska pravda* displayed the results of the exit poll most sympathetic to Yushchenko as well as detailed news about allegations of fraud. The website also provided all sorts of practical information to protestors.

Ukrainska pravda may have been the most important source of news for opposition-minded Web surfers, but other portals also provided critical information that helped to make the Orange Revolution. The Maidan site was a clearinghouse of information and coordination for protestors. Pora and Our Ukraine also had important websites and webmasters that blasted informational and motivational emails to supporters and observers all over the country and all over the world (including to this author) during the critical moments right after the vote. Text messaging was also an essential coordinating device for those in Maidan and in the tent city, who did not have access to email.

Eventually, a more traditional technology—television—also played its role in the Orange Revolution's success. Realizing that limited access to television with a national reach was going to hinder Yushchenko's campaign, multimillionaire and Our Ukraine supporter Petro Poroshenko bought a small television station in 2003, which he soon renamed Channel 5. Amazingly, the state authorities allowed this sale to be completed. Yushchenko ran his television spots on Channel 5, but even at the end of the campaign, the station continued to reach only a small portion of the country. Channel 5's central role came after the vote, when the channel's management decided to provide twenty-four-hour coverage of the protest in downtown Kyiv after the results of the falsified election were announced. Like Rustavi 2 in Georgia, these broadcasts helped to increase the number of protestors, especially when people saw the peaceful, festive nature of the crowds in Maidan. By the end of the demonstration, Channel 5 catapulted from thirteenth to third place in the national ratings. Channel 5 coverage also put pressure on other national channels to stop spewing propaganda. By the fourth day of protests, the staff at most other stations had joined forces with the street demonstrators.

In Kyrgyzstan, the state's dominance of national media outlets grew during the 1990s, earning the country a not-free rating from Freedom House in the final years of Akaev's rule.[19] Private owners had established several television and radio stations, including Piramida Television and Radio, Independent Bishkek Television, and Asman Television, but most of these firms kept close ties to Akaev's regime. Kyrgyz media, therefore, did not play the same mobilizing role that independent media played in the other breakthroughs. Once mobilization in the south began, however, a few media outlets, including the newspaper *My Capital*, Radio Azzatyk, and BBC Kyrgyz service, together played a vital role in helping to spread the news of events in Jalalabad and Osh to the capital.

Mobilizing the Masses

As discussed by Pavol Demes and Joerg Forbrig in chapter five, another critical factor for a democratic breakthrough in Ukraine was the opposition's capacity to instigate significant numbers of protestors to challenge the falsified electoral results. The same was true in Serbia and Georgia. In all three cases, newly formed student groups—Otpor, Kmara, and Pora (both the black and yellow versions)—provided logistical support. In the case of Ukraine, the Pora constituted the first wave of protestors. In the final phase, however, these student groups worked together with both the main opposition parties and other NGOs to move the tens of thousands, and in Serbia and Ukraine, the million, needed for success.

In Serbia, the opposition had planned for street resistance well in advance. The night of the election, after Kostunica claimed victory in the first round, Serbia's democratic opposition stitched together a broad and highly motivated coalition of people ready to take to the streets to make sure their votes were counted. Otpor, DOS, regional government heads, trade union leaders, and civil society organizers coordinated their popular resistance efforts, culminating in the million-strong march on Beograd on October 5, 2000. As columns of protestors approached the capital, they met police barricades. But when tested, not one police barricade seriously tried to stop the caravans. When the advancing columns reached Beograd, the number of protestors exceeded one million, making the state's defense of parliament futile. Within hours, the opposition had seized parliament, police headquarters, and the national television station. The next day, Milosevic resigned.

In contrast to Serbia, Georgia's protestors seemed less organized and fewer. By Georgian standards, the mobilization was coordinated, well organized, and massive, involving not only citizens of Tbilisi, but people from all parts of the country. Modeled after Otpor, Kmara spearheaded the civic resistance movement.[20] Kmara was a new organization and did not play the same mobilization role that Otpor had in Serbia in the months leading up to the election. After the vote, however, Kmara played a more central role than Otpor had in promoting street protests. As in Serbia, however, the principal figure in Georgia's popular resistance was politician Mikhail Saakashvili. Once the protests had begun, Saakashvili's charisma, boldness, and oratory skills made him the focal point of a new and well-coordinated United Opposition coalition, which brought together opposition parties (the National Movement, Burjanadze Democrats, and Unity), Kmara, and other civil society organizations. As in Serbia on October 5, 2000, the number of Georgian protestors eventually reached such a critical edge that suppression by police forces would have ended in massive casualties, an outcome that no one in the old regime, including Shevardnadze, wanted.

Compared with their counterparts in Serbia and Ukraine, Georgia's demonstrators (or at least their leaders) were more radical both in their demands and actions. In Serbia, protestors took to the streets to press the government to recognize the results of the presidential election. In Georgia, Saakashvili called for and succeeded in obtaining not only recognition of the parliamentary election results, but Shevardnadze's ouster, even though the Georgian president was not standing for reelection at the time. The demand was clearly unconstitutional. Moreover, in contrast to the Ukrainian demonstration, Georgia's protestors initiated physical contact with the ancien régime by storming the parliament.

In Ukraine, Our Ukraine, in coordination with Pora (the yellow branch), planned to take immediate action should Yushchenko not win the election. The morning after the second round of voting, Pora activists erected hundreds of tents on the main street near Maidan, where Our Ukraine activists—under the supervision of Our Ukraine ministers of parliament—were already busy erecting a large stage to accommodate a massive protest in Maidan. Truckloads of tents, cushioned mats, and food supplies soon appeared as well, clearly demonstrating the opposition's preplanning.

Our Ukraine and its partners made preparations for tens of thousands to protest a rigged election. They did not anticipate that their act of civil disobedience would swell to hundreds of thousands and eventually more than a million people. As the numbers escalated, the logistical challenges of running the equivalent of a major city soon became overwhelming. The protestors succeeded in keeping the crowds who joined them in the square fed, warm, clean, and peaceful only because thousands of small businesspeople contributed to the efforts and because the city of Kyiv supported the Maidan action. In fact, support from city hall was critical not only in Kyiv, but also in Beograd and Tbilisi. Such support may even constitute another necessary condition for success.

In Kyrgyzstan, demonstrations against the regime started in Osh, not in the capital. Local elites spearheaded the effort. Over time, protestors in this southern city gained strength and boldness, especially when their activities met no state resistance. They eventually seized government offices in Osh and Jalalabad, creating a tense situation in which two "governments" claimed authority over two separate regions of the country. Demonstrators then marched on to the capital. Kel Kel, a Kyrgyz student group modeled after Kmara, Otpor, and Pora, planned to occupy the main square in Bishkek, but its plans were preempted by events as the Akaev regime dissolved on the first day of public protest in the capital.

Splits among the Security Forces

A seventh and final necessary condition for success is a split in security forces, that is, of those actors within the state, such as the ministry of the interior or the armed forces, that wield coercive power. A segment of these forces must defect from the ancien régime, making the option of using force risky if not untenable.

In Serbia, Milosevic called upon local police officials to undertake increasingly violent actions against young Otpor protestors, a policy that many law enforcement officials did not support. Demonstrations throughout the year had grown in size and intensity, fueling doubt in the security ministries about the long-term sustainability of the Milosevic regime. The massive demonstrations that took place after the falsified vote convinced many police and intelligence officials that violent repression was no longer an option. On October 4, 2000—the day before the million-person march on Beograd—Zoran Djindjic conducted a lengthy set of negotiations with Yugoslav army chief of staff Nebojsa Pavkovic that ended with an agreement that the military would not intervene to stop protestors on the following day. In return, the new government would not purge the ranks of the power ministries. This agreement guaranteed that October 5 did not turn violent, an outcome that many had feared since some of the demonstrators had come to Beograd armed and prepared to fight.

In Georgia, well before the 2003 election, the opposition had also courted favor with key ministries with coercive capacity. Once demonstrators took to the streets, several important government officials connected to security structures, including the secretary of the security council, Tedo Japaridze, deserted Shevardnadze, while the minister of security, Valery Khaburzania, stayed but made it clear that he would not allow his units to be involved in arresting, let alone shooting, protestors. The defection of the Gulua unit, an elite paramilitary group within the ministry of the interior, to the side of the protestors spurred other military units to switch sides. The memory of the heroic roles played by Georgian police in trying to protect civilians during the violent repression of a 1989 demonstration by Soviet forces also played an immense role in stimulating defection and keeping the protest peaceful.

Compared with his counterparts in Serbia and Ukraine, Shevardnadze had a more legitimate reason to use force against the rebellious opposition. They, after all, had stormed parliament and then demanded his resignation, not simply the recognition of the true results of the parliamentary election. The act was a coup, even if the overthrown leader was, in fact, corrupt and had not followed democratic procedures. Shevardnadze, however, did not use force, in part because he may not have had enough reliable forces to carry out such an order, but also because he did not want to use force against civilians. Because of his role as the Soviet foreign minister, Shevardnadze had a positive reputation in the West, which would have been severely damaged by bloodshed after a falsified election.

In Ukraine, communication between opposition leaders and intelligence officials also helped to remove violent suppression as an option for the Kuchma regime.[21] On the street, where protestors and special forces stood eye to eye for days, Pora demonstrators deliberately used humor and placed young women in the first row opposite the police lines to defuse tension. As in Georgia, the defections of several Ukrainian police and intelligence units made clear that the guys with the guns could not be trusted to carry out a repressive order. A week into the Maidan protest, special troops from Ministry of the Interior did arm and mobilize, but Orange Revolution sympathizers from within the intelligence services warned the Maidan organizers of the impeding attack, while commanders within the regular army then pledged to protect the unarmed citizens if these special forces tried to clear the square. The result of these splits was no serious attempt to use armed force to stop the demonstrations.

In Kyrgyzstan, the police and soldiers put up little resistance. In Osh, the government authorities melted away almost immediately. In Bishkek, after one attempt to push back the crowds, the armed forces fled.

In all four cases, however, the heroic role of defectors from the ranks of the military, intelligence, and police has been overplayed. A commitment to inaction from the guys with the guns emboldened protestors and also made it easier for less politically motivated citizens to join the demonstrations.[22] At the same time, except for Kyrgyzstan, the size of the crowds, not the goodwill of the armed forces, was key in removing violent suppression as an option for the ancien régime. Smaller, less organized crowds would have tempted state officials to act more aggressively. A protest of ten thousand can be dispersed with tear gas and armored cars. A crowd of one million cannot.

The External Dimension

Most accounts of these democratic breakthroughs, including this book, discuss domestic factors first and separately and then add international factors, so that the narrative reads something along the lines of the following: "Four internal factors and one external factor caused democratization in country X." In fact, in only the rarest of cases (as in Iraq today) do external factors act independently in cases of democratization or democratic breakthrough. Most external factors have only a casual influence by strengthening or weakening the value of domestic factors.

When understood within this analytic framework, external actors in all four cases played a facilitating role in changing the value of the seven variables just described. Space does not permit a full accounting of all these external factors for all four cases, especially when this volume already contains two excellent and detailed accounts of the role of the West and Russia in influencing the Orange Revolution. But a few general patterns are worth noting.

Western actors played an indirect role in sustaining competitive authoritarianism and preventing a full-scale dictatorship from consolidating. The leaders of the ancien régime had varying levels of autocratic tendencies, but all refrained from attempting to construct truly repressive tyrannies because they each wanted cooperative relations with the West and member status within the world community of democracies. Even Milosevic wanted his country to be considered a democracy by the outside world. Foreign assistance and moral support also helped to sustain pockets of independent, opposition actors. Russian leaders, to varying extents, played the exact opposite role and encouraged autocratic methods as an effective strategy for holding on to power, especially for Milosevic and Kuchma.

Western actors played only a marginal role in eroding popular support for incumbents. In Serbia, sanctions and the promise of lifting them after Milosevic's ouster helped the opposition's cause, but the NATO-led bombing campaign against Milosevic's regime boosted his popular standing in the short run. Western support for Shevardnadze and Akaev for much of the 1990s may have helped to prolong the reign of these leaders. The causal impact of external actors on Kuchma's popularity is difficult to measure. His own failures, not the West's reaction to them, were the real drivers in the decline in his popular standing.

Western actors played some role in helping to forge effective oppositions in each of the countries, but only indirectly. Secretary of State Madeleine Albright was keen on strengthening Serbia's democratic opposition, so she and her staff engaged directly in pushing the case for a united opposition. The National Democratic Institute (NDI) of the United

States also provided polling data that demonstrated conclusively the benefits of uniting behind Kostunica. Although their friends in the West nudged them from time to time, the Serbs themselves did the hard work of forging an effective and united coalition. The same was true of the successful coalition building in Georgia and Ukraine. Kyrgyzstan had much more limited success in building ties between opposition groups before the spring 2005 election.

Western democracy assistance played an essential role in providing the technical assistance and financial support needed to run effective electoral monitoring efforts in Georgia, Kyrgyzstan, Serbia, and Ukraine. All the major electoral monitoring organizations in each of these countries were trained and underwritten in part by Western sources. Western organizations also facilitated learning between monitoring organizations in the countries, including the deployment in Ukraine of the European Network of Election Monitoring Organizations (ENEMO), which comprised electoral monitoring organizations from countries in the former communist world. Without this form of assistance, these monitoring efforts would have not occurred.

Western sources also provided vital support to key independent media outlets. The West did not play a decisive role in funding independent television stations. Rustavi 2 in Georgia and Channel 5 in Ukraine received no serious support from Western government sources or private donors (although Western sources subsidized the production of individual programs on each channel). Key radio stations and critical print and Internet outlets such as B–92, the ANEM network, Radio Index, *Ukrainska pravda*, Maidan.org, *My Capital*, and Radio Azzatyk did rely, to varying extents, on Western support.

The same can be said about Western assistance to the nongovernmental groups that organized mass protests. All three effective student organizations—Otpor, Kmara, and Pora—received grants from various American and European governments and foundations.

The West did not play a major role in causing divisions in the security forces before mass mobilization began.[23] Once troops and citizens took to the streets, however, Western leaders were active in all the cases except Serbia in encouraging compromise and preventing conflict between those on different sides of the barricades. As discussed by Oleksandr Sushko and Olena Prystayko in chapter seven, the Western effort in diffusing the crisis in Ukraine was particularly active and effective because the United States and the major European powers acted swiftly and in unison. In all four cases, U.S. government officials clearly signaled that they would not condone the use of violence as a means for staying in power.

Factors Not Present in All Cases of Breakthrough

Highlighting these seven factors suggests that other factors were not as important. For instance, the state of the economy or level of economic development did not play a uniform role in these cases of democratic breakthrough. The literature on democratization posits two arguments—one long term, one short term—about the relation between economic development and democratization. In the long run, modernization theorists have identified a positive correlation between the rising wealth of a country and (in particular) the emergence of a middle class and democratization.[24] In Ukraine, recent economic growth and an expanding middle class were causes of the Orange Revolution. Åslund has noted, however, that the real class drama in that breakthrough was the clash between billionaires and millionaires. This class dimension cannot be observed in Georgia, Kyrgyzstan, or Serbia, where populations had experienced real economic trauma before a breakthrough occurred.

Nor, however, can economic crisis be cited as the spark of breakthrough in all these cases.[25] Economic hardship most certainly figured in undermining the popularity of Shevardnadze, Akaev, and Milosevic, but an economic meltdown was not the trigger for transition in any of the cases. Rather, the trigger was a manipulated vote. And in Ukraine, the economy had grown 12 percent in 2004.

Nor was the resolution of border disputes or the clear stipulation of who was in the polity and who was not a precondition for a democratic breakthrough in any of the countries. In his influential article, Dankwart Rustow argued that "national unity must precede all other phases of democratization" and that it works best as a precondition for democracy "when national unity is accepted unthinkingly."[26] Although this dictum has stood the test of time globally, it cannot be considered a necessary condition for this set of cases. Ethnic conflict and elite-manipulated disputes about the boundaries between ethnic groups resulted in interstate and civil war in the Balkans and in civil war in Georgia, developments that delayed democratic consolidation.[27] Yet the status of Kosovo, Montenegro, South Ossetia, and Abkhazia did not have to be resolved before a democratic breakthrough could occur in Serbia or Georgia. Nor did tensions between ethnic Ukrainians living in western Ukraine and ethnic Russians living in eastern Ukraine become the destabilizing, antidemocratic factor that some Ukrainian elites had hoped for. The north-south divide in Kyrgyzstan was critical in setting in motion the ouster of Akaev, but border disputes and ethnic divisions were not key to democratic development and did not require resolution beforehand.

Nor did a split between hard-liners and soft-liners within the ancien régime figure prominently as triggers for democratization.[28] In several respects, this split had taken place years before, so that the opposition was dominated not by civil society leaders or dissidents, but by former reformers from within the regime. In all these cases, the opposition comprised politicians who had previously served, in some capacity, in the regimes they were now trying to depose. Of all the cases discussed, Serbia's opposition had the least common history with Milosevic, yet Kostunica, Djindjic, and other DOS leaders had served in the parliament before, side by side with Milosevic's party members. In other words, they were not revolutionaries who had always opposed the regime, but had spent many years abiding by the political rules of the game of the Milosevic regime. In Georgia, Kyrgyzstan, and Ukraine, all the major leaders of the opposition were former government officials.

The relationships between the ancien régime and the West follow a single pattern in these cases. Milosevic obviously had the most adversarial relationship with the West, and with the United States in particular. In the year before his ouster, NATO aircraft had bombed Serbia for several weeks. Whether the NATO campaign helped or hindered democratization is still intensely debated among Serbia's democratic activists and their supporters in the West.[29] Compared with Milosevic, Shevardnadze enjoyed much better ties with Western leaders, but his good standing in European capitals and Washington did not help him to stay in power. Kuchma and Akaev endured strained but cordial relations with their Western counterparts, relations that did little to help them stay in power but may have pushed them to do the right thing in stepping aside when the potential for armed conflict became serious. Because the range of relationships of the four leaders with the West varied, tracing a single causal role for Western diplomacy is difficult.

Finally, campaign slogans and techniques deployed by the opposition do not appear to have played an independent or significant role in any of the campaigns. In all contests, these were campaigns *against* unpopular incumbents, not campaigns for a set of positive policies or reforms. Campaign programs, therefore, never figured importantly in any of these contests. Even the function that democratic ideas had in activating voters first and then protestors is not uniform across the cases. Rather, all four successful movements constructed compelling ideologies of opposition whose main message was that the people had had enough of the current regime.

Even the pivotal role of the opposition leader is not easy to discern in all four cases.[30] After the breakthrough, it seems as though no other leader could have united the opposition and toppled the regime. But this "fact" seems obvious only after success had been achieved. Immediately after victory in 2000, Kostunica seemed to be the only moderate nationalist who could have defeated Milosevic in a free and fair election, yet Kostunica's limited skills as a politician have subsequently diminished his heroic status. The diabolical tactics of the Kuchma regime, including most obviously the poisoning of Yushchenko, transformed him into an indispensable hero of the Orange Revolution. Yet, just months before victory, several leaders within the Ukrainian democratic movement questioned whether Yushchenko had the political and campaign skills to win. In Georgia, Saakashvili became essential and one of a kind only after he had ordered the storming of the parliament and Shevardnadze's ouster. Yet, had the opposition maintained more modest objectives—a new parliamentary vote or the recognition of the real results of the vote—Saakashvili's place in Georgian history could have evolved into a very different narrative. Kyrgyzstan had no single figure leading the opposition yet still managed to topple the regime. Whether great men and women make history or history makes great men and women is not a debate resolved by these cases.

In seeking to learn lessons from these democratic breakthroughs, it is important to realize that the list of necessary conditions is long. The presence of only a few factors is unlikely to generate the same outcome. A more popular or more ruthless autocrat might have been able to outmaneuver the democratic opposition. A less organized electoral monitoring effort in any of the three countries might not have been able to convince people to take to the streets. Thousands in the streets, instead of tens of thousands or hundreds of thousands, might have produced a very different outcome. The stars must really be aligned to produce such dramatic events.

Path-Dependent Legacies

Democratic breakthroughs or revolutionary outcomes do not ensure success in consolidating democracy. These instances of breakthrough

disrupted the antidemocratic status quo and jump-started stalled democratic transitions. Yet renewed stagnation in democratic development
and even democratic reversal are still possible outcomes.

Moreover, the different modes of transition in each of these cases
have produced path-dependent consequences. In Serbia, Djindjic and
Pavkovic cut a deal on October 4 that kept those with arms from firing
on demonstrators but also allowed senior leaders in the ministries to
remain in power. Three years later, the very general who had negotiated with Djindjic appears to have ordered his murder. Corrupt officials remain ensconced in the ministries of interior and intelligence and
still impede deeper democratic development within Serbia—a linger-
ing legacy from the kind of transition that transpired in October 2000.[31]

Georgia's breakthrough was not agreed upon or negotiated. Rather,
one side seized power, which is a mode of transition with both positive
and negative consequences. In the plus column, Saakashvili owed no
favors to leaders of the ancien régime. He could clean house, and he has
tried to do so. In the minus column, the lack of constraints on Saakashvili
has some worried that he will use his mandate to resurrect yet another
form of autocratic rule.[32] Similar to the way in which Shevardnadze first
came to power a decade earlier, Georgia's mode of transition reinforced
a dangerous, nondemocratic precedent for changing leaders. Georgia
has yet to transfer executive authority between individuals through an
elected, rule-based process.

By contrast, with the assistance of international mediators, Ukraine's
leaders eventually agreed to negotiate an arrangement by which Kuchma
and his side allowed the second round of the presidential election to be
rerun. In return Yushchenko and his side agreed to changes in the constitution that will give parliament and the prime minister more powers
and the president fewer. At the time of these roundtable talks, some
leaders of Ukraine's opposition wanted to end discussions, follow the
example of the Rose Revolution, and simply seize power. Yushchenko,
however, rejected these calls for storming government buildings and
insisted instead on the path of negotiation. Yushchenko's decision will
constrain his presidential powers in the short run but help to consolidate democratic practices of compromise and checks and balances between government branches in the long run.

The Kyrgyz mode of transition was the least structured, most violent, and most chaotic. Akaev's grip on power disappeared faster than
the opposition had anticipated, creating a lack of agreed-upon procedures to guide the country from the destruction of the old regime to the

construction of a new regime. To its credit, an interim government did form and eventually established a timetable for electing a new president. Yet continued squabbles over who was elected to parliament and who was not in the spring 2005 vote, rivalries among those in the new leadership, and the presence of clan-based networks seeking to influence the transition behind the scenes all suggest that the final outcome of Kyrgyzstan's breakthrough is far from certain.

Was the Orange Revolution Really a "Revolution"?

The events that unfolded in the fall of 2004 in Ukraine were dramatic, abnormal, pivotal, and exceptional, causing both friends and foes of the final outcome to label the drama a revolution. Both sides of the barricade had an interest in deploying this grand term to describe events; the "revolutionaries" wanted to underscore the break with Ukraine's past and codify the glory and greatness of their achievement. They succeeded. The very act of labeling their successful efforts at mass mobilization and reversing a falsified vote a revolution did much to codify the Orange Revolution as a fundamental event in Ukrainian history. This positive image of the revolution also won the day in the West. The "antirevolutionaries" and their friends in Russia wanted to emphasize the illegality of the hotheads and the threatening nature of their actions. This negative image of the revolution played well in Russia and in those post-Soviet states still ruled by autocrats.

For analysts, however, a term like *revolution* marks a category of events deployed to signal those cases that should be compared and those that should not. When understood as an analytical category, the label *revolution* has both limits and benefits in describing Ukrainian politics in the fall of 2004. To date, the Orange Revolution falls short of more comprehensive and complex definitions of *revolution* championed by structural theorists. At the same time, the Orange Revolution most certainly meets the minimalist definition of *revolution* as advanced by political-conflict theorists who see all struggles between two or more political groups fighting for sovereignty over the same territory as revolutionary situations.[33]

In several important ways, the drama that unfolded on the streets and in the corridors of power in Kyiv in the fall of 2004 does not resemble the social revolutions begun in France in 1789 or in Russia in 1917.[34] Most important, those who took to the streets to defy Kuchma's regime did not seek the destruction of Ukraine's existing political institutions or the rewriting of Ukraine's political rules of the game, although changes in those rules—from a presidential system to a parliamentary system—were an unintended consequence of the protests. There were no demands to replace democracy with a fundamentally new and different form of government. Rather, Ukrainians protested in order to guarantee that the rules and institutions of democracy—formally outlined in the constitution and other documents but informally undermined by corrupt government practices—were followed.

Nor, in contrast to many other revolutionary movements, did Ukrainians demand a fundamental redistribution of the country's property or the wholesale transformation of Ukraine's economic institutions. Rather, those in Maidan wanted a less corrupt, more efficient form of capitalism. They wanted an economy based on markets and private property, not a new form of economic organization altogether. After all, many of the leaders of the revolution had served in the Kuchma government just a few years before. (The same was not true of Robespierre, Lenin, Mao, or Khomeini.) A few previous transactions involving the redistribution of property during the Kuchma era may have been so corrupt that they must be reversed to allow the postrevolutionary government to maintain legitimacy. Yet neither leaders nor followers of the Orange Revolution have pressed for a fundamental reorganization of the institutions of the Ukrainian economy or for a radical redistribution of property. Eventually, the consequences of the Orange Revolution could be dramatic for Ukraine's economy and society, but they are unlikely to generate new social classes, let alone a new economic system, as has occurred in other social revolutions.[35] More generally, the economic, political, and social changes unleashed by the Orange Revolution are unlikely to replicate the scale and scope of transformation or the stages of revolution observed in earlier revolutions.[36]

In the means they used, Ukraine's demonstrators also departed from a common "revolutionary" practice in refusing to use violence or even provoke violence as a strategy for toppling the old order.[37] For some theorists, the absence of violence means the absence of revolution. As Chalmers Johnson has written, "'nonviolent revolution,' so long as these words retain any meaning whatsoever, is a contradiction in terms."[38]

At the same time, the events that unfolded in Ukraine in the fall of 2004 were not a typical election or a normal transfer of power from one leader to the next. Instead, it was a revolutionary transfer of power in that extraconstitutional means had to be deployed and the creation of a situation of dual sovereignty had to crystallize before the leaders of one regime stepped down and another took over. When Kuchma and his regime declared Yanukovych the winner of the November election, Yushchenko countered by declaring himself the winner. In parliament, Yushchenko even held a swearing-in ceremony, meaning that for a time Ukraine had two groups of people, each one claiming sovereign authority over the same territory, which is one of the classic definitions of a "revolutionary situation."[39] Not all revolutionary situations produce revolutionary outcomes; incumbents often reassert their sovereignty and quell those making alternative claims to rule. Ukraine's upheaval, however, did end in a revolutionary outcome—the "displacement of one set of power holders by another."[40] Moreover, this process of displacement included mass mobilization, another key attribute of revolutionary change.

Those who took to the streets and then remained in the streets for more than two weeks primarily comprised socioeconomic groups formed and strengthened by Ukraine's change from communism to capitalism. In the language of Karl Marx and Samuel Huntington, they were new classes pushing up against antiquated political institutions.[41] Finally, the Orange Revolution included moments when there were threats of extraconstitutional means from those on both sides of the barricades, which is another classic attribute of a revolutionary situation. The Orange Revolution, therefore, was an event that included attributes of a revolutionary change of power but with two distinct and laudable features: mass mobilization without violence and social protest triggered by a falsified election. These features affirmed in practice the democratic institutions that in form were already codified in the Ukrainian constitution.

The very presence of the latter phenomenon underscores the continuity or, at least, the connectivity between the Orange Revolution and Ukraine's transition from communism fifteen years earlier. At the time of independence in 1991, Ukraine was midstream in a social revolution, which was beginning to redefine the borders of the state and nation, undermine Soviet political and economic institutions, and start to create new market and democratic institutions. The emergence of an independent Ukraine by peaceful means was the monumental and underappreciated achievement of the previous decade. With less success, Ukrainian leaders in the previous decade had also managed to dismantle most Soviet-era economic practices and create the permissive conditions for a form of capitalism (however flawed) to take root. Yet the collapse of communism did not lead smoothly or quickly to the consolidation of liberal democracy either in Ukraine or throughout the region.[42]

The political transformation from communist autocracy to liberal democracy stalled in the 1990s. Before the Orange Revolution, Ukraine's regime—like many others in the region between the consolidated democracies in East Central Europe and the full-blown autocracies of Central Asia—seemed stuck somewhere in the twilight zone between democracy and dictatorship.[43] By the close of the century, the prospect of further democratic gains in Ukraine seemed unlikely.

The Orange Revolution, however, fundamentally shattered the alleged stability of the old order and created the prospect of further democratic gains, that is, the completion of the political transformation that had really begun fifteen years earlier. In a sense, then, the Orange Revolution represented a second wave of democratization, or democratic breakthrough, in Ukraine, and perhaps the completion of the triple transformation of borders, polity, and economy launched with the collapse of the Soviet Union in 1991.

The final word, however, on whether the Orange Revolution was a "true" revolution rests with the people of Ukraine. That so many immediately adopted the phrase *Orange Revolution* to describe the tumultuous events of the fall of 2004 suggests that the term will stick, whether Western academics like it or not.

Notes

1. In important ways, Slovakia in 1998 and not Serbia in 2000 may have been the first case of a democratic breakthrough in the region.
2. Guillermo O'Donnell and Philippe Schmitter, *Transitions from Authoritarian Rule: Tentative Conclusions about Uncertain Democracies* (Baltimore, Md.: Johns Hopkins University Press, 1986).
3. To have real confidence that these factors were all necessary would require expanding the number of cases examined, including, most important, a selection of "failed" cases in the data set, which is a topic for future research.
4. Daniel Brumberg, "Liberalization versus Democracy," in Thomas Carothers and Marina Ottaway, eds., *Uncharted Journey: Promoting Democracy in the Middle East* (Washington, D.C.: Carnegie Endowment for International Peace, 2005), 15–36.
5. On this regime type, see Larry Diamond, "Thinking about Hybrid Regimes," *Journal of Democracy*, 13(2) (April 2002): 21–35; and Steven Levitsky and Lucan Way, "The Rise of Competitive Authoritarianism," *Journal of Democracy*, 13(2) (April 2002): 51–65.
6. Charles King, "Potemkin Democracy: Four Myths of Post-Soviet Georgia," *The National Interest* (Summer 2001): 93–104.
7. Alexander Motyl and Amanda Schnetzer, *Nations in Transit 2004: Democratization in East Central Europe and Eurasia* (New York: Freedom House with Rowman and Littlefield, 2005), 238.

8. Zeljko Cvijanovic, "Belgrade Opposition Upbeat," *Institute for War and Peace Reporting*, BCR, 160 (July 28, 2000).
9. Office of Research, Opinion and Analysis, Department of State, "Georgians Fast Losing Faith in Shevardnadze and Their Democracy," M 238 01, December 3, 2001, 1.
10. National Democratic Institute, *Serbia Issues Poll* (prepared by Penn, Schoen and Bergland Associates, October 24, 1999).
11. The failure of Shevardnadze's government to fight corruption prompted the International Monetary Fund to suspend its programs in Georgia two months before the revolution.
12. Interviews with CeSID officials Zoran Lucic and Marko Blagojevic, Beograd, Serbia, January 13, 2005.
13. Ibid.
14. Interview with Anna Tarkhnishvili, the director of the Business and Consulting Company, one of the three firms involved in the exit poll, Tbilisi, Georgia, October 14, 2004.
15. Interview with Igor Popov, the chair of the Committee of Ukrainian Voters, Kyiv, March 10, 2005.
16. Interview with Ilko Kucheriv, the president of the Democratic Initiatives Foundation and the organizer of this exit-poll consortium, Kyiv, Ukraine, March 10, 2005.
17. Interview with CEC member Roman Knyazevich, Kyiv, March 12, 2005.
18. On B–92's history, see Matthew Collin, *Guerilla Radio: Rock 'n' Roll Radio and Serbia's Underground Resistance* (New York: Nation Books, 2002).
19. Motyl and Schnetzer, *Nations in Transit 2004*, 301.
20. On the Serbia connections, see the interview with David Zurabishvili, the former head of the Liberty Institute, in Zurab Karumidze and James Wetsch, eds., *Enough: The Rose Revolution in the Republic of Georgia 2003* (New York: Nova Science Publishers, 2005), 61–68; and Peter Baker, "Tbilisi's 'Revolution of Roses' Mentored by Serbian Activists," *Washington Post*, November 25, 2003, A22.
21. C. J. Chivers, "How Top Spies in Ukraine Changed the Nation's Path," *New York Times*, January 17, 2005, 1.
22. Timur Kuron, "Now out of Never: The Element of Surprise in the East European Revolution of 1989," *World Politics*, 44(1) (October 1991): 7–48.
23. There is evidence that Ukrainian and Georgian officers who participated in Partnership for Peace programs may have played a role in diffusing these crises in 2003 and 2004, but the evidence marshaled to date is anecdotal.
24. Seymour Martin Lipset, "Some Social Requisites of Democracy," *American Political Science Review*, 53 (March 1959): 69–105.
25. On the importance of economic crisis for democratic transitions, see Stephan Haggard and Robert Kaufman, *The Political Economy of Democratic Transitions* (Princeton: Princeton University Press, 1995).
26. Dankwart Rustow, "Transitions to Democracy: Toward a Dynamic Model," *Comparative Politics*, 2 (1970): 350–51.
27. Michael McFaul, "The Fourth Wave of Democracy and Dictatorship: Noncooperative Transitions in the Postcommunist World," *World Politics*, 54n(2) (January 2002): 212 44.
28. These actors and this framework for understanding democratic transitions, which in many ways has become the model for analyzing transitions, come from O'Donnell and Schmitter, *Transitions from Authoritarian Rule*.
29. Interviews with several democratic activists involved in the anti-Milosevic campaign in 2000. Polls show that Milosevic benefited in the short run from the bombing campaign, although, ironically, this spike in popularity may have caused him to miscalculate his chances of winning a direct election.

30. On the misplaced emphasis on leaders more generally in such situations, see Kurt Schock, "Nonviolent Action and Its Misconceptions: Insights for Social Scientists," *PS: Political Science and Politics*, 36(4) (October 2003): 705–12.
31. Helsinki Committee for Human Rights in Serbia, *Human Rights and Accountability: Serbia 2003* (Belgrade, 2004), 163–66.
32. Interviews with several Georgian NGO leaders, Tbilisi, Georgia, October 12–14, 2004.
33. On these varying definitions of revolutions and theories of revolution, see Jack Goldstone, "Theories of Revolution: The Third Generation," *World Politics*, 32 (April 1980): 425–53.
34. Theda Skocpol, *States and Social Revolutions: A Comparative Analysis of France, Russia, and China* (Cambridge, U.K.: Cambridge University Press, 1979).
35. Barrington Moore, *Social Origins of Dictatorship and Democracy* (Cambridge, Mass.: Harvard University Press, 1966).
36. On the stages of revolutions, see Crane Brinton, *Anatomy of Revolution* (New York: Vintage Press, 1938); and Vladimir Mau and Irina Staradubrovskaya, *The Challenge of Revolution: Contemporary Russia in Historical Perspective* (Oxford, U.K.: Oxford University Press, 2001).
37. For a different view, see Michael McFaul, "Revolutionary Transformations in Comparative Perspective: Defining a Post-Communist Research Agenda," in David Holloway and Norman Naimark, eds., *Reexamining the Soviet Experience: Essays in Honor of Alexander Dallin* (Boulder, Colo.: Westview Press, 1996), 167–96; and Peter Ackerman and Jack Duvall, *A Force More Powerful: A Century of Nonviolent Conflict* (New York: Palgrave, 2000).
38. Chalmers Johnson, *Revolutionary Change* (Stanford, Calif.: Stanford University Press, 1982), 7.
39. On the definition of a revolutionary situation versus a revolutionary outcome, see Charles Tilly, *From Mobilization to Revolution* (Reading, Mass.: Addison-Wesley, 1978), chapter 9. The idea of dual sovereignty as a definition of a revolutionary situation comes originally from Leon Trotsky's *History of the Russian Revolution*.
40. Ibid., 192.
41. Samuel Huntington, *Political Order in Changing Societies* (New Haven: Yale University Press, 1968).
42. McFaul, "The Fourth Wave."
43. The image of the twilight zone comes from Larry Diamond, *Developing Democracy* (Baltimore: Johns Hopkins University Press, 1999). The idea of a static quality of regimes stuck between dictatorship and democracy comes from Thomas Carothers, "The End of the Transition Paradigm," *Journal of Democracy*, 13(1) (January 2002).

Acknowledgments

EVEN AS IT WAS TAKING PLACE, Ukraine's Orange Revolution was an earth-shattering event. For one month, its minutiae dominated the international media. It stands out as the greatest political upheaval in East-Central Europe since 1991, but also as the major postcommunist revolt in favor of democracy in a series of events that started in Slovakia in 1998, followed by Serbia in 2000, Georgia in 2003, and Kyrgyzstan in March 2005. The natural question is, which country is next?

Whatever follows this upheaval, the Orange Revolution was a great historical event. We therefore decided to write a book about the Orange Revolution as soon as it ended with the inauguration of Viktor Yushchenko as the democratically elected president of Ukraine on January 23, 2005. Our purpose has been to analyze this revolution to show why it happened and the contribution of various factors.

We chose to do a compilation, with a chapter for each major aspect of the revolution, selecting the best expert for each issue. Two leading Western political scientists, Adrian Karatnycky and Taras Kuzio, focus on Ukrainian politics, covering the emergence of the political opposition and social attitudes, respectively. Nadia Diuk, a longtime specialist on Ukrainian affairs and the director for the region at the National Endowment for Democracy, took on the evolution of civil society. The activist group *Pora* played such a major role in the revolution that we asked Pavol Demes and Joerg Forbrig of the German Marshall Fund, who had worked with Pora, to tell us their story. Considering the enormous importance of the Internet newspaper *Ukrainska pravda* in the revolution, we were happy that its editor-in-chief, Olena Prytula, agreed to write about the impact of the media. To avoid Western biases, we wanted a Ukrainian to write about the role of the West in the elections. Fortunately, two persistent students of this topic, Oleksandr Sushko and Olena Prystayko, respectively, the director and project director of the Center for Peace, Conversion, and Foreign Policy of Ukraine in Kyiv, agreed to give their perspectives. To have the curious role of Russia in the revolution illuminated, we asked our colleagues from the Carnegie Moscow Center, Nikolai Petrov and Andrei Ryabov, to delve into the topic, which has already generated a huge amount of writing in Russia. We are deeply grateful to all our authors for their diligent and conscientious work. Finally, for ourselves we chose the topic of the old regime and the Orange Revolution from a comparative perspective, respectively.

We asked everyone to write quickly, and on March 10, 2005, we organized a full-day book workshop at the International Renaissance Foundation in Kyiv. Most of the authors presented their papers in draft form. The discussion was intense.

Apart from gratitude to the authors, we want to thank the following people for their active participation (in alphabetic order): Stephan Bandera, Markian Bilynskyy, Alexander Bogomolov, Tatyana Boyko, Yevhen Bystrytsky, Valery Chaly, Iryna Chupryna, Juhani Grossman, Chris Holzen, Andriy Ignatov, Vladislav Kaskiv, Ilko Kucheriv, Sally Kux, Masha Lipman, Inna Pidluska, Dmitri Potiekhin, Oleksandr Potiekhin, Oleksandr Solontay, John Somers, Kathryn Stevens, Mykhailo Svystovych, Yaryna Yasynevych, and Sergei Yevtushenko.

This book is a product of the Carnegie Endowment for International Peace. We want to thank our management and colleagues at the Endowment for their moral, intellectual, and financial support for this project: Jessica Mathews, Paul Balaran, George Perkovich, Carmen MacDougall, and Carrie Mullen. Marina Barnett, Matthew Gibson, and Roman Ginzburg have assisted greatly in editing the manuscript, Daria Khabarova provided first-rate research assistance, and as always, Ann Stecker has provided excellent secretarial support.

In addition, we are grateful for financial support from the Law Reform Institute, the German Marshall Fund of the United States, the International Renaissance Foundation, and the Chopivsky Family Foundation.

—Anders Åslund and Michael McFaul

Appendix: Election Results

Table A.1. First-Round Presidential Election, October 31, 2004

	Yushchenko	Yanukovych	Moroz	Symonenko
Ternopil region	87.5	5.5	2.0	0.5
Ivano-Frankivsk region	89.0	4.5	1.4	0.7
Lviv region	87.3	5.8	1.6	0.8
Volyn region	77.2	10.5	3.2	2.1
Rivne region	69.3	16.1	5.2	2.3
Vinnytsia region	59.7	16.0	12.8	3.9
Kyiv region	59.7	16.7	9.4	3.3
Khmelnitskyi region	57.9	21.1	7.1	4.1
Chernivtsi region	66.6	17.9	2.7	2.6
Sumy region	52.7	25.7	7.3	4.0
Cherkassy region	57.7	17.9	11.8	4.3
Kyiv	62.4	14.6	5.4	3.1
Chernihiv region	43.4	24.5	16.3	5.2
Zakarpatska region	46.6	37.8	2.0	1.5
Zhytomyr region	43.5	29.2	10.3	6.3
Poltava region	43.6	26.0	15.4	5.6
Kirovohrad region	39.0	30.8	12.5	7.0
Kherson region	32.1	37.4	7.3	10.0
Dnipropetrovsk region	18.7	49.7	5.3	10.6
Mykolaiv region	17.9	54.0	5.4	7.8
Odesa region	17.3	53.4	8.5	6.7
Kharkiv region	15.4	57.4	5.3	7.9
Zaporizhzhia region	16.6	55.7	5.3	8.8
Autonomous Republic of Crimea	12.8	69.2	1.0	6.7
Sevastopol	6.0	73.5	1.2	8.8
Luhansk region	4.5	80.0	1.9	5.8
Donetsk region	2.9	86.7	1.3	3.3
Total	**39.9**	**39.3**	**5.8**	**5.0**

Note: Voter turnout was 74.5 percent.

Table A.2. Second-Round Presidential Election, November 21, 2004

	Yushchenko	Yanukovych
Ternopil region	93.5	5.2
Ivano-Frankivsk region	93.4	5.1
Lviv region	91.8	6.6
Volyn region	85.8	11.9
Rivne region	76.7	20.1
Vinnytsia region	75.9	21.1
Kyiv region	76.4	20.0
Khmelnitskyi region	71.5	24.9
Chernivtsi region	74.5	21.7
Sumy region	69.1	26.4
Cherkassy region	71.9	24.1
Kyiv	74.7	19.9
Chernihiv region	65.7	30.0
Zakarpatska region	55.0	40.0
Zhytomyr region	60.4	40.1
Poltava region	60.9	34.5
Kirovohrad region	47.1	46.5
Kherson region	42.3	52.3
Dnipropetrovsk region	29.6	63.6
Mykolaiv region	25.4	69.6
Odesa region	26.1	67.8
Kharkiv region	24.1	70.3
Zaporizhzhia region	24.1	70.3
Autonomous Republic of Crimea	14.6	82.0
Sevastopol	7.6	89.0
Luhansk region	4.8	92.7
Donetsk region	2.0	96.2
Total	**46.6**	**49.5**

Note: Voter turnout was 80.4 percent.

Table A.3. Rerun Second-Round Presidential Election, December 26, 2004

	Yushchenko	Yanukovych
Ternopil region	96.0	2.7
Ivano-Frankivsk region	95.7	2.9
Lviv region	93.7	4.7
Volyn region	90.7	7.0
Rivne region	84.5	12.3
Vinnytsia region	84.1	12.9
Kyiv region	82.7	13.8
Khmelnitskyi region	80.5	16.0
Chernivtsi region	79.8	16.4
Sumy region	79.5	16.9
Cherkassy region	79.1	17.4
Kyiv	78.4	17.5
Chernihiv region	71.2	24.2
Zakarpatska region	67.5	27.6
Zhytomyr region	66.9	28.9
Poltava region	66.0	29.2
Kirovohrad region	63.4	31.8
Kherson region	43.4	51.3
Dnipropetrovsk region	32.0	61.1
Mykolaiv region	27.7	67.1
Odesa region	27.5	66.6
Kharkiv region	26.4	68.1
Zaporizhzhia region	24.5	70.1
Autonomous Republic of Crimea	15.4	81.3
Sevastopol	8.0	88.8
Luhansk region	6.2	91.2
Donetsk region	4.2	93.5
Total	**52.0**	**44.2**

Note: Voter turnout was 77.2 percent.
Source: Central Election Commission of Ukraine, available at www.cvk.gov.ua/pls/vp2004/WP0011.

Index

About the Contributors

Anders Åslund is a senior fellow at the Institute for international Economics, former director of the Russian and Eurasian Program at the Carnegie Endowment for International Peace, Washington, D.C., and adjunct professor at Georgetown University.

Michael McFaul is a senior associate at the Carnegie Endowment for International Peace, Peter and Helen Bing Senior Fellow at the Hoover Institution, and associate professor of Political Science at Stanford University, Washington, D.C.

Pavol Demes is the director for Central and Eastern Europe with the German Marshall Fund of the United States, Bratislava, Slovakia.

Nadia Diuk is the director, Central Europe and Eurasia, at the National Endowment for Democracy, Washington, D.C.

Joerg Forbrig is a program officer with the German Marshall Fund of the United States, Bratislava, Slovakia.

Adrian Karatnycky is a counselor and senior scholar at Freedom House, New York.

Taras Kuzio is a visiting professor at the Elliott School of International Affairs, George Washington University, Washington, D.C.

Nikolai Petrov is a scholar in residence at the Carnegie Moscow Center, Moscow.

Olena Prystayko is the project director of the Center for Peace, Conversion, and Foreign Policy of Ukraine, Kyiv.

Olena Prytula is the editor-in-chief of *Ukrainska pravda*, Kyiv.

Andrei Ryabov is a scholar in residence at the Carnegie Moscow Center, Moscow.

Oleksandr Sushko is the director of the Center for Peace, Conversion, and Foreign Policy of Ukraine, Kyiv.

The Carnegie Endowment for International Peace is a private, nonprofit organization dedicated to advancing cooperation between nations and promoting active international engagement by the United States. Founded in 1910, Carnegie is nonpartisan and dedicated to achieving practical results.

Through research, publishing, convening, and, on occasion, creating new institutions and international networks, Endowment associates shape fresh policy approaches. Their interests span geographic regions and the relations between governments, business, international organizations, and civil society, focusing on the economic, political, and technological forces driving global change. Through its Carnegie Moscow Center, the Endowment helps to develop a tradition of public policy analysis in the states of the former Soviet Union and to improve relations between Russia and the United States. The Endowment publishes FOREIGN POLICY, one of the world's leading magazines of international politics and economics.

2002

2004

August 18, 2004
Putin declares his
support for
Yanukovych's
candidacy during
a meeting with
Kuchma in Sochi.

004

December 8, 2004
Changes are
made in
parliament to the
electoral law to
ensure fairer
voting. Parliament
simultaneously
votes to reduce
presidential
powers.

ull
ets
as

nd

**December 26,
2004**
Voters turn out
across Ukraine
for a rerun of the
second round of
presidential
elections.
Yushchenko wins
with 51.99
percent,
compared with
44.2 percent for
Yanukovych.

2005

's

arch 31, 2002
rainian
rliamentary
ction:
shchenko's
r Ukraine bloc
ns the most
ats (114 of 450).

vember 21,
02
chma appoints
vernor of
netsk
nukovych to
e post of prime
nister.

July 26, 2004
Putin meets with
Kuchma and
Yanukovych in
Yalta.

**September 5,
2004**
Yushchenko is
poisoned.

004

om
rt
h,
ing
ith

ole
t
ate

**December 11,
2004**
Doctors in Austria
say that
Yushchenko had
been poisoned
with dioxin earlier
in the campaign.

**December 31,
2004**
Yanukovych
resigns the
premiership.

January 23, 2005
After the
Supreme Court
rejects final
appeals from
Yanukovych,
Yushchenko takes
the oath of office
and is sworn in
as Ukraine's new
president.

y

er the Orange Revolution: Strengthening European and Transatlantic
/downloads/aussen/gmf%20hbs%20Ukraine%20book%20final.pdf; and

Oleksandr Moroz, presidential candidate and leader of the Socialist Party of Ukraine.

Viktor Pinchuk, prominent businessman from Dnipropetrovsk. Owner of Interpipe and three television channels. Son-in-law of Kuchma.

Petro Poroshenko, prominent businessman and major Yushchenko sponsor. Owner of television Channel 5.

Petro Symonenko, presidential candidate and leader of the Communist Party of Ukraine.

Yulia Tymoshenko, leader of the Yulia Tymoshenko bloc in parliament since March 2002. Deputy prime minister for energy, 2000–2001. Former gas trader.

Viktor Yanukovych, presidential candidate. Leading politician from Donetsk. Prime minister, November 2002 to December 2004. Former governor of Donetsk region.

Viktor Yushchenko, presidential candidate. Chai of Ukraine cent bank, 1992–199! Prime minister, December 1999 April 2001. Lead of Our Ukraine faction in parliament, March 2002.